W0017231

CITIZEN BY CHOICE

MY JOURNEY TO THE AMERICAN DREAM

ROLANDO BERNUI,
D.D.S., COL., USAF (RET)

978-1-09835-901-0

CONTENTS

This book is dedicated to my wife, children, and grandchildren

Today, genealogy is an important subject to the family. The basis of this book is my personal story. But it has been a joint effort of my wife and me from our own recollections and recollecting the data from family members who are still alive in Peru and other family members and friends.

INTRODUCTION

There are probably millions of stories told by immigrants who have come to this country telling their personal reasons for leaving their homeland. Most of them have left all their belongings and perhaps, most sadly, they have left their families and social ties along with the love that unites them. Today, it is evident to me that many of their descendants, not familiar with their parents' or parents' homeland, are curious and wish they knew their story. This thought emanating from my children in earlier years, is the moving force that motivates me to write my life story. I realize with the passing of time, memories get fuzzier, and sources of information disappear with the passing away of relatives and friends due to aging, relocating and other common life events.

I have been very fortunate in being able to achieve most of my life goals. Even if they were modest in scope, they have been enormously fulfilling spiritually. We often hear the expression time flies, and my experience confirms it. It appears that I frequently find myself starting new projects, while neglecting some important family projects. Some of these projects have been generated by the questions of my children and other immediate family members. Many of their questions remain unanswered or just keep being added to the pile of unfinished personal projects. As time takes its toll on my life, I see the need to start prioritizing my projects, and stop thinking that "Tomorrow" is still a good option. For me that means anything involving my family should come first. As children mature, their questions just keep growing in scope.

From simple questions, such as, "Daddy, where are your Mommy and Daddy", and "why don't we see them?" Some of their questions about things that feel as if they were just recent happenings or lifelong mature historic details, often stop me in my tracks and send me looking for easy answers that children can understand.

Justifiably, the questions regarding their ancestry seem to be the first. Similar adult questions started from my wife during our courtship days, and became more frequent after meeting her parents as we began to get serious. The curiosity of family and friends keep on adding and grow with time. Soon the questions jump from the children to the grandchildren, and along with them a larger circle of family and acquaintances that continue to add up. To give everyone a better perspective, I decided to start my story with a geographical reference to where I was born, grew up, went to school, etc. most of it probably only interesting to the immediate family members. I have been able to go back to Peru on several occasions, and God willing, I would like for most of my immediate family to visit the land of my ancestors and perhaps savor some of the life style of our family and friends there.

It was not political persecution, religious oppression, or financial hardship that forced me to make my final decision to leave Peru. It was the limitless opportunity that AMERICA offered its people to make their own decision to better themselves. As for me, it was the search for opportunities to fulfill larger dreams rather than just to obtain a degree at a national level. My dreams included traveling to other countries, regardless of the time it took. Travel to places where as long as I was within the law, ownership of my possessions would not be arbitrarily taken away by unscrupulous people or by local or national government.

In retrospect my living conditions and the way of life for most people around me at the time were enviable, for the most part, to my peers. Working for Cerro, was my first experience working for a living. Being appreciated by my peers, and working together with people of over 20 nationalities, in addition to the local population, gave me the opportunity to learn much more about other countries. Observing human relations events arising in the work place or locally, helped me to create my own opinion, from an impartial point of view, on laws, regulations and different cultures and how they impacted the human spirit.

My exposure to people of different ages and other nationalities and cultures, became a reality in my being granted a fellowship by the Guggenheim Foundation to specialize in Pediatric Dentistry and experience life in America first hand by actually living in this country. Americans started having a more positive impact and offered me more possibilities when I had the opportunity to experience life in America.

I was a well-adjusted Peruvian with no political aspirations or even interest, in the aches and pains that political situations were bringing to the country. I just adjusted to them. I can only explain it with the everyday minor pains and aches we all experience as tolerable in our daily lives. You tolerate the chronic discomfort until for some miraculous reason you move to another region where the climate agrees with you. Suddenly you feel better and express it to others in words such as "I did not know how sick I was until I started feeling better".

Many aspects of living conditions that Americans take for granted are not appreciated because they never had to work or fight to get it; obstacles in everyday life, if you are born in certain environments, you just deal with them. My competitive nature and knowledge taught me that there were other nations that could prepare professionals to be trained beyond the average. The realization that hard work and sacrifice pays off, was the fueling reasons that I came to America to get better prepared than most of my peers in the practice of my profession. But achieving my first goal was just like climbing a mountain, when you reach the top, you see other even higher tempting mountains. While living and practicing my profession for a year in New York City, the sincere appreciation expressed by my patients was intoxicatingly enjoyable.

The title of my position as "Chief Dentist" of a giant Industrial Company, and other opportunities available opened my eyes, and the experiences had a deep impact on me. I had given my "All" and felt blessedly rewarded. So I got in the habit of attending "Continuing Education Courses" during vacation periods from work, in La Oroya, Peru. The repeated visits to the States for graduate courses, at different Universities, and my interaction with patients of 20 different nationalities, molded a new way of thinking in my life. Also, my expectations of the "future" began to emerge.

I began to fall in love with America, and I could have decided to live here permanently on that first time visit, but I was not quite sure because I also love my homeland, Peru. As my training in Pediatric Dentistry was ending soon, practice opportunities became available both here in the U.S. and abroad.

A great and generous report from Dr. Daniel F. Tobin, the director of the Guggenheim Dental Clinic in New York City opened the doors for me. I realized that people needed me here more than in my country, and also made me aware of other opportunities abroad as an American trained dentist. Ironically, one of the offers came from a Huge American Mining Company called Cerro that had large operations in Peru. Hired in New York City, I signed a four year contract to return to Peru and occupy the position of Chief Dentist of their Dental Division. My duties would be primarily the care of English speaking patients, and some administrative duties supervising other dentists working in other Camp Sites away from the main Camp with its headquarters in La Oroya, Peru. It offered many perks including my returning to the U.S. for additional courses of my choice. Personally, for me taking this job was a no brainer. It would give me the opportunity to experience the life style of both countries and practice high level dentistry, without the concerns of personal cost to me. I could provide high quality service without the limitations of materials or labor costs often involved in providing excellence in care.

I had fallen in love with New York City, and the American people that I had come across both professionally and socially. Six decades later, I feel that I have been blessed to have had the opportunity to practice Dentistry in a variety of settings, Institutional, Military, and Private Practice dentistry, as well as serve as teacher, instructor during my years as a student. While practicing full time in the USAF, I had other related assignments in teaching some specialty aspects to Graduate Military officer students. Later, upon retirement from active duty and private practice, I was offered a teaching position at Meharry Medical College School of Dentistry in Nashville, Tennessee. Following my retirement from private practice, I accepted the position and initiated the undergraduate training program of Dental Implantology. I was promoted to the rank of Associate Professor.

I am Board Certified in the specialty of Prosthodontics and Qualified in two other specialty fields of Dentistry. Probably an even greater professional accomplishment is having served in the USAF and achieving the rank of (06) Full Colonel. As a family man, my biggest pride is being blessed with an ever loving family, who have supported me in every way and often sacrificed because of my decisions. My selfless wife and four loving children deserve all the credit for my success. Again, the true treasures I have accumulated are "MY FAMILY". Four top notch professional children who in total have given my wife and me fourteen beautiful and intelligent grandchildren. Should I have had another opportunity to choose a path for my life, I would make the same choices. Hopefully at lesser pain and sacrifices for my family.

For a person interested in the experiences of a naturalized citizen from my part of the world, in this book I will try to include illustrations via photographs, short movie clips or whatever means available. There may be people who are in similar circumstances and are contemplating becoming an American "Citizen By Choice".

CHAPTER 1

WHERE IN THE WORLD IS YAUYA THE TOWN WHERE I WAS BORN

Geographically, Peru is subdivided into Departments, Provinces, and Districts.

The Continent is South America, the country is Peru, the Department is Ancash and the town is Yauya.

Yauya is in Nothern Peru, in the Department of Ancash, just east of the Pacific Ocean and just beyond the area called "Callejon de Huaylas" and its capital Huaraz.

"Callejon de Huaylas" is a wide valley, some 200 km long, it is split by the Santa River and fringed by a picturesque group of towns and villages. From east to west, and from the highest altitude down to sea level, are the cities of Ticapampa, Recuay, Huaraz, Carhuaz, Yungay, Caraz and Huallanca. It is a land where time appears to have stood still. Wedged between two soaring mountain chains, the Cordillera Negra, the black mountains and the Cordillera Blanca, the white mountains. The Callejón de Huaylas gave rise to the ancient Chavín civilization, which has left a legacy in the Chavín de Huántar temple, just hours from the city of Huaraz.

The Cordillera Blanca includes the 4th, 5th, 6th and 7th highest mountains in the world, The Huascaran, with its impressive height of 6,768 meters, being the highest. Alpamayo, named by UNESCO as the most beautiful mountain in the world, is nearby. There are a number of other cities, such as, Huari, Chavin, Chacas, San Luis, and Yauya, spread along the eastern slopes and the plains, extending beyond the Cordilleras toward the Jungle.

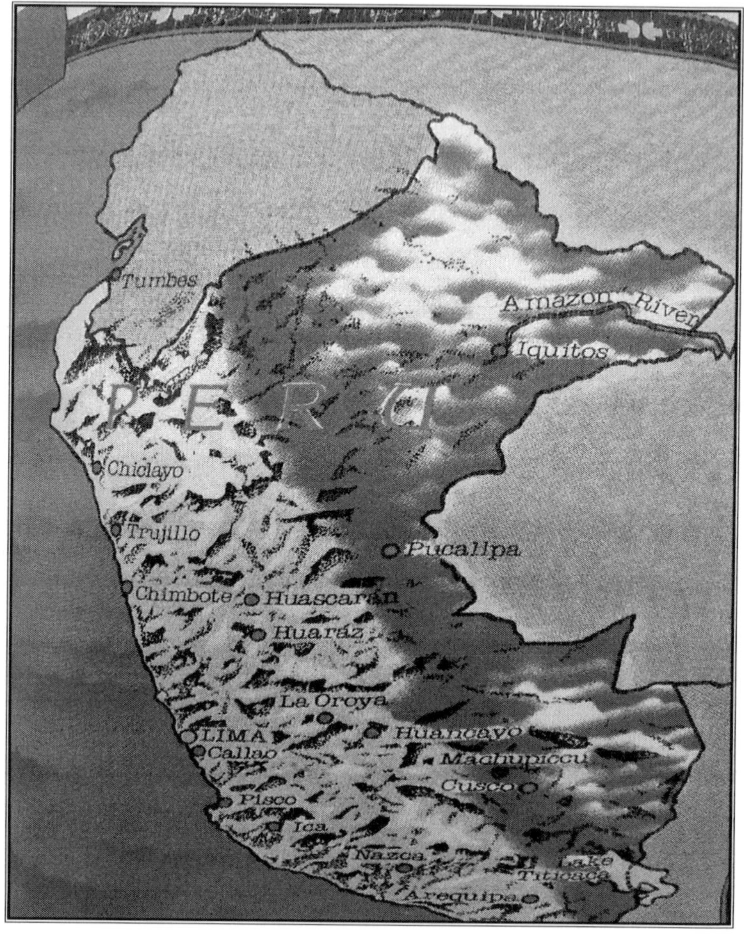

A map of Peru.

CHAPTER 2

HOW POLITICAL AND SOCIAL STRUCTURE IN PERU INFLUENCED MY EARLY CHILDHOOD DEVELOPMENT

My early childhood was spent in Yauya, a small self-governing town in the northern part of Peru, South America. The local officials were elected in town hall meetings and it was more like dividing the jobs among volunteers without much help from the national government except, of course, on major projects. They all tried to impress the nationally appointed officials in order to get federal help for major community projects. Politically divided according to their own prejudicial beliefs, they tried to rally behind their own candidates who they thought would do the best for the local community. They ended up supporting more the national political figures, who of course espoused the same international politics of today's world. Some had socialistic or left wing overtones and some were right wing conservatives. Each side would give away lavish empty promises, but no realistic plan for the best interests of the country. They never mentioned that the country could not afford these things and was already in debt to other countries. There were also foreign interests promoting their candidates which at the end divided the country even more. People aligned themselves with only their personal interests at heart striving to attain government positions. Corruption was a way of life. In other words pretty much as world politics is today.

It appeared to me that the nation was always divided into two sides. I was very disappointed that there was no middle of the road candidate who would not espouse any form of ideology, except as to what was best suited for the nation. Locally, however, in small towns like Yauya, this was not the major issue because no one was aspiring to become national figures, they were all busy worrying about their own personal problems or the problems of the town. Positions for running the affairs of small communities were not paid positions. They were selected by committees formed by the people of the town, who would then ask the chosen person to accept the position. It was considered an honor to be nominated, and although the nominee could decline, they seldom did.

The appointed person then formed his own group to see ways of generating the necessary funds to accomplish a project towards which everybody could cooperate. For example, to build a church in a certain location, a group of people, usually people with some stance in the community, would ask a land owner to donate or sell a certain piece of land for the church, or whatever project was to be built on it. Once the land was secured, the plans would be drawn, and a materials list prepared. To generate funds, events would be planned for the whole year taking advantage of official holidays, nationally recognized and local traditional celebrations that attracted people of nearby towns. Events such as soccer games, bullfights, dances, dinners, bake sales, jousting contests, beauty pageants, etc. were some of the activities.

In Yauya, there were a couple of large General Stores where goods were sold, but they were also liquor stores where they served alcoholic drinks over the counter. Occasionally on weekends men would gather around to share news with each other or tell tall stories. They avoided open political confrontations, but they were always looking for a harmless way to express their views. The homes in town were usually two stories with balconies facing the street, sitting next to each other. Some had a store on the first floor and living quarters above. One of my uncles owned one such store. It was a two story building. The first floor of buildings like this was usually dedicated for businesses, such as bakeries, post office or any type of stores. My Uncle Federico Palacios had a general store. The streets were a common playground for kids, pedestrians or horseback riders.

One Sunday afternoon a couple of us kids (ages 4 or 5) entered the store to buy candy and found ourselves amidst a group of drinking people. They all stopped and got quiet, they looked at us and asked what we were doing there without a parent. "To buy candy we replied." They all laughed, and one older man with a long white beard picked me in his arms and said I'll buy you a big candy bar if you go out to the street and yell at the top of your lungs "Viva Sanchez Cerro". I happily obliged! As I turned around I saw my friend who had been coaxed by another man with opposing views, run out the door and shouted "Viva Leguia". In doing so we had spooked the horse of a rider who was passing by throwing the rider to the ground. The man was not hurt but it was a kind of funny scene.

There are three layers of noticeable groups of people in Peru:

The upper class composed mostly of very wealthy people who have made their fortunes either in the business world, or those who have inherited fortunes from their ancestors. Many of these families dated back to the early days through Spanish nobility classes who acquired huge amounts of prime land through special land grants. Most of them were Europeans and people who were descendants of the Inca Empire. They called themselves "the cream".

The middle class is comprised of people of lesser wealth, such as merchants, small business people, and budding entrepreneurs. Most of them were constantly active in business and were always trying to gain some economic supremacy. Racially speaking they are a more diverse group which includes children of immigrants who married local people of multiple ethnic descent. The most predominant mixture was of Spanish and those of Inca Indian descent commonly referred as "mestizos". Spain colonized and governed the Inca Empire, for over 300 years, the native population dwindled to 20%. Today, other groups include a multitude of European immigrants. In later years hard working Asians emerged.

The lower class is primarily composed of people without much education, who are attached to the land and Inca traditions. Unfortunately, this last group includes the native Peruvian population, most of whom do not speak Spanish, but only their own native language or a dialect. They are composed of those who work as mining laborers, farm workers and tradesmen. Ethnically, they are the result of the mixture of the above two groups, but are still predominantly Peruvian natives who are descendants of the Incas. They are the most attached to the land areas where they were born. In spite of the government's efforts of compulsory education and compulsory active military service, for the most part they restrict themselves to their own little communities and do not attempt to incorporate themselves into the main stream. Many have proven themselves during the wars with neighboring nations, and become well known heroes. In spite of such successes many return to the villages where they were born. Few take advantage of the opportunities in the Armed Forces. Some did advance in rank and some of them achieved high ranking grades in the Armed Forces and even became Presidents of the nation. As a group however, they feel more comfortable wearing their own traditional clothing, living in small huts and speaking their own native language or dialect.

The Assumption of Mary procession in Yauya, Peru.

Rolando's mother, Guadencia Bernui Vidal

Rolando's home and birthplace (first house on the left). Yauya, Peru

CHAPTER 3

MY BIRTH AND EARLY CHILDHOOD

On August 15, 1929, a Holy Day in the Catholic Church, my Mother, Gaudencia Vidal de Bernui was laboring to deliver me. She had been in labor for a long time and the midwives were worried that there were going to be complications. In Peru, on Holy Days, there are usually big celebrations with Processions and bands accompanied by fireworks including sticks of dynamite, called avellanas, being exploded. As the procession passed by someone detonated an avellana, that shook the house and out I popped, feet first! My Mother was very happy to have me. My Father was away working in the mines and came to see us as soon as he could.

My life story begins with my early recollections of life in Yauya. Much of what I remember, I learned from my mother about herself, and from what family members told me about myself and my Mother after her death, when I was almost seven.

My mother was an only child from the Vidals, a well-established, well-known family in our part of the country. Although rooted in a deep traditional Catholic, Peruvian family, my mother grew up as an independent and well-schooled young woman. She was gifted with a strong independent character, which was not really common for those days, nor approved by the family or society at large.

Her independent and rebellious personality, as related by other family members, manifested itself first when she married my father without the approval of her mother. Her father had died when she was young. She loved and respected her mother but she did not feel that parents should arrange their children's marriages, as often happened in those days. So she married my father without her approval. Her mother likewise loved and respected her and she maintained that relationship until she also passed away, at an early age. My mother was only 19 years old when her mother died. My father's name was Gregorio Bernui, a miner, the son of another miner. Even though he was born in Peru, he was considered an immigrant because his father was an immigrant from Italy and they moved to the area because of the mines. They both worked at nearby silver mines owned and operated by families of Italian descent. The names of the mines were "Pompey" and "Vesuvio". I can only assume that they were named after the well-known volcanoes in Italy. The owners were the Caferata family who were a well-stablished family from the nearby town of Chacas.

The families of the men who worked in the mines lived in the nearby towns of Chacas, San Luis, and Yauya. The mines were closest to Chacas, some 3 miles from the mining camp, which was located four to five hours away, travel time on horseback, from Yauya.

My mother was living in Yauya when she met my father. I was told that after my parents married and I was born, my father came to Yauya as frequently as he could to see us. I was told that I had a sister who was born when I was about a year old. Her name was Aida and she died before I was three. My mother and I lived in Yauya in my mother's house.

One unfortunate day, when I was about three years old, my mother was notified by a messenger that a portion of the mines where my father worked had collapsed, burying a good number of people, among them my father. Rescue attempts were unsuccessful. It was an impossible task in those days, and the rescue attempts were eventually abandoned and the mine operation activities were stopped for a period of time.

The Vidals were compassionate, and united in being supportive of my mother's situation, a young widow with a three year old child. But they wouldn't do anything to help her unless she apologized for getting married without the family's approval and requested their help. My father's side of the family who lived at the other side of the cordilleras, in the town of Carhuaz, had asked my mother and me to join them and live with them in Carhuaz, but my mother did not want to choose sides and create animosity between the families. My father, an only child as well, had also lost his father in a mining accident many years earlier, when he was still very young.

My father's mother, Braulia Mejia, my paternal grandmother, survived two other husbands. Grandmother also came from an old family of Spanish descent, the Mejias, who lived the established life style of those days. She was very sympathetic to my mother because she had also experienced similar disapproval from her family on her first marriage to my Grandfather because he was an immigrant.

After my Grandfather passed away, my Grandmother married her second husband, Manuel Broncano. He was a well-known cattleman, who had a colorful history and told some exciting stories about fighting cattle rustlers. He died at an early age, leaving Grandmother a widow again with another son, Roberto.

There were colorful stories about Grandmother, as well. It was said that she was a very beautiful woman, but was feared by many to be a death wish for potential suitors, because she had lost two young husbands. The family members were all devoted Catholics. It was not long, however, before a younger man, Lizandro Obregon, would decide to take his chances and succeeded in marrying her and fathering three more children; a long awaited girl, Estella, and two boys Samuel and Moises. Following the Spanish tradition, she decided to educate her four surviving children by devoting the first son, Roberto, to God, by sending him to the seminary to become a priest. Roberto, was eventually appointed custodian for me and the rest of the family. The second, Samuel, went to medical school to become a doctor (physician) and the third, Moises, was to become a lawyer. The first two fulfilled her wishes, the third was the only one left to run the farm. He couldn't go to college because farming was the support of the family and it was too extensive an operation to be done part time. He later decided to study Agricultural Engineering to learn how to run the family farms more efficiently. He could not complete that degree because it took too much time. He married one of my mother's relatives, whose family lived near Yauya. He fathered thirteen children.

CHAPTER 4

MY MOTHER'S LIFE AS A SINGLE MOTHER

My Mother was a very happy, spirited person, a great dancer, had a great voice, loved music and frequently played the mandolin. She was always ready to have a good time or entertain others, wherever time would find us. She was never heard complaining and never engaged in self-pity saying "poor me". She would frequently say that "Poor only applies to people who have lost the grace of God, and as far as I know God still loves us". I had a nanny, Julia, who lived with us until my mother's death. She went with us everywhere. After mother passed away, she went with me to live with my aunt Abigail, who was to take care of me during my childhood years. Aunt Abigail would frequently comment to Julia about how difficult it must have been for my mother during all the years that we had lived alone. Julia, answered, "Ms. Abigail, I never heard Mrs. Bernui complain and I was as close to her as any flesh and blood relative could have ever been".

My mother's life was characterized mainly by fond memories of her childhood and a strong determination to be self-sufficient, almost to a fault. Family members expected her to run back to them, repentantly, after my father's death. But it did not happen that way. Her behavior was more as if she was telling friends and family "I'll survive and I'll show you that I don't need anyone's help or pity. All that I ask of you is either like me or dislike me with a good reason. I am who I am, and I don't need the families' legacy, money, or even what was legitimately mine by inheritance from my parents. Although she never expressed this verbally to me, that I remember, she did share her feelings with her friends and to some family members.

I knew that she felt that the family had distanced themselves from her for marrying my father against their will and they thought that sooner or later she would go back to them, with apologies, asking for help.

Mother survived by managing some extensive farm lands that she and my father had either inherited or purchased. Farming is particularly hard in the mountains due to the rough terrain and total absence of mechanization. You have to rely heavily on manual labor and an assortment of mules, horses, donkeys, and oxen to do the plowing, carry cargo, etc., and sheep, and cattle for food, clothing and cash. There was an absence of trustworthy managers, thus, the management of the farm demanded the total personal involvement of my mother.

A great many business transactions are carried out without much use of cash currency, both for goods and services. Bartering is a big part of it and leasing out farm land to be paid with labor is another part. Another common arrangement for farm land is share crop farming. In fewer instances, farm rentals were paid with hard currency, gold and silver coins, rather than paper money. This is how my mother supported herself and me. She had inherited a good deal of property, so she had parts of it in different types of contracts. The end result was that we always had plenty of food, clothing, cash and help around the house. Unfortunately, this changed when the government started over-taxing properties and appointing an ever increasing number of administrators, allowing increasing rights to tenants, farm workers, and corrupt government officials, to enforce government regulations and to gain popularity with the masses.

There was a scarcity of commercial professional merchants, so privately organized bartering for goods and services were big. For example, my mother had arrangements with family friends living in other parts of the country, who produced other varieties of foods, to exchange goods. To give you an idea of the needs of people living in different climates I will describe a little bit of the geography of the area where we lived and what our needs were, not only to sustain ourselves but to fill the basic needs of the population.

Peru is divided into three major geographical areas: The coastal region, a narrow strip of desert land that runs north and south, is much like what you see portrayed in the movies about deserts in Arabia. It has sand dunes, sand storms, absolutely no vegetation, except an occasional green valley, which are irrigated by small rivers which flow from the western slopes of the western range of the Andes Mountains.

Then comes the Sierra region which rapidly emerges at the east side of the coast, and also runs the whole length of the country from north to south. The sierras are composed of three ranges of the Andes Mountains, running almost parallel to each other, but merging at some points known as Knots. This very rugged area boasts having some of the highest mountains in the world, in fact next to the Himalayas the highest mountains in the world are, the second highest, Chimborazo in Ecuador, in third place Aconcagua in Chile, and the next three, ranking fourth, fifth, and sixth are in Peru. These snow-capped peaks are named, Huascaran, Hualcan, and Huandoy. Next to them are also some of the deepest canyons in the world. The world famous Colca Canyon is in southern Peru. The rugged topography with mountains that emerge straight up, deep valleys with rivers, volcanoes, and the proximity to the equator, of course allows for an infinite number of climates within short distances from each other. It is also the area where the Inca subcultures existed and flourished during the Inca civilization. Going eastward, the mountain ranges diminish in height, and the tropical Amazon region, known as La Selva, begins and extends all the way to the frontiers with Brazil, Ecuador and Colombia.

Since no single region was completely self -sufficient, products typical of each area had to be transported from one region to another, thus trading, frequently became more extensive. The lack of good roads and other means of fast transportation caused lack of merchants. Very few merchants would take risks and make it convenient for small consumers so the demand was there for many families to have their own trade agreements with people of other regions and make trips back and forth from time to time.

We had friends who were living in the foothills of the eastern range of the Andes. They made their living by farming cocoa, tea, coffee, rubber, coca, and dried fruits. Our crops were potatoes, wheat, corn, textiles, etc. Since there were no highways, the only means of transportation available were horses, donkeys and mules. Most perishable goods were just lost.

In 1934 and 1935, when I was 5 and 6 years old, I was included in the yearly, five to eight day trips over the mountains to the jungle side, to trade crops with them. Since I was so young and my legs didn't reach the stirrups, they tied my legs to the saddle with pieces of soft fabric so that I wouldn't fall off of my horse. I would sometimes fall asleep as we rode. That trip would be quite an adventure even these days. It resembled what you see in the movies of the early Americans going west.

Our expedition would start in Yauya with a 20 or 30 mule train carrying our cargo of salt, sugar, bread, assorted flours of wheat, peas, etc., medical supplies such as aspirin, anti-malaria products etc. The food we brought with us consisted of, beef jerky, cancha (roasted corn kernels), boiled eggs and a mixture made with lard that had pieces of pork in it, pea flour and salt. After it was made at home it congealed and when we were on the trail at dinner time all they did was add the mixture to boiling water and we had pea soup. Sometimes the guides would shoot a rabbit or other small animal and roast it over our campfire. Our personnel consisted of two mounted trail riders, and two guides on foot. Our journey was up and down the mountains heading northeast looking for pastures and less demanding passes for crossing the cordillera. The trail riders would pick the suitable places for camping, depending on the availability of pasture and day light time before dark. Sometimes we would ride for 10 to 12 hours, and sometimes for only five or six.

My mother was an accomplished horsewoman and sharpshooter, who had a keen sixth sense. She only rode side saddle. In those days ladies did not wear pants or slacks because it was considered inappropriate. On long trips, she would carry a small rifle and an umbrella within easy reach in the front part of the saddle. She also had a small silver revolver hidden in a handbag on her person. Fondly engraved in my memory is our last trip to the jungle when we had two experiences that were so exciting that I remember them vividly. On our third day we broke camp quite early in the morning. We had spent the night in a cave entrance at the foot hills of some snow-capped mountains before the mountain pass. The trail riders were busy rounding up the horses and mules, getting ready, reloading the cargo and fixing breakfast by the camp fire. The cave, as it usually happens had previously been used by other travelers as evidenced by the layers of "Ichoo" a high altitude grass similar to hay. It is customary to have the help gather up bundles of this hay with a sickle, the hay is spread out on the ground in abundance to provide a soft warm and insulating layer on which to spread our blankets and other bedding paraphernalia for the night. At some point I must have rolled out from the blankets, and the cold woke me up. I called my mother and I told her that I was very cold, and that Julia, the nanny, who would sleep with us by my side, was as cold as ice. My mother replied, "Julia did not come on this trip", and that I probably had been having a bad dream. With that I cuddled up to my mother and went to sleep.

When I woke up in the morning almost everyone was just about ready to get started on our journey. I remembered that my mother had told me that I had probably had a bad dream, but it appeared so real that I decided to check it out. As I combed the hay I was shocked to see the body of a person, so I yelled for the trail riders and my mother who rushed to my aid and discovered the frozen body of a human being buried in the hay. The trail riders carried the body somewhere nearby and buried it in the ground, placing a cross as a marker in case someone came by in search of the person. We did not stay around to investigate, but the trail riders later told me that it is not uncommon for people traveling alone to suffer a colic or heart attack, or be killed by robbers who leave the bodies with a scanty cover of hay. Although I was intrigued, my mother and other adults brushed away my questions, and I never found out any more details on the matter.

Another excitement occurred two days later on the same trip. We were riding on the big plains at the foot hills of the eastern slopes of the snowcapped mountains, grazing grounds for fierce wild cattle, and breeding grounds of fighting bulls. My mother and I along with one of the trail riders were at the tail end of our mule train. Suddenly the trail rider alerted us to a fast approaching bull that had broken off from its herd. Before we knew it the bull was about 30 feet away from my horse when my mother turned her horse around towards the bull and clicked opened a large black umbrella. The bull skidded and stopped dead in its tracks as I galloped away. The trail rider galloped towards my mother's horse encircling her while she had already gotten ready to fire her rifle. The surprised bull just watched us and eventually turned away and headed back towards its herd. Cattle and sheep are afraid of condors. These giant birds fully grown may have an average wing span of 16 to 18 feet and can pick up sheep and baby cattle and carry them away to inaccessible places to feed on. Apparently the bull thought that my mother's umbrella was a Condor. Two days later we arrived at our destination and visited for a week before we started back home with our cargo of traded goods. My favorite gifts from our friends were two rubber sling shots, a rubberized poncho and a rubber ball.

Wild cattle on the way to the jungle where the brave bulls are raised in Ancash, Peru.

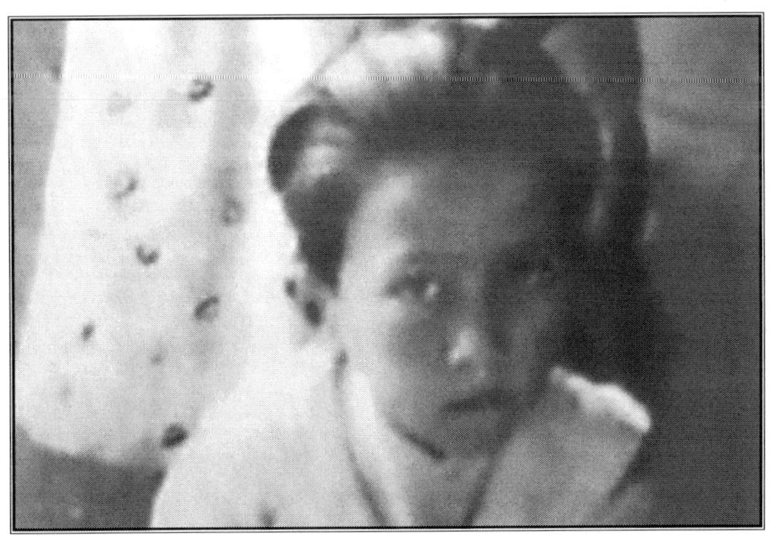

Rolando, about four years old.

CHAPTER 5

OUR MOVE TO THE CAPITAL OF THE DEPARTMENT: THE CITY OF HUARAZ

Running a farming operation in our area was needless to say exhausting. Most of our labor force was composed of farming families whose family members would pay for the use of certain parcels of our land with manual labor. Depending on the amount of land leased they would work one, two or three days per week in lieu of payment in money.

Although they were paying us with work for the use of the leased land, we had to provide them with sleeping quarters, meals, and a ration of coca daily during the time that they worked for us. It became increasingly challenging because there was no strict way to enforce the agreements, so there was a lot of non-compliance. Because of this and other problems beginning to sprout, in 1935, my mother decided to lease the whole farm to share croppers, sell the cattle, sheep and other farm operation equipment, and the animals we had, to traders and move to the city of Huaraz, capital of the Department of Ancash. (Peru is divided into 21 departments like the U.S is divided into 50 States, each Department being the equivalent, politically, to a State) Although officially my mother claimed that the move was prompted by my educational needs, I knew that secretly, she just wanted to get away from it all.

My mother had home schooled me from a very early age. She also taught me everything I would need to know about religion, etiquette, generosity, respectfulness, responsibility, compassion, cleanliness, and how to treat other people, especially ladies. When we would go to parties at homes of friends, I was expected to announce our arrival by saying, "good evening Ladies and Gentlemen", and then go around the room shaking hands with the men and boys and bowing and kissing the hands of the ladies and girls. I hated it, especially the hand kissing part, but, Mother insisted. At age six I was tested and admitted to second grade, bypassing kindergarten and the first grade of primary education.

Life in the city of Huaraz, was completely a new world to both my mother and me. It was even more shocking being in a large school with classes of 25 or 30 students per grade.

I had never seen a motorized vehicle before in my life, and I was fascinated with cars and trucks. The city had several large stores with all kinds of merchandise, several restaurants, two movie theaters, five neighborhood churches and one main cathedral. There was also an ice cream and soda shop that later on would become one of my favorite treat spots.

The family house in Huaraz.

My mother had purchased a nice large house in a nice neighborhood with enough room to ride into the courtyard on horseback, it had its own water well and a bathroom which was a small detached room adjacent to the main house. It had a canal of fast running water passing under the toilet seat which was a regular wooden box with a circle cut out in the center and no bottom. On the back wall of the room, above the seat there was a wire hook with cut pieces of newspapers or magazines on it to be used as toilet paper. The box was built on top of the canal where you had to sit to go to the bathroom, and the running stream of water would carry away the waste, pass thru other houses until it emptied into a large river. The small squares of old used papers and magazines were deposited in a waste basket to be burned up later in the day in a burning barrel, whether it was full or not! My first modern bathroom! ….For those years, in that part of the world, it was rather a luxury. No more plant leaves or rough corn cobs to do the job in the fields.

From early childhood my mother started teaching me to draw objects, shapes of letters, numbers, etc. as an entertainment game. As time went by, the games gradually became more complicated. My nanny carried on with the exercises and told my mother how grown up and smart I was, when she was the one who had done most of the work, holding my hand and guiding it while writing letters or drawing pictures. Fortunately for me, it began to give good results in time with the constant repetition of the games. By the time I was 5 years old I had mastered my A,B,C,s and numbers including some math games. The games were concocted using real names and real life events from our life in Yauya or the farm, i.e. "Pedro, our foreman at the ranch, had a female shepherd dog that has had six puppies. Pedro already had two other dogs and my mother told him he could keep only one puppy, so Rolandito (that was me) tell me how many dogs will then Pedro have, and how many of them he'll have to give away?" or "One of the hens had laid 8 eggs in a nearby bush and only 5 hatched, how many were lost?" etc. I enjoyed those games because I could see it visually, and had experienced the scenarios.

By the time I was enrolled in school, I already was keeping a note book of my own, very simple things of course, with letters and numbers, sometimes drawn backwards, but good enough for my teacher. That was why, after two months in kindergarten I was advanced to second grade. The same teacher taught me up to the 3rd grade. The classes were very small, seven to ten students per grade. She was very strict and quick in using a paddle. She had a young assistant following her around, and she was a tattle tale.

Farming in the Peruvian Andes

CHAPTER 6

THE PAINFUL YEARS

All was going great from my point of view. I had a new house, a great new school and new friends and relatives whom I had never met. In 1935 sometime after my birthday in August, my mother had started dating a childhood friend of hers. He was from our hometown, Yauya. He had been in love with mother even before she married my father. After a time, he asked for her hand in marriage. Mother's side of the family, however, did not approve of him, either, but that did not stop her before, and would not this time either.

In the following months, she became pregnant. In May, unaware of her condition, she signed up for an event called "Carrera de Cintas", Jousting. In that condition she continued training hard for a charity event. She had been riding an unfamiliar horse, and one afternoon she took a tumble. She did not think much of it because she had been thrown off a horse many times in her life. Early that evening, she started hemorrhaging, there was only one doctor in the town. When they finally got the doctor, after searching for a couple of hours, nothing could be done for her. As she felt her young life slipping away from her, she told Julia, "my poor son, take care of him," closed her eyes, and passed into the arms of the Lord. Julia later commented that that was the only time she had ever heard my mother say the word 'poor' in regard to herself or me.

Early the next morning following my mother's death, one of my relatives from the Santillama family, picked me up and took me to her house telling me that my mother had been taken to the hospital ill, that she might have to stay there for some time, and that my mother had asked her to take care of me in the meantime.

I was almost seven years old in May of 1936, when my mother passed away. She was only 28 years old.

A few days later, Uncle Roberto came to visit me. He hugged me tightly and sobbed for long time without saying a word. That is when I felt that my mother had probably passed away, but no one had said so. I was very upset and angry that I could not visit my mother, but I was always told that my mother's instructions were specific. My nanny had been left taking care of the house, but I was not allowed to see her or go back to our house or go to the hospital.

I was not openly aware of the animosity between my father's and mother's side of the families, but I knew Uncle Roberto was held in high esteem by both sides. He was respected as a priest, was chosen as a mediator between both sides and was appointed as my guardian. In that position, he guarded my financial interests as well. I continued to live with the Santillama family for a year or so. Uncle Roberto, had me enrolled in a religious, private, coed school that I was not very fond of. I would frequently get in trouble for not paying attention during class or when saying our prayers, or teasing some teacher's pet girls. He would come to visit and it was obvious to me that I was not getting good reports from the principal, who had suggested to Uncle Roberto that he should send me to an all-boys school where they would be better equipped to handle me.

At first I was very joyful. My prayers had been answered. I would not be sent to the chapel to say 30 or 50 Hail Mary's every time I got in trouble.

Then, in 1937, a decision had to be made as to which side of the family I should live with. Uncle Roberto had been avoiding getting caught in the middle. Aunt Estella, the next sibling on my father's side, and my grandmother had violently opposed the idea of my returning to Yauya. In their view, my mother would have never suffered or died, if it had not been for their unfounded prejudices. For them I was a Bernui, the only one to carry on the Bernui name.

A few months later, just following the end of the school year, in 1937, I was taken to the farm of my father's family, where I lived until 1938. This farm was run by my youngest uncle, Moises. He had six children at the time and a new baby on the way. It was a great environment to have playmates and have lots of activities with which I was familiar, farming, horseback riding, hunting, cattle ranging to name a few. One of my favorite times was watering the horses at a nearby small river later in the day. At least one of my cousins and I would mount the horses bare back with no bridals or ropes. When the farm hand would open the gates of the pasture the horses literally stampeded for the river, and we just held on to the horse's mane till we reached the river about 10 minutes away. We developed sores on our seats from the horse's back rubbing the insides of our legs and seat, but we could not complain. We just bore the pain, walking bow legged until it got well.

Not far away, (three hours by horse back) there was the smaller bustling town of Carhuaz, where my Uncle Samuel (the physician), Aunt Estella, and Uncle Roberto lived.

In 1938, after living with Uncle Moise's family for about a year, Uncle Roberto received a surprise visit in Carhuaz, from one of my uncles, Samuel Vidal, from my mother's side who told them, "I have come to take Rolando to live with us, where he belongs." Uncle Roberto immediately intervened to calm things down before it could end in a bitter show down. He started by asking everyone to hear Samuel out. He also invited Samuel to have dinner with the family. The dinner was cordial, and everyone was civil with each other. Never-the-less, after dinner, I understand they argued vehemently about what was best for me. They agreed that I would go back to Yauya, live with my mother's side of the family for a while, and see how things would work out. At the end of the dinner, my mother's side Uncle

Samuel, thanked them for the dinner, and asked them to bring me in to him. He was told that I was not there, but that I was at our farm a couple of hours away. He did not quite believe them, he hesitated for a few seconds and then called the stable man and asked for his horse. He got on his horse, pulled out a concealed gun from his saddle bag to show them that he was armed and told them, “I have six mean riders, heavily armed, staying at a ranch 30 minutes away. We are not going back empty handed after a three day journey, so please bring the child to this house by tomorrow afternoon. If we have not heard from you by then, we will either come here or go to your farm to pick him up, forcibly if necessary”.

He was under the impression that the reason why Uncle Roberto tried to keep me with my father’s side of the family was because he was only interested in my inheritance from my parents. As a guardian, he could dispose of it without having to account to anyone for the portions belonging to my father’s side, and those from my mother as well.

Uncle Roberto, by virtue of being a highly respected priest and the only one who was credible and respected by the Vidals, was an effective negotiator and peacemaker. He convinced my rescuers-to-be, to give him 48 hours so that he could have a chance to talk to me first and prepare a more favorable scenario. That way, I could go with them without giving the impression that I was being kidnapped.

Uncle Roberto showed up on the farm unexpectedly and he told me that one of my mother’s cousins had come to town requesting that I spend the summer vacation with them in Yauya and that all my cousins and other relatives from my mother’s side were anxious to see me. I agreed enthusiastically and went to town to meet my new uncle. They had brought me a lively young white horse because they knew that I was a good rider.

We left Carhuaz at 5:30 in the morning so that we could cross the pass through the Andes by 2:00 pm. We passed two beautiful glacier fed lakes called Llanganuco before reaching the mountain pass which is at the foot hills of the Huascaran.

Lake Llanganuco

We spent the night in the caves at the other side of the white cordillera pass where there was good pasture for our horses. The ride was basically uneventful. Occasionally we would cross paths with travelers going the opposite way. As soon as we sighted them in the distance, my companions would huddle on their horses and some precautionary protective moves were put into effect being careful to not appear unfriendly. One exciting thing happened when a rider going in the opposite direction, broke away fast and galloped toward us waving his hat. When he reached hearing distance from us he asked if we had some colic medicine with us. One of their riders was having a terrible stomach ache and he did not know if he could survive for the time it would take for him to go through the mountain pass where he could get help. One of our riders reached into his saddle bag and pulled out a small medicine bottle and said, "this is paregoric (a well-known colic medicine) take no more than three to four drops every four hours". The rider thanked us and offered to pay, but he was told "today for you, tomorrow for me, go in peace". With that the man sped away with a grateful expression on his face. The second day we started with a couple of riders lassoing a wild mother cow and getting some milk. We drank the milk raw and still warm, accompanied with "cancha" (roasted corn), the favorite snack of the Indians. Later we stopped briefly to water the horses, while we snacked on cancha, beef jerky and hard boiled eggs from our saddle bags. Early in the evening we could see the flickering of lanterns and candles and kitchen chimney smoke at a relatively short distance away. We were approaching a small town called Yanama where we spent the night at the home of some friends and relatives. The following day we left after an early, hearty breakfast and continued our trip to Yauya. By 2:00 pm we arrived at one of the Vidal's farms called San Nicolas. The riders stayed there while Uncle Samuel and I continued our trip to Yauya, after eating some fruit from a cargo of figs and other fruits freshly picked at the farm. We arrived into town late in the afternoon. Word had gotten around that we were on our way and we had a fabulous reception from families and friends who were eager to see me.

Yauya was, at that time, a small but unique town. As I recall the homes were mostly furnished with heavy European style furniture. It must have been brought there from the port in Lima on mule trains, since there were no roads or trucks at that time. It had a self-motivated population where everybody knew just about everyone. Most of the people were ranchers, who instead of living in isolation on their ranches, lived in town with their ranch homes short distances away. Yauya had one school that went only to the third grade with only one salaried teacher and two or three volunteer teachers assisting. The school was in a two story building where the downstairs was used as jail that was seldom occupied.

Most local authorities were locally elected or held volunteer positions in public works, such as road maintenance, maintenance of public facilities such as an arena used for parades, bull fights, celebrations, the church building, etc. In essence it was like a large family congregation with less than two thousand people. Most families had a home away from home in larger towns or cities where their children attended school beyond the third grade. Public works and civic activities were performed by the local population involving whole families. When I returned to Yauya, it was like coming home to an extended family. There were two surviving brothers and a sister of my maternal grandparents, from the Vidal side of the family. Since my mother's father had passed away during her early childhood, she had little recollection of him, therefore, she had never told me anything about him.

Most of the children, of my mother's cousins, with the exception of the younger ones, were all away at schools in larger cities. I was taken to the home of my mother's Aunt Pastora, who lived with her daughter Abigail Palacios, her husband Federico and their children, Hugo, Federico, Dora, and three or four younger ones. Among the other children were the Ames children, Augusta, Honorina, and Federico, the Pasco brothers, Victor, Luis, and Demetrio, the Munoz brothers, Manuel and Ricardo, we were all related to some degree. Some of them had older or younger siblings. We had a group of about 20 children around my age all related to each other either by blood or marriage. The other children were children of other family friends who lived in town.

Rolando with a puppy, age eight.

I spent the summer and the next school year attending school with other children about my age. Some of them were children of more distant relatives and public officials living in Yauya or nearby villages. It soon became obvious that some families were moving out of Yauya to larger cities, such as Huari and Pomabamba or Huaraz, where the schools were more advanced, searching for better educations for their children. Huaraz was considered the Mecca, being the capital city of the Department of Ancash. It had both private and public schools, Catholic Seminaries, Convents, Sports teams, Police Force, and a Government provided home for the appointed chief government representative.

By the end of the school year in Yauya, Uncle Roberto had convinced the Vidals that I should return to Huaraz to attend school. So in 1939, I was enrolled at the Sacred Heart Primary School, a school with boarding facilities run by Catholic nuns of the same religious order, as a compromise not to be living with either side of the family in Yauya or Carhuaz.

Huaraz was known as a very cosmopolitan and prosperous city of its time. It was a center of tourism, mining companies' headquarters, agricultural centers, and great educational facilities where many parents would send their children for better educations.

Huaraz was and still is the gateway for an entire area known as "Callejon de Huaylas", nicknamed the "Switzerland" of South America because of its scenery, which resembles the Swiss Alps. The natural beauty of the area is enhanced by the presence of the 4th, 5th, 6th, and 7th highest mountains in the world stretched along approximately 120 or so miles of the western range of the Andes mountains. It is a valley between two mountain ranges that run parallel to each other eventually converging towards each other to form a very narrow canyon with a river at its depth which grows in volume with tributary waters from the glaciers and rain fed small rivers along the way.

At the beginning of this valley the mountain ranges may be as much as 50 miles apart. A valley that begins at approximately 15,000 feet elevation has a small lake and swampy terrain called Lake Conococha. This lake is the origin of the Santa River which runs the whole length of the valley and ends at sea level with a great waterfall. Today, this waterfall is partially used for one of the largest hydroelectric plants in Peru, and empties its waters into the Pacific Ocean in the coastal city of Chimbote. To see this valley the most popular trips are by bus or private vehicles. Traveling along the valley, you will go through areas where it is hard to breathe because of the thin air at that altitude. There are mountains covered with perpetual snow and wild grass on the slopes of one side named the "white cordillera", and on the other side another mountain range of mountains which is mostly dry, dark green or barren contrasting in color to which they owe their name "black cordillera". It is thus described as the valley of the "black and white cordilleras". The entire area is sprinkled with some of the richest gold and silver mines in the world, which are actually in operation even today.

Lake Conococha at the beginning of the White Mountains on the road to Huaraz.

Cañon del Pato, Ancash Peru

Cañon Del Pato, Ancash, Peru

The richest gold mine today, is owned and operated by a Canadian company. I am told that the gold is of such purity that, in spite of good existing surface roads, the gold is flown out by helicopters or small planes due to safety concerns.

In the "Callejon de Huaylas", there are basically only two seasons, the dry season from approximately May to October and the rainy season the other half of the year. The temperature will vary according to the height of the location from sea level. There is sunshine year around, and as you descend in the valley toward sea level, the vegetation gets richer and the towns exhibit an array of palm trees and tropical fruits and flowers. Although tourism is not developed to its potential, it is a popular destination for Europeans and Americans, and has recently been discovered by Asian tourists, as well.

Huascaran Mountain 6,767 meters above sea level, fourth highest mountain in the world.

CHAPTER 7

THE PAINFUL YEARS IN SCHOOL

Upon my return to Huaraz, in the fourth grade, I was enrolled in a public school upon my own pleading. The private school I had attended so far was co-ed and was attended mostly by people of a little higher economic status. The children from the private school were known by the public school children as sissies. When I returned from Yauya, there were some children who knew I had attended a private school, and I was frequently teased by my new schoolmates. That was when my problems began. I could not tolerate anyone calling me names and in particular a sissy. To make matters worse for me, I was the smallest kid in my class—partly because I had skipped a couple of grades and partly because of my genetic make-up—and my uncommon names. My registered name was Rolando Bernui. Most Peruvians feel proud to be of Inca Indian descent. My name didn't indicate that I was of Inca descent.

I was picked on by just about everyone, but particularly by the bullies in class. Some of them already had the reputation of being bullies. They had had instructions at home from older brothers and even parents about different types of street fighting, from the regular fist fights to Roman Fighting and Kickboxing. I had none. However, since I was never a push over, I was engaged in fights almost daily. Unfortunately for me, I spent most of the time kissing the ground. Seldom a week went by that I did not come home with bruises and/or black-eyes.

When questioned by the family I always offered some type of explanation from blaming it on accidents to the result of rough play in soccer. I was not about to be pushed out or quit school, but there were times that it got so bad that I could hardly wait for school vacations or the end of the year. Sometimes I would lay awake at night crying myself to sleep or praying, but I always hid it from everyone in the family and my friends. Frequently, I drew strength from memories of my mother and I felt that someday I would have the upper hand in the fights.

One day I overheard one of my aunts, who was visiting, say to the relatives I was living with, that it is not normal for a child to be so bruised up so often. She demanded that someone go to speak to the school authorities, to which my other aunt answered, "Rolando is his mother's son, feisty, undisciplined and stubborn, and I would not be surprised if most of it is due to well-deserved disciplining by a teacher." My aunt insisted that she should go and find out anyway. As soon as I had a chance I rushed to my aunt and told her that I had heard her talking to my other aunt, and pleaded that if she really loved me not to go to my school. I played down the events and told her that if she went to the school and talked to anyone, sooner or later the story would come out and it would just make matters worse for me. I would be accused of being a no guts sissy and a helpless cry baby. She smiled and promised me that she would not go to the school if I promised her that I would spend at least part of my summer vacation in Lima with her. I enthusiastically agreed, (anything to get away from school and the town for that matter). Lima, the capital city of Peru, with fun places to go and many beaches to choose from, would be the icing on my cake.

Once vacation time came, I went to Lima, historically known as "The Pearl of the Pacific". It is a much bigger city than Huaraz, and had endless places to go—nice beaches, museums, and international soccer games, just to name a few! I was a very good soccer player and soon had an army of friends in Lima. We played soccer in the streets using rubber balls to prevent (really, minimize) breaking glass windows. Fortunately in Peru, most windows have wrought iron works around them!

Soccer games would frequently get heated, and players of the opposing teams would try to take me out and we would wind up in free-for-all fights. But this time they were fights between two groups of kids rather than one-on-one. Some of my teammates were accomplished fighters and they taught me how to fend off or reverse situations. For the first time I learned how to use my head and my feet in a fight, with the same skill and accuracy as in soccer. I already was familiar with the hillbilly fighting styles, like holding a rock inside your fist to make it heavier or pick up sand or dirt to throw into the opponents eyes, if you hit the ground during the fight.

I did not look forward to going back to the mountains, so I asked to be enrolled in one of the best known public high schools in Lima, Guadalupe. It was also known for trying to be too progressive, which was a negative factor for traditionalist parents. The school was also a boarding school for out of towners like me, or even if you had family living in town. I really liked the idea because it presented me with another option as to where and with whom I would live.

Unfortunately for me, two months after school started, the boarding school students went on strike, (can you imagine anywhere in the world, high school students going on strike?) demanding better food, more facilities, and more free time. The school authorities dismissed their demands and laughed it off as an insane student attitude. Obviously, there was outside influence caused by government political groups trying to interfere. Unfortunately, the student groups had been infiltrated by some older trouble makers with political agendas. They were attempting to embarrass the school authorities with political appointments, which consequently affected the country's government.

My family, being very strict disciplinarians, decided that enough was enough with that kind of nonsense and dragged me back to Huaraz to finish High School at the Colegio Nacional, "La Libertad", where I had started as a freshman.

Although high school would open a new chapter for me with new friends and teachers, I soon was faced with the same dilemma, the presence of some bullies. By this time I was considered to be a good little athlete, had friends on my side, and I was better prepared to protect myself.

School fights for the most part were arranged by other students almost as a means of entertainment. There were some unwritten rules for the events. Fights were all arranged to take place out of school hours and school classrooms if possible, fights took place in areas such as playgrounds, empty lots, park grounds, etc. and in front of a crowd. No weapons or objects of any kind, just bare hands and fists. No kicks in the abdominal areas or below the waist, and no hitting if the opponent was on the ground. Any infraction of these rules, and the culprit got a bad beating from the crowd.

There were times that I spent mostly laying on the ground eating dirt again, perhaps crying, but never giving up, to the point that I would win by default. They would think that I was growing mad, and some kids began to be afraid of me. The crowning episode came one day in the classroom just after the teacher had stepped out and we had a 25 or 30 minute break before the next teacher would come in. In my class there was a well-known bully who was also known for mouthing off at the teachers. He stood about 4 to 5 inches above the next tallest student in class and would roam the classroom picking on, hurting, or just plain abusing other kids. His name was Hidalgo. I tried to stay away from him.

I was known to be very sensitive about keeping my clothes, as well as my desk, clean. The teachers liked me and frequently made comments about how I always looked well-groomed and clean. Our desks had ink wells and the old style pens that you dipped in them. One day, as Hidalgo passed by me, he said, "Look here everyone the teacher's pet. Doesn't he look neat and clean? Gosh, today his mother must have forgotten to comb his hair." He messed up my hair, took my pen and dipped it into the ink well, and shook it all over me and my clothes. I looked at him, mad, and the room got painfully quiet. I pushed him away and called him an SOB. He got his balance back and asked me what had I called his mother? (In those days anything said about their mother or even just implying something, were the biggest insults ever and always led to a bitter fight). I was still so mad and ready to cry and I repeated it even louder. "You are son of a bitch." He came running at me and I climbed on top of my desk, he came after me chasing me from desk top to desk top. He yelled for me to say my prayers because even the approaching next teacher wouldn't stop him from killing me. I got to a corner desk and when he thought he had me cornered, he reached to grab me and pull me down. At that time I kicked him with a scissor kick landing one foot in his extended arm pit and landing another kick on his jaw. He landed on the floor, unconscious. It scared me to death! I jumped down from the desk, put my arms around him and with tears streaming down my face I fanned him with my hands. I apologized to him and tried to help him to regain consciousness. My classmates and I thought that I had killed him. In the middle of the commotion the teacher came in and asked what was going on. The teacher called for help from the school nurse, but by the time she got there, he had gotten up, and told the teacher "I fooled everybody, I was playing with my friend Rolando and I pretended that I fainted," and everyone laughed. No one ever told the real story to the school authorities. The classes ended for the day. Nobody knew what would happen next. My classmates quietly huddled around me. No one condemned me for it, quite to the contrary, I felt they all were ready to come to my help and jump on him should I have needed it.

Days went by and then weeks, and no challenges. The word got around that I had floored Hidalgo. On one occasion a small group of us had gotten into a heated argument that had become loud, over a foul in a soccer game. Hidalgo rushed over and asked what was going on? No one answered him, so he said, “If anyone has a beef with Rolando, he will have to answer to me as well.” We all got speechless and as he walked away, the rest of us just had a small chuckle. As time went by Hidalgo and I became good friends and occasionally he would ask me to help him with some of the school work. From then on nobody else picked on me or arranged fights for me. Years later I heard that he had become a very popular Physical Education Teacher. I went on to college with the intention of becoming a physician or a dentist. I have not heard about him since.

CHAPTER 8

TRYING TO MAKE MONEY

Since Uncle Roberto, was my guardian in charge of all my financial needs after my mother passed away, he collected the money from all the sources of my inheritance. Yauya was three days away by horseback, and Uncle Roberto was very busy with his work. His Parish was composed of a variety of towns and hamlets three to eight hours away from each other by horseback. He would frequently let people get away without paying rent and other payments that needed to be made to him on my behalf. These payments were to take care of all my educational and personal expenses. He either sent the money to me personally or he made direct payments for all of my expenses. So, every now and then, when he had not collected the money or he was in some remote location in his Parish, he was late in sending me money for my personal expenses. Much like my mother, I never asked for money from anyone, so when I needed money badly I always seemed to find a way to earn enough money to hold me up during tough times.

When I was 10, selling newspapers was the first thing I learned. I had to have some money for the deposit, to get the papers. Five Soles was a lot of money for me then, and that was the minimum deposit for a stack of 100 copies. I also had to get up at 4:00 a.m. to get to the bus station on time to pick up the newspapers brought from Lima to Huaraz. I would hit the streets running in my play clothes, and I had figured out the best streets and places to sell. I discovered that businesses, stores and restaurants were great! Usually by 7:30 a.m. or so I was done selling. Weekdays and Saturdays, my classes did not start until 9:00 a.m. so I had enough time to sell before school. I was the youngest, and only occasional paper boy. Everybody was nice to me.

Another time I found a recipe for making shoe polish. I thought that since everyone wanted their shoes to look nice, that making and selling shoe polish would be a good way to make money. I bought all of the ingredients and mixed up a batch. I had some containers to put it in, but I didn't realize how much this recipe made. So I had shoe polish in every empty container I could find. Then I had to market it and found out that selling it wasn't as easy as it sounded. So I ended up with enough shoe polish to last me a lifetime!

During this same time period, I heard about the carrier pigeons that were used by the Army to send messages during World War I. It sounded like it would be fun to train some pigeons to send messages to my friends. So I caught some pigeons and my cousin Hugo Palacios and I trained them and it worked pretty well. I didn't earn any money from it, but it was fun!

At one time, we had a large house in Pariahuanca, (a little town near Aco), the last access point for trucks to Aco and points beyond. We raised and sold chickens, eggs, grains, and potatoes to visiting merchants (road salesmen). We also sold other products like coca leaves to local workers in the area, mostly Indians who did not speak Spanish, only Quechua, which I spoke fluently.

One time when I was 11, Aunt Luz, who used to live in the house in Pariahuanca most of the time, was away, and I was left alone in charge of the maids and a couple of farm hands. One day an elderly Indian lady showed up, and asked to buy some potatoes, corn, and some coca. She untied an old handkerchief that she had used to hide a bunch of coins, and opened it to pay me. I realized that she did not have any idea of how much she had, but it was obvious to me that she did not have enough money to pay for even part of it. I felt so sorry for her, that I added a few more things for her, a couple of brown sugar cakes, called chancaca. I told her that was her yapa, which means bonus. She then checked her purchased items and did not see the coca leaves. She insisted that she needed the coca leaves that were not there, and pushed back the wheat. I asked her to forgive me for overlooking it and added it to her bag. I picked only a few silver coins from her handkerchief and told her that it was all that she needed to pay. As she wrapped up the rest of her coins, she picked up a large copper coin, nicknamed un gordo, and put it in my hands, and folded hers over mine. She said, in broken Spanish, "Que Dios te lo pague" (it literally means "May God pay you," but it is interpreted as "May God bless you"). She kissed my hands as she left, pulling her little burro with her small load.

Towards the end of another week, a merchant pulled up in a small truck, asking to buy some chickens and eggs. He went to a small barn and garden we had across the street from the house to assist in catching 10 chickens, and gathering about two dozen freshly laid eggs from under the bushes in the garden. He had neatly tied up 5 chickens each by their feet on a string. I had been wondering how in the world he was going to carry 10 chickens without using cages. Soon after paying me, he asked if we had ever considered taking the chickens to Lima to sell, which of course we had not. He offered to provide the transportation on a profit sharing basis, and to contact him if we were interested. The idea kept bugging me, and I tried to analyze the possibility of doing it. I knew that right after the high school term ended, I had to go to Lima to look into applying for exams to gain admission to the University of San Marcos. Since I had to go to Lima anyway I could have free transportation and make some money at the same time if I took the merchant up on his offer.

So, I contacted the merchant, and after finishing the plans I was picked up in Pariahuanca by the merchant/truck owner, who already had almost a truck full of goods loaded up. I was a little put off when I saw him, and I asked him where we were going to put the 40 chickens, and other stuff. He replied not to worry! While I was making arrangements with the workers and locking up, he had put the cargo on metal frames on top of the cargo area, and put a tarp on top. He had already finished putting everything neatly and securely and was ready to roll.

After a long six hour drive we came to a point on the road near Lima called Pasamayo. This area is constantly menaced by sand storms. The highway is reduced to one lane in each direction and traffic is reduced to about 10 miles an hour, with road crew workers sweeping the road surface from constantly falling sand. The road at one point has a deep and sharp cliff down to the raging waters of the Pacific Ocean, and a solid rock formation covered with sand at the other. It was very dangerous, but we made it through there. We finally arrived in downtown Lima and headed directly to the City Central Market. (Mercado Central). After a couple of hours of calm, the action starts with vendors and buyers arriving. My partner the driver and his helper, rolled up one side of the truck's tarp cover to expose to view the chickens and whatever else he was selling. It did not take very long to sell everything and divide our profits, and then he drove me to my home in Lima. When I got home I was so tired that I think I slept for 12 hours straight!

After a few days of calm, I started to evaluate my recent venture. I came to the conclusion that what appeared to be a great profit maker upon my initial evaluation, would not be so great if I had considered the initial costs of raising the chickens. It was a great experience, but I decided that I would not be doing it for a living, under the conditions that I just described.

Since I did not need extra money badly, I decided to be more frugal and manage my money better by putting some aside for those harder times. I concluded that I should put all my energy into my studies, to the point that I became too competitive later on during my professional career.

CHAPTER 9

SUMMERS ON THE FARM

Summer was a busy time in the rural areas of the mountains. Everyone was busy with farm related activities, planting some crops and harvesting others, farming is year round due to the moderate climate there. Recreational activities are centered on summer events. Male children help to oversee the farm workers. In our family we had 15 to 20 workers, who lived in small huts on the farm. They would come early in the morning for their meal and for their ration of coca leaves before going to perform their assigned chores. They had an assigned cook, usually one or two of their wives, and we supplied the staples. They cook the food in large clay pots using wooden utensils. The food was served in dishes made out of gourds, called mates, and eaten with wooden spoons called weeshllas. They would sit on the ground, on rocks or wood stumps in a circle-like manner. The food depended on what was in season, such as in corn season, corn was used as the major ingredient, in potato season potatoes were the main ingredient. The dishes they prepared were never dull, the cooks were ingenious in using wild plants and spices. For lunch, the workers carried a small pouch which the cook would fill for them, usually with some roasted cereals such as corn, peas or lima beans. The most popular was cancha, the roasted corn like we carried on our trail rides.

The evening meal was similar to the early morning meal. At both meals, soups were the main dish. Most of the meals were boiled or roasted over an open fire with very little fried food. Meals were early morning, a break at noon and in the evening at sunset, before dark. Our family meals were breakfast around 8:00am, lunch at 12 noon, tea at 3:00 pm and dinner at 8:00 pm.

My main job was as an overseer, but I was also responsible for dispensing a handful of coca leaves to each worker into their upside down hats. The workers were all very nice people. They liked me because I spoke Quechua, their language, and I played soccer with their children using balls made with rags and strings. I often lined up with the workers to get food, and sat on the floor to eat with them. Sometimes the family would be looking for me at meal times and find me eating with the workers. The Indians would just laugh when I was whisked away from them.

I learned a lot from them, they are very resourceful in every aspect of life. I learned a fast and simple way to build a hut as a shelter for sleeping or as a mobile home using materials which are readily available in the wild. I also learned how to repair or sew clothing without the use of thread and needle, how to cut, grind or liquefy things using different types of stones without appliances or tools, how to dress and stop the bleeding of a wound using herbs. I learned how to use different types of cactus for making ropes, light weight beams for construction, floor mats, and detergent for washing hair and clothing. They also taught me how to use cactus as a source of food and water for the animals and people, how to trap and hunt with cloth slings, using a waraka. I learned how to make clay vessels and baskets using bush branches, carrizo, and bamboo and many more useful things. Most of my friends and relatives never learned any of these things. For fun, I learned their music and dancing, making music and rhythm with readily available objects. I also learned about their fears, demons and superstitions.

Much of this is hard to put in writing for a two finger typist trying to learn modern technologies in his 80s and still trying to learn easier ways to earn a better living.

Huaraz after reconstruction from the disaster in 1941

CHAPTER 10

THE WORLD WAR II DAYS

I was in high school during the World War II days in Huaraz, but I usually spent most of my summer in the city of Carhuaz with my Uncle Samuel, who was a physician. We lived in the old, large family home of my grandparents along with my aunt Estella. From time to time Uncle Roberto would come and stay with us for a few days when he wasn't riding, on horseback, to the small parishes he served. Uncle Samuel had two children, Victor Samuel known mostly by the nickname, Polo, and Mercedes, whose nickname was Meche and their mother, Uncle Samuel's wife, Haydee. Aunt Estella had a son, Silvino, who was older than most of us children. He was an accomplished soccer player and had just graduated as a teacher, eligible for a position as a School principal. He would also come and live with us from time to time. Life with the family was interesting. Most of the men spent much of their time with farming related matters. The wives and children spent much of their time with social and church related activities. One of the things I enjoyed the most was riding my horse to Huaraz, a 2 to 3 hour ride, to go to the movies. Uncle Samuel's daily routine included Hospital rounds starting at 6:30 a.m. every morning, till 9:00 a.m. followed by breakfast and getting ready to see patients at his private office at 10:00 a.m. He had me following him around everywhere and explained to me, to the extent of my ability to understand, the different ailments and possible causes for his patients' conditions. After a while I was allowed to work with the medical technicians drawing blood and helping run some basic tests at the Hospital Lab.

Lunch was usually at home, served between 12:30 p.m. to 1:30 p.m., for the entire family which included his two children and his wife. Starting around 2:00 p.m. in the afternoon he made house calls while we children, along with other children of friends and relatives in town enjoyed playing soccer, table tennis, volleyball or other activities. There was also a small club house where we hung out playing chess, card games or spinning records. Around 5:00 p.m. was tea time. The whole family gathered again mostly at home, but frequently at one of our relatives or friends families' homes. My favorite place to go for tea was to the home of the Aunts Mejia, who along with the tea, served coffee, or hot chocolate with small sandwiches and pastries. At around 6:00 p.m. we all returned to our work related activities, visited with friends or shopped. At home dinner was served after 8:30 p.m. or 9:00 p.m. with the whole family present. The conversation at the dinner table focused on news we all had gathered during the day and kind of an update on our activities and plans. After dinner we would break-up into small groups to pursue conversations on subjects of interest to the individuals, or dig deeper into people's stories, or current events.

Uncle Samuel would frequently persuade me to listen to the world news on the radio with him. With a large map of Europe and the world we followed the developments of World War II, which was raging on at that time. We would listen to radio BBC from London followed by Radio Berlin from Germany and The Voice of America from the U.S. We had huge world maps hanging on the wall on which we would follow the war. The large newspapers published in Lima would reach us early in the evening with big headlines that were not necessarily the same as the news we had heard on the radio.

At the beginning of the war, it appeared that Germany had gone mad and was committing suicide by going against giant and powerful Russia, the preparedness of the French army and the mighty power of England on the seas. The giant strides and fighting power of the Germans captured the attention of most. It is common for people to root for the underdog, in this case, Germany. Local children of German ancestry made news volunteering to join the German army. In a short period of time Russia was converted into a paper tiger, that had it not been for the severe winter, they would have fallen miserably to the Germans. The famous French "Maginot Line" was taken without much effort. London was being bombarded with rockets from across its oceans. Then the Japanese made the big mistake of "waking up" a sleeping giant, "The USA", on December 7, 1941, when they bombed Pearl Harbor. The massive transformation of the USA into a war machine would soon, not only impress all the powers of the world, but also change the odds of the war with the final triumph of the Allied Forces.

CHAPTER 11

SURVIVING A DEVASTATING AVALANCHE

In Huaraz on December 13, 1941, one week after the bombing of Pearl Harbor by the Japanese, early in the morning on my way to school, a deafening thunder and dark clouds and smoke started rising on the western side of the city. People were running in panic shouting, "the Japanese are bombing us in retaliation for abuses and internment of their people. Run towards the mountains and hide". People were yelling at the top of their lungs. A nearby sawmill blew its alarm whistle constantly until it suddenly stopped. Along with others, I ran toward the nearby mountain and reached there just as some of the dust and smoke began to settle down. Rumors ran rampant, but nobody knew what was really happening. Some said that a new volcano was erupting from one of the nearby mountains and judging by the devastation, it seemed to originate at the level of the glaciers. Others still attributed it to a bombing of the lakes at the foothills of the snow-capped mountains. Whatever started it, it caused a massive avalanche which wiped out ¾ of the city. At one point, we all saw clearly in the distance, a massive concrete and stone structure, it was a tourist hotel which had just been completed and was the pride of the area. The people staying there, and others who had taken refuge inside, had all crowded on the roof top. For a short time it appeared that they might be spared, but then a giant second avalanche wave of rocks, mud and water lifted the hotel from its foundation, much like a ship emerging from the ocean. It was carried downstream where the previously small river merged with the Santa

River like a letter T. We could see the desperate people perched on the roof top while it was being carried away down the river perpendicular to the black mountain range. It then collided with the massive black cordillera wall and disappeared leaving just dust, smoke and muddy water.

Most of us spent two days and nights just waiting to find out what kind of phenomenon had occurred and waiting to see whether it was safe to go back to our homes. There was plenty of clean water coming down from the glaciers, but for food, people just grabbed whatever was in the immediate vicinity, sheep or fowl, then slaughtered them and roasted them over open fires, which also kept us warm at night. Some people were afraid to go back to their homes because there were fears that the avalanche might have been caused by earth tremors common to the area. On the third day it appeared to be safe to return just to find the heart breaking realities of flood damaged homes at the edges of the avalanche and over half of the town gone. Homes were buried by mud and giant granite stones leaving that part of town at a much higher elevation than it had been. Previously, it was considered the lower elevation of town. Finally, massive help started arriving. The army corps of engineers arrived as part of a rescue plan by the government. They built temporary small bridges and cable chairs over small ravines and small, swollen rivers which crisscrossed the affected area. I attempted to get to my house to no avail. It had been completely wiped out, along with everything we owned, without a trace. Nearly 70% of the city was gone. Family members had scattered and only weeks later we would find out each other's whereabouts. The massive avalanche had continued from Huaraz downhill following the course of the Santa river bed towards a canyon and eventually the Pacific Ocean destroying towns, farms and industry in its wake. Thousands of people were left homeless, penniless and in despair. The world was in the middle of the Second World War, so we could not expect much help from any nation.

Although I am sure there might have been some token help, my family and I saw none. Worse, we couldn't locate each other or the land where our house had stood. The avalanche brought down rocks the size of buildings, and the muck that came along had changed the location and the course of the river. The old river bed was 20 to 30 feet higher than it had been previously and the surrounding banks had been overrun. Since I had no place to live and was unable to find any relatives, I decided to walk to Carhuaz.

I stopped at night when I would see a house or a hut and ask if I could stay until morning. Everyone was very helpful and invited me to eat with them. After 2 ½ days of walking alone along trails up and down mountains, I arrived in Carhuaz where my family was distraught for not having heard from me or anyone in our house. An aunt who was living in the house with me had gone to Lima just a few days before the avalanche and two house keepers were eventually found alive and in good health. Nothing seemed to matter anymore. But, the joy of being with the family again made all the bad memories and pains slowly go away.

My high school had sustained minor damages, and reopened its doors six months later. I was unaware of the missing students in the whole school, and only three students from my class did not return. I never found out if they had been killed or just gone to schools elsewhere.

The school year usually ended between December 10th and 15th, and students were allowed to go home until the 1st week in April of the following year. I spent most of the time at our houses scattered in Carhuaz, Pariahunca, Aco and Huaraz, all of them were within 40 miles of each other in The Callejon de Huaylas. The only organized sport was futbol (soccer) and teams from each town traveled to play each other, usually for some kind of festival.

The country homes have a walled area where there are mixed activities, such as, herb gardens, fruit trees, flowers and bushes and in some places there is just grass and wild vegetation. We had a flat area where we used to raise one or two lambs for consumption when they were big enough.

We boys enjoyed training the rams to charge with head butts, to simulate bull fights. After the ram was trained, when anyone entered the Huerta, the ram would run to meet them, but would not attack you unless you waved a towel in front of him. If you accidentally or purposely did that, the ram would back up about 10 or 15 feet and come at full speed to head butt the towel with full force. So we used to play bull fighting to amuse ourselves, friends and family. Most of our friends and family who had never lived in the country had never heard of such a thing. One vacation time when I was staying in Pariahuanca, a lady friend of the family from Lima came to visit Carhuaz. She wanted to visit the farm and spend the night in Pariahuanca to enjoy some time in the country, where food is prepared on wood stoves, bathing and laundry are done in the creek and for the bathroom you go behind rocks, bushes or anything that would offer some privacy. Well, the lady arrived with a family member late one afternoon and we gave her a short walking tour of the house and garden. As daylight began to give in to the darkness of night, we first lit candles and later on some kerosene lamps to increase light, because at that time there was no electricity in the mountains. After finishing dinner we sat on the porch telling or listening to someone's ghost stories that never fail to come up. Then we all said our goodnights and went to our beds for the night.

The next morning everyone got up quietly in their own time to start gathering around the dining room table for breakfast that was prepared by Aunt Luz and the cooks. There are a couple of wash bowls on stands, each with a large jug of cold water and a bar of soap on the stand and a towel next to it for anyone who wants to use them. The lady guest emerged from her room and rushed to the housekeeper and asked where the bathroom was, the housekeeper pointed to the door to la huerta. She went into la huerta and came out shortly after to ask someone else, who explained that there was no bathroom and that she should go to the back part of the garden and find a spot that was behind the bushes. Well, she didn't. Instead she raised her skirts in a rather clear area, the ram grazing nearby saw someone waving a towel, so to speak, backed up and charged, hitting her with full force with its head! We all heard a bloodcurdling scream and as we were rushing to her aid, she got up and the ram seeing her skirts again, hit her again. Most of us children laughed, but the adults were occupied helping the lady, whose major injury was to her pride. Uncle Roberto ordered that the lamb be slaughtered. We children were all upset, and the lady guest refused to eat anything and asked to be returned to Carhuaz as soon as possible so that she could return to Lima.

As we grew older the children of the family began to disband going to different schools. For me it was Huaraz. I already had some friends from my elementary school days. We were all fanatic fans of American western movies, such as, The Lone Ranger, Roy Rogers, Gene Autry, etc. Whenever possible, when I was visiting Carhuaz, that's the kind of games we played. The family of one of my friends, the Valdarama's, lived on the outskirts of town and had lots of horses. One time we decided to play cowboys and Indians with real horses, riding bareback and using ropes for lassos. At one point one of the "Indians" caught me with a lasso and pulled me off of the horse landing me on by butt. It happened near their house. I could barely stand up as he passed me going fast because he was being chased himself. I crawled into a small adobe building where the family used to store newspapers and magazines, which in those days, were prized possessions. As I was hiding I came across another friend, who was also hiding. He told me he didn't want to play anymore. By then, the boys who were playing Indians had discovered our hiding place. Since we were well barricaded, there was only one door and one small window, they broke the window and started shooting flaming arrows through it. One of the family's servants, who was living there, had a lot of authority over the children and he told the brothers to stop immediately and that he was coming out with his whip to take care of all of us. I quietly skipped out and went back to Pariahuanca and never told anyone. A week later, I went back to Carhuaz. I still didn't tell anyone, but quietly I inquired about any news around town. I didn't hear anything about a fire until just before I returned to Huaraz to go back to school, I heard the story, like old news, that the Valderama boys had almost burned their father's prized collection of old newspapers that were in a small storage shed near their house, but the fire had been extinguished by the house staff with buckets of water. The boys had gotten a whipping from their father that they will never forget!

CHAPTER 12

MY JUNIOR YEAR IN HIGH SCHOOL

Chacas is a city the size of Carhuaz, with a similar layout located on the eastern side of the white cordillera. It was a prosperous city due to its two small silver mines located at the foothills of the cordilleras. There were no highways or roads for motorized vehicles. The silver ingots from the mines were brought to Carhuaz or Huaraz by mule, donkey, horse or even llama packs, for transfer to the seaports of Chimbote, Casma or Callao by trucks or trains, depending upon to which seaport they were going.

Like most towns in Peru, Chacas had a special Fiesta Week, filled with special events. Most small towns have a fairly well equipped brass band. The musicians are local people who volunteer to practice year round to play at events organized by either civic or church event organizers. These events included a soccer game on Saturday, a High Mass at the Cathedral on Sunday morning and a bullfight on Sunday afternoon. The fiesta celebrations usually started early on the preceeding days with dinners, dances and other celebrations. Local residents are very hospitable and invite people from all nearby towns. Because there were no hotels or restaurants to accommodate large groups of people, all visiting guests are housed in private homes with whom they had made arrangements ahead of time. My high school class soccer team, (School Champions of the year), was invited to play the local team of the city of Chacas that week. Our team was invited to be housed by local families who volunteered to accommodate us for the week.

The local soccer teams for events like this are composed of the best players in town, (supposedly students) regardless of who they were. Some of them were obviously well over our age. Their objective was to win at any cost! As scheduled, on Saturday afternoon, the band was playing cheerful warm up songs when our team entered the soccer field. The local team's cheering groups were on one side and the visiting team fans, most of them from nearby towns and visiting family members on the other side.

At about 2:30 p.m., the local government authorities and town dignitaries and other celebrities, entered and took their seats. By then the anxious soccer fans started getting louder. Some of them were even dancing on the bleachers or in any open space near them, including portions of the lined playing field, until the referees, linesmen and some elected authorities marched to the center of the field. The participating team members were called and the coin was tossed to determine who kicked off first and which side of the field they would defend first. Shortly thereafter the game began. There were two 45 minute halves to be played with a 20 minute halftime intermission. The first half went rather smoothly. The second half began to get heated fast when one of our team members got injured and there was no sanction from the referee. Our team's fans started to get louder and louder and the players became more aggressive. Fortunately, the game ended in a tie, before anyone else was injured. The evening came and each one of us went with our hosts for our evening meal, which is usually characterized by the polite behavior of all guests and the cordiality of the hosts.

On Sunday morning, there is usually a light breakfast, or no breakfast for those who are planning to receive communion during the High Mass at church, which starts at 11:30 a.m. Lunches are a big deal, but are supposed to end by 1:30 p.m., or so, in order to have enough time to prepare for the Bull Fight event.

Most small towns do not have the resources to hire professional bullfighters or the special breed of bulls that major cities have. Major Bull

Fights are international events in many Latin American countries, with finals in Mexico, Peru and Spain.

In Peru the small towns do not have special bull fight arenas like major cities do, so the events are frequently held inside a fenced-in part of the soccer fields. The bulls are usually young, wild bulls that have been rounded up from nearby pastures. The bull fighters are all local aficionados, and/or spectators, who jump into the ring from behind the fence. On one occasion I was one of those adventurous spectators. After watching a couple of volunteers and watching the way the bull charged, I felt confident that I could do better than the previous bull fighters. The brass band had started playing a new inspiring song and encouraged by friends, I jumped in with a borrowed cape in hand. I started to walk toward the bull and called, "Toro", the standard bull call, to get its attention. The bull noticed me soon enough and as I stopped, it charged at a fast speed. I made a clean pass and the spectators cheered. I followed with two more passes. I noticed that the young bull was kind of tired, so I decided to try one last fancy pass called "La Veronica". Unfortunately, I had gotten a little too close to the bull and the horn closest to me hit me slightly on the hip bone. That sent me spinning to the ground. People standing around the fence jumped in to distract the bull and some even grabbed the bull by the tail and turned him around, while others helped me get to safety. The first aid team examined me, I had a small cut a couple of inches long, but no stitches were necessary. I was bandaged up and given a seat on the bleachers to watch the remaining two bulls that were scheduled for the afternoon. That was the end of my bullfighting career!

Plaza de Armas Chacas, Peru

Chacas Cathedral

CHAPTER 13

SHOWERS AND BATHING

When I was growing up, and before I went to Lima to go to college, bathing was not something we did daily. Saturdays were bathing day! We did not have modern bathrooms with fixtures like toilets, showers, or built in lavatories. We had chamber pots under each bed for night needs.

What we had in every house was an S shaped iron stand with a large bowl holder on its top and a smaller ring in the center to hold a large water jug. It had three legs and had a holder for a bar of soap attached to the top bowl holder ring. There was an empty bucket beside it into which the soiled water was emptied when we were finished. The whole exercise was more like taking a sponge bath. First, in the case of children and women, you poured enough water into the bowl to wash your face and hair, then you wet all skin surfaces thoroughly. Then you wet a wash cloth and saturated the entire cloth thoroughly with the bar of soap, and then you scrubbed your face, arms, neck and arm pits with it. Then you rinsed the cloth in the bowl of clean water, and went over the scrubbed areas to remove the soap scum. When you finished you scrubbed the bowl with the cloth and emptied the soiled water into the empty bucket. Then you repeat if necessary. If you wanted to wash your hair, that's what you did first, before washing your face. You could ask the maid for an extra jug of hot water to mix with the cold water. The rest of the body (lower half) was washed in the same manner. We only washed the top half daily, the whole body was deferred for Saturdays. Some of my friends and I would skip some days, washing only the face, hands, and wetting our hair for combing. Some schools had "Inspectors" whose only job was to maintain order and discipline with the students. They also periodically inspected for hygiene by checking your ears, nose and fingernails.

For showers, we had in the house backyard garden a wooden rectangular platform with a soccer goal, where an S shaped iron hook, in the middle of the horizontal bar hung down a large tank with a specially designed chain to pull the shower head, and let bath water from the tank rain down on the bather. The whole exercise was in the open.

Depending on the school year period, this aspect of my life changed periodically. If I was in Aco, Carhuaz, or Huaraz, taking a good bath was a big event. We would gather in a group at mid-morning on Saturday and hire a passenger truck to take us to the nearby hot water spring bathing facilities. In Huaraz we had the hot springs at Monterey, which had belonged to, and had been the home of, my mother's grandparents at one time. It had private rooms and cabins with hot water cement pools the size of an extra-large bathtub. The tub had two small canals, one with hot, and the other with cold running water to refill the pozo (tub), as they called it. It also had a concrete bench built inside the pool to sit on and a plug at the bottom at one end to drain the soiled water after finishing bathing. Inside each cabin there was a large wooden bench and a clothes rack where you could hang towels, hats, shirts, etc. while you were bathing. The ceiling was unfinished with exposed wooden rafters. These resorts are in the middle of some small farming areas in the countryside. It was not unusual to find a snake hanging on the rafters, and on more than one occasion we would notice that someone, in the middle of their bathing would run outside without much cover on them.

Monterey is between the cities of Carhuaz and Huaraz about seven km. from the center of Huaraz going west on the Callejon de Huaylas road.

Chancos, the other hot springs that are nearby, is about seven km. from Carhuaz on the road to Huaraz. The road turns towards the snow-capped mountains after five km. on the way to Huaraz. It is all paved today and what used to take one and a half hours walking, just takes a few minutes now. From Aco and Pariahuanca it's about the same distance.

Neither of the two spas are busy year around. In slower times, mice and snakes find their way into the cabins. The mice are attracted by left over snacks on the cabin floor or in waste containers nearby. Snakes are attracted by the moist, warm air and the mice! More than once I have seen bathers jump out of their cabin after discovering these pests inside. One time one of my female cousins and her friends had just gotten undressed and were ready to get into the tub when a snake dropped down from the ceiling into the water. You have never seen anyone get out of a cabin so fast, screaming and trying to cover themselves with their towels or whatever article of clothing they could get quickly! The snakes are not poisonous, but they certainly can scare you. So it was a good idea to check the rooms and ceilings before preparing to bathe.

In the dry season in the Callejon de Huaylas, we used the creeks or the Santa River to bathe. Creeks usually had some slow areas where the water pooled creating shallow ponds where we'd jump, or swim. Primarily we just had fun in the water until our skins turned pruney and purple. If we wanted to soap up and rinse we used to go to small waterfalls nearby. In Carhuaz our favorite water fall was called "El Chorro" which was about 30 feet high. At its edges it was barely a mist that intensified as you approached the mass of water with a nearly vertical fall. The water was crystal clear and pleasant when the sun was shining. As the rainy season approached we would see heavier clouds and rain at higher altitudes in the mountain chains above "El Chorro". The water would then start to turn murkier as the intensity of the season progresses. On one occasion when a group of us were rinsing off, one of the boys, wanting more water impact stepped into the main bulk of the stream, it was the beginning of the rainy season, and soon we saw him bleeding and got him out of the water. We assume that a small rock carried by the water current fell on his head.

On other occasions during the dry season, we would go to the river to swim. We had some favorite areas that we were familiar with, where the water ran slower and was spread over a wider surface. This one particular area had a huge flat rock near the edge of the opposing shore line. We used to swim to the rock, and sun ourselves before swimming to the other side. I had been swimming there with my friends several times, so I felt confident enough to join the fun. I used to estimate very closely as to where the rock was, and seldom opened my eyes to locate it. Once in the water, I realized that the current was running a little faster, so I tried longer and more frequent strokes. When I got to the rock I realized that there was not enough rock to grasp and it was slippery, so I missed the rock and was too tired to press on to the other shore. The river current increased outside of our usual swimming area, and I remember floating up and down. The friends who had already reached the shore line began to run alongside the river's edge near me trying to reach for me, when suddenly I felt something large just below me; it turned out to be a tree washed down by the raging waters following an earlier storm up the river. I grabbed a branch that was barely visible near the surface and held on tight until I regained my senses. I realized that I was only about 15 feet or so from the shore. One of my friends was near me, encouraging me just to jump towards the shore and that he would catch me, but I would not do it. In the meantime others had gotten long pieces of drift wood for me to grab and then they would pull me to the shore, but I still would not do it. The water current was too fast and I thought that it would drag me down. Finally one farmer nearby had noticed us and ran down to help with a rope. He threw the end of a lasso that I got hold of and I looped it around my chest, I jumped into the water and they pulled me out as I tried to swim. That was the last time I swam in that river.

Rolando in front of Monterey, the former home of his maternal great grandparents, 1944.

Waterfall shower in Peru.

CHAPTER 14

EXPLORING MY INHERITED PROPERTIES AND ENCOUNTERING A COUGAR

High school in Peru lasted for 5 years. During my long vacation from December 15th to April 1st, between my 4th and 5th year of High School, I decided that I should check into the properties that I had inherited from my mother. So I made arrangements to be picked up from Pariahuanca by an "Uncle", German Vega. About six years earlier, when I was about 9 years old, he had offered to buy my mother's house for forty dollars. That seemed like a lot of money to me so I signed the sales papers he gave me and sold it to him. He was now interested in some of my other properties that were away from town. They were down towards the Black River Canyon in an area called "El Temple" where the weather was hot all year around. His property adjoined mine. He had a nice, large house with a large back porch that extended the whole length of the house. It opened into a fenced in area where the cows with calves were kept at night. Beyond the fenced in area were trees, bushes and a cattle grazing pasture. There were probably five or six cows with their calves that were kept there, mostly for the protection of the calves, which were frequently killed and carried away by cougars during the night. When Uncle German and I arrived there, the family was away, probably in Huarmey, a small, oceanside, fishing town. They went there during school vacation where they spent time salting and drying fish to take back to the mountains, particularly for Lenten meals.

As soon as we arrived at the house, we were met by the housekeepers and a couple of workers, who were all excited to tell us that for the last two nights, a cougar had tried to attack the calves and they were certain that it would probably be back that night. So they had moved their own bedding into the house. My uncle had a couple of shotguns in the house, so I volunteered to sleep on the porch that night on a sheep skin with a poncho overhead like a tent, armed with one of his shotguns. I was at one end of the porch near the woods.

It was a bright, moonlit night and I remember waking up with my heart pounding fast because it appeared to be too quiet. The cows were restless and had moved closer to the house, and had surrounded their calves. They were keeping very quiet except for occasionally shifting locations nearby and stomping on the ground. I was fully clothed, clutching my double barrel shotgun, when it got completely quiet for just a bit. That was when I noticed the cougar jumping over the fence towards the calves. But it noticed me and as it turned its head towards me I fired my first shot. The cat fell and as it started to get up, I fired the second shot to its head. My uncle, loading another shot gun and all of the help, armed with machetes, suddenly were all around me. We all kept an eye on the cat, but nobody wanted to get close to the beast. So, holding my reloaded shot gun, I got closer to the animal, whose entire body seemed to be quivering and shot it in the head again at close range. The farm workers skinned the cat for me and stretched it on the adobe walls on the porch to dry. (I kept the skin for several years, even after I married and had children.) We spent the rest of the week visiting small patches of cleared and cultivated land down towards the big, fast running Rio Negro River. It had some short stretches of quiet water which was used during the dry season to pull cattle roped by their horns to the opposite shore to sell for meat to the nearby villagers.

CHAPTER 15

HIGH SCHOOL GRADUATION AND NEAR DROWNING AGAIN

While the academic year, as a rule, in the U.S. is from September of one year, and extends to June of the following year, the academic year in Peru is from April to December of the same year. I graduated in 1945 in December and moved to Lima where summer was just beginning. It was time to cram and prepare for admission examinations to San Marcos University, which took place in March.

This time I was staying with my uncle Gerardo Carrion, who had three children, two boys and a girl, whose nicknames were Tuto, Pina, and Kiko. The oldest boy, Tuto, was one or two years younger than I was. They lived in a residential area where there were very few cars and almost no traffic to worry about, so we played soccer on the paved street. But the grownups did not like it very much. The children were all born in Lima and had lots of friends, but I felt older since I was already a college student. I felt that they expected more of me, so I behaved more seriously and composed at home and in the neighborhood. Besides I had a lot of studying to do for the exams and I was scared to death to fail the entrance exams to the University, because it was extremely competitive. About six blocks or so from the house ran a tranvia (Linked electric buses that run on rails similar to railroad tracks) line that stopped near two of the most popular beaches called "Agua Dulce" and the "Regatas" in nearby Chorrillos. The populated areas in the nearby towns of "Miraflores", "Barranco" and "Chorrillos" ended just before a cliff that dropped to the sandy beach. There were some quite shallow abandoned caves on the cliffs that I found ideal for studying, so I used to get a ham sandwich and some fruit along the way and spent hours reading my books undisturbed.

The lower sandy beaches would soon get crowded in January, February, and March, as summer heat started to intensify. On weekends I used to go to the beach with a group of friends. People would change into bathing suits either in their own private tents or in the beach house. My friends and I usually went walking into the ocean and wave run or swim ashore. As usual, one Saturday morning I went to the beach with my friends. Although there were life guards around, we usually just relied on each other. As we entered into the ocean we used to keep an eye for waves to catch to take us ashore. In one of those times, a friend running a little behind me was yelling for us not to go too far because we were diving to avoid being hit hard by the surf. At one point someone yelled to watch out, and while I turned my head to look I was hit by the wave that carried me to the shore tumbling over and over. I was trying to get my head out of the water, but I couldn't tell which way was up. When I hit my head on the bottom I realized that I was going down instead of up. The next thing I saw was a life guard's face trying to get me to cough. My chest and arms were sore, so I just pushed him away and turned around to lay on my stomach to rest. My friends were all around me trying to talk to me. After a little while it was time to get our towels and go to the beach house to rinse and change into our regular clothes, and go home.

At home the big thing on Sundays was to dress up and go to the main mass at church, and come home for a big lunch. After lunch, we all had different activities, Uncle Gerardo liked to get comfortable, on his rocking chair and read the newspaper, while listening to a soccer game on the radio. Earlier that morning, I got ready for church, and got the newspaper from the front porch for Uncle. Much to my surprise I recognized myself lying on the beach with people all around me. The caption was, "Careless student caught by strong wave nearly drowns". I immediately got a little spit on my finger to moisten the picture and with a small wood stick I carefully removed my face, and put the folded newspaper on the coffee table in the living room. There was a big soccer game to be broadcast by radio that afternoon, so casually I got a chair near the radio. Uncle Gerardo came in and sat in his rocker as usual, got his glasses on and started to read his paper. Squinting his eyes as if he wanted to recognize someone in the picture, he said, "I have to have a talk with the newspaper man to make sure that he doesn't give us newspapers with holes in them", and pointing to the picture, he exclaimed "see, the face is missing here and the other side of the page there are words missing" and just shook his head. Whew! I told myself, I just missed getting a big lecture! But it was not completely over, my younger cousins were trying to recognize some in the picture, and the youngest one said look Rolo, this guy looks just like your friend, and I said, no, it can't be him, he was gone further south to another beach with his family..... another sigh of relief after they abandoned the paper!

Rolando, age fifteen, in Pariahuanca

CHAPTER 16

HIGHER EDUCATION, MEDICINE OR DENTISTRY?

San Marcos University in Lima is the oldest University in the Americas, and the best known in Latin America. It offered a wide variety of fields of studies, but was best known for its first class medical and dental schools. Gaining admission to the partially subsidized government institution with very astringent and difficult admission tests and policies for Dentistry and Medicine were my challenge. The entrance exams were over in early March, and the results published on bulletin boards at the University. When I went to check it, the listing was in alphabetical order, my name was the second on the list. I went home with the news to celebrate and arrange my trip to Carhuaz to inform the family and friends there. After a few days of celebration in Carhuaz and Huaraz, I had to return to the University to register for courses in Pre-Med, since that was the family plan.

San Marcos University in Lima, Peru (Parque Universitario)

Commuting to school was a big problem for those of us who lived in the suburbs. We had to connect with 2 or even 3 bus service lines to get to classes, which were conducted at different locations in town. Because of that my family made arrangements for me to have room and board with the Soliz family, who were originally from Huaraz, and now lived in Lima. Their younger son, Jorge had enrolled into Pre-Dental. He had an older brother, Oscar and two sisters, Dora and Alina. Oscar and Jorge were a little older than I was, but we got along very well.

The huge student population was almost overwhelming to me at first. In time, it began to be less crowded as the student population dispersed into the different professional schools, branching out for specific classes for the different professions. Although I was admitted as a pre-med student, classes were held in conjunction with pre-dent students. I soon found myself leaning more towards Dentistry.

While studying at the University, I went home to Carhuaz for a couple of months or so, every year. All of my childhood friends and relatives lived there, and there were a lot of fun activities not possible in a large city like Lima. My Uncle Samuel would take me to the hospital with him to follow him around during hospital rounds. He was preparing me for my professional life as a physician. I did what was necessary but I did not really like dealing with sick people, nor babies. I did enjoy most of the small surgeries that my Uncle performed, but not the smell of the ether that was used to put patients to sleep. I remember getting very sick at my stomach just from the smell of it.

The big thing that bothered me to no end was how to find a gentle way to let the family know of my feelings in an environment where the norm is to accept the recommendations made by the elders in the family. Uncle Samuel, especially, who had grown closer to me and kind of groomed me to follow in his footsteps would not only be disappointed, but hurt, so once I started my studies in Lima I decided not to go home for the summers. My excuses were that my courses were too demanding and I also had summer classes to attend. I attended all the required courses for medicine and dentistry because I had a very difficult time in making my final decision. One influential fact was borne from my summer time activities and life in general in Huaraz and Carhuaz, the towns where I had lived. It kept coming back into my mind over and over. Our family's social circle of friends included other professional people, among them a young dentist, who would often invite me to his office to observe him in his practice, just to have a broader idea of the health fields. He was not a recruiter for the profession, but was romantically interested in Meche, my cousin, the daughter of my uncle the physician. He became a close friend of mine and visited me occasionally at my uncle's home, where I was living at the time.

From my observations of both a medical and a dental practice, one aspect became obvious to me from the very beginning. My uncle's medical practice seemed to be either older people or the very sick including in his private office. He seldom saw healthy or younger people, with the exception of victims of accidents, or people suffering from acute illnesses. They all reflected their conditions in the way they dressed and their general appearance and attitude. There were few healthy or happy looking patients because in my area, people did not go to see the doctor for minor illnesses until all home remedies were tried and the condition kept getting worse. Uncle Samuel worked extremely long hours and practically seven days a week. The dentist worked only from 9 to 5 and could close his office at will, or take a vacation any time to spend a week or more taking trips in or out of the country. My poor uncle could not. However, I must say that Uncle Samuel thoroughly enjoyed his practice and never complained. Socially and politically he was very influential and was well known in the community and the region at large. My memories of his practice were people's faces. In Uncle's waiting room or in the hospital, reflections of sadness and at times despair, even on the patient's accompanying family members, were on their faces.

A clear contrast to the medical waiting room, was the dental waiting room. It was always full of smiling people, and in general a younger crowd. Even if you could hear some short lasting screams from the adjoining treatment rooms, no one seemed to panic. In fact some would make some funny comment like "oops, that tooth must be wrapped around the patient's jaw bone", or "the doctor needs a softer shoe so as not to hurt the chest, when he needs to put his foot on the patient's chest to pull the tooth out"...and giggle. All and all, and joking aside, I came to the conclusion that I could bear a little less fame and fortune in exchange for a little more fun in life, which would be more suitable to my personality.

CHAPTER 17

GRADUATION AND OPENING MY OWN DENTAL OFFICE

When I was 21, in December of 1950, I graduated and received my two diplomas a B.S. from the Faculty (School) of Sciences and D.D.S. from the Faculty (School) of Odontology (Dentistry). I took my boards in June of 1951.

Rolando's dental school classmates in Peru.

Rolando, and classmates at dental school graduation luncheon, 1950

World War Two had ended in 1945 and thousands of refugees from Europe and other parts of the world had begun to pour into Peru by ship loads. Most Europeans easily adjusted and were hard workers, hungry, and ready to take any job that was available to them, from domestic positions, rural jobs, factory workers to farm settlers. Many of those who were familiar with Peru's geography, opted to receive land and some farming equipment from government agencies and settle in the Amazon region. Many war widows and orphans went to live with families that would take them. Many took jobs below their skill level. Peru is not an industrialized nation thus employment opportunities with industry were hard to come by, so many began to open their own businesses, while others just used Peru as a stepping stone to come to the U.S.

A few cottage industries were born and the country benefited by the influx of the much needed human capital. However, the lack of financial resources limited the potential for large scale industrialization. Although, Peru is a nation rich in natural resources, and intellectuals, it has never attracted the right people to the political arena. It seems that it has often been the victim of inept and corrupt politicians, whose only ambition has been their own personal financial gain. Their shortsightedness and support from people with vested interests, both national and international, soon killed the opportunities for true national progress.

Shortly after I passed my boards, I found a location in downtown Lima, and equipped an office for my practice.

A person who is 5'2" in height and 120 lbs. in body weight, soaking wet, with a baby face to boot, is not exactly an impressive person in the dental professional world where most of the people frequently judge you on their first impression. Unless you come highly recommended by a former patient or someone else that they trust, you don't have much of a chance. An older, heavier and experienced looking professional usually inspires more confidence initially to prospective patients. So I tried to gain weight and even grew a mustache trying to look older to impress prospective patients.

My areas of interest within dentistry were to be able to perform complete transformation procedures for patients with poor appearance due to poor dentition or deformities, such as, cleft palate and prognathic patients, who were often victims of ridicule and frequently characterized in cartoons. These conditions could impact their lives. This type of dentistry involved surgical, prosthetic, and restorative procedures. It didn't take me long to realize that people seeking this kind of service would rather choose professionals who inspire them with confidence and maturity. On the other hand, I experienced that children did not have the same prejudices as their parents and that many of them were more comfortable with me than they were with their previous older dentists. This of course was flattering to me and was a confidence builder and opened the doors in my mind towards the little known field of Pediatric Dentistry, known as Pedodontics at that time. The U.S. was the top nation for graduate training centers of the world, but I had only a very limited knowledge of the English language other than what I learned in High school which was not enough.

Since my practice in Lima was going nowhere, I sold it and moved back to my small town of Carhuaz, up in the mountains, where Uncle Samuel had practiced medicine for many years, and I myself was not an unknown. Uncle Samuel was delighted to see me and the local community received me with open arms when I started my own practice.

My family had frequently encouraged me to consider taking some time to travel abroad for advanced education. I thought that perhaps this would be the best period of my life to do so before settling down completely into a private practice. Most of the professionals that we knew had gone to Europe and had very successful practices when they returned. The few who had come up to the United States of America for specialization never returned. The most popular countries for post-graduate studies before the war were Germany, France, England and Spain. Unfortunately, all of those countries had been involved in the long devastating war and were practically destroyed, so going to Europe was out of the question. In the Western Hemisphere, the U.S. had begun to make headlines in the scientific and literature fields and had colossal military power. A new radio station made its appearance, The Voice of the United States of America" and in the movie theaters a very popular feature was the "Movietone News". The "Movietone News" showed clips of actual war events. The newsmen, and especially the cameramen, were admired for capturing action events that rivaled the Hollywood movies. My friends and some family members frequently attended the movie theaters regardless of the movie feature, just to watch the news which was presented just before the feature film.

In Europe, an exodus was taking place and homeless Europeans were leaving their countries in large masses. Most top German scientists were being snatched away by Russia and America. Others settled in Brazil, Argentina, or wherever they might have had relatives or acquaintances.

The less notable Europeans migrated to our continent just in search of new and peaceful lives in whichever country welcomed them. The war had destroyed their cities, killed their people, and in many cases, had broken their spirits and destroyed their hopes.

During the war years, the U.S. had gained industrial, scientific and military power second to none. The country's image worldwide began to improve year by year, as they helped war ravaged countries to rebuild their economies and their people's lives. That is one thing that separated Americans from most other nations. The Marshall Plan of the American government and a variety of other ambassadors of goodwill, independent of government sponsored programs, enhanced the image of a great nation. There were religious organizations and philanthropic organizations, which sent their people to help enroll American students in foreign schools and universities, in order for them to learn about the lifestyles, cultures and motivational behaviors of people from other nations.

Other such organizations offered scholarships and fellowships at American schools and universities for foreign students to come to America to learn about their lifestyles cultures and motivational behaviors.

An American-Peruvian Cultural Center in Lima, Peru was a cultural exchange center open to the public, where anyone who was interested could learn more about the U.S., their educational system and educational opportunities. This center was a place where both American and Peruvian young people could meet. They also offered free classes in English, as well, for those who were interested. Philanthropic organizations, such as The Fulbright Foundation, the Kellogg Foundation, and The Guggenheim Foundation offered educational opportunities for which anyone could apply.

During my last year at the Dental school, I learned about these three American Foundations that offered fellowships to Peruvians for advanced education in the United States. There was only one slot for dental students in each one of these organizations, so it was very competitive.

I submitted applications to the Kellogg and Guggenheim Foundations in the fall. The application task was enormous. There were many pages to complete in the application forms that I received, in addition to writing my curriculum vita. There were several follow up communications ahead with both institutions, which I continued from Carhuaz. Applicants were supposed to hear from them sometime in the Spring. In the Spring my best friend and classmate, Bernardo Rojas, was notified that he had been accepted by the Kellogg Foundation and I was notified that I had been accepted by the Guggenheim Foundation.

The Guggenheim Fellowship was in the field of pediatric dentistry, and although this was not my primary field of interest, the positive experiences I'd had treating children compelled me to actively pursue this opportunity to come to the United States. So I immediately began to brush up on my very limited proficiency in the English language. I did not have a working knowledge of English, so I knew that I needed to prepare myself before I came to the U.S. so that I could communicate enough to survive. My English was very poor, probably equivalent to that of American high school graduates in any foreign language.

While living in Carhuaz, I had become very good friends with some of the students of a Cornell University group working in the nearby village of Vicos. Vicos had an unusually unchanged population of native Peruvians, which had peaked the interest of Dr. Alan Holmberg, the head of Cornell University's Anthropology department. The population of this small village was unique. Most of the people who lived in Vicos were Indians who only spoke Quechua rather than Spanish. They lived in small huts, made their own clothing, including very heavy weight wool hats, and mostly restricted themselves to their own little community. They are free to leave, but if they want to return to the community they must abide by the customs of the community. They frown upon marriage to anyone outside of their own village. They had maintained their own poetry, customs and language for many generations. There were no industries of any kind or size and they earned their living by working as farm hands at nearby farms owned by middle class people who were bilingual. They did their own small farming, raising a few sheep, chickens, guinea pigs (a delicacy for many Peruvians), cattle, donkeys, etc.

The Cornell project, as I understood it, was to teach the people in this community better ways to take care of themselves. They wanted to teach them to be more self-sufficient, maintain better health habits, manage their resources, get better educations for their children and in general teach them to become part of the larger community where they lived, worked and worshipped.

Most of the members of the Cornell group were about my same age, so they felt it to be safe to become friends with me and become involved in some of our local activities. The younger group of Peruvians were incredibly hospitable to the Americans, while some of the older people in the area were somewhat suspicious of what they might be doing there.

I eagerly sought opportunities to see my young American friends who were living in Vicos to practice my conversational English. I also knew that some of them wanted to practice their Spanish and Quechua with me.

I had already shared with some of the members of the Cornell University group that I was applying for a fellowship at the Guggenheim Foundation in New York City to come to the U.S., and all of them were very supportive. What I did not know was that one of the students was from New York City, and was the daughter of a very successful dental practitioner in the City. Her name was Joan Snyder. She had lived in Mexico for a while, and spoke Spanish fluently. She was very nice, and although she did not need anyone's help in Spanish, she was eager to learn Quechua, the native language of the Indians of the region. She did that by moving into their village and living with them. This surprised a lot of families and land owners living in the area, when they saw a highly educated young woman do that. Some were suspicious that she and other members of the group were members of a communist group engaged in promoting subversion against local land owners. Uncle Samuel, as a physician, and I, as a newly graduated dentist, got to know some of the Cornell people very well. Some of those concerned people did not hesitate to ask if we knew anything about their activities. We told them that as far as we knew, they were here to educate some of the native groups, and we thought getting educated would not change their way of life. It would also help them to find ways to integrate themselves into the society in which they lived. Everyone that I know of had a pleasant experience with them and liked them. In time, two young members decided to live in Carhuaz for a while and so I rented them an empty room next to my dental office. In spite of our reassurances, few local people had invited them to their homes. The American group maintained their distance and most of their families preferred to live in the group compound in Vicos. They were generous with their help, whenever solicited. When Ms. Snyder learned that I had applied for a fellowship at the Guggenheim Dental Clinic in New York City, she helped me with my application follow-up and other related paper work.

CHAPTER 18

FELLOWSHIP AT GUGGENHEIM AND LIFE IN THE U.S.A., (THE BIG APPLE!)

Once I was accepted and traveled to New York, Ms. Snyder's parents took me into their home and helped me to get my own place and settle down. My studies in Pediatric dentistry included a heavy clinical practice which I enjoyed very much. I found that American children were non-judgmental and enjoyed friendship with foreign people.

Among the activities I enjoyed the most was going to the elementary schools in the City in the Guggenheim Clinic bus with the team that offered free dental examinations to students in Public Schools. Upon completion of the examination, Dental Clinic staff would send the results to the children's parents. They were also informed that if they could not afford dental services for financial reasons the clinic might be able to help, and encouraged them to apply. Many of them qualified to receive the necessary dental care at the Guggenheim Dental clinic at no cost to them. Otherwise, most of them probably would not have received any care because of the cost involved. I was proud to be a member of the Guggenheim staff, and admired the Foundation for their thoughtfulness.

Another interesting aspect was the educational, and multicultural diversity of fellows that composed our dental staff. There must have been at least 15 to 20 countries represented, Americans, Europeans, South Americans, Asians, Carribeans, etc. This gave each one of us an opportunity for self-evaluation in preparedness in our own countries. And of course our teachers probably had a good data base on which to judge the preparedness of the applicants from each country.

After I was notified that I had been accepted for the fellowship in Pediatric Dentistry at the Guggenheim Dental Clinic in New York City, I tried to learn as much English as possible, not only to do well at school, but also to be able to communicate and survive in the activities of daily life. I got to the point that I could do fairly well in expressing myself, but being able to understand what other people were telling me, was quite a different story.

I came to the States a few weeks earlier than my reporting date to Guggenheim so I could brush up on my sprouting conversational English. Miami was my port of entry, so I decided to spend a little time getting acquainted there so I could speak a little more fluently in a more comfortable environment heavily populated with Latin Americans. I thought that since in Peru everyone could speak a little English, that surely in the powerful country of America it would be the same. I soon learned that this wasn't the case! I had a hard time telling the taxi driver from the airport where I wanted to go. Then when I went to a restaurant, the only thing I could read on the menu was "Chili con Carne", I knew that was a meat dish so that's what I ordered. For the next week in the heat of Miami, that was all I ate! Finally, I made friends with some Cuban Americans who spoke both English and Spanish. I thought, "it is going to be a snap to get along in this country being able to speak both languages". Unfortunately for me, I found myself speaking Spanish with them and my English improved very little.

Learning single new words daily increased my vocabulary but did not help me too much in constructing phrases properly. For example, "Yo voy a ir a ver la Casa Blanca, the literal translation word for word would be "I am going to see the House White", but most commonly used colloquial expressions cannot be translated word for word. Rather, they are translated by words that convey whole sentences.

I like music and I liked to listen to the radio, or juke boxes, etc., all the time so I decided that learning songs would be a more enjoyable way to try to learn to express myself. So it came easy to me to learn the English lyrics to some of the most popular songs of that time. I thought songs could help me to learn phrases already properly constructed rather than just isolated words. I bought myself a record player and began to buy some 45s to spin. I tried to learn the TOP TEN of the hit parade. Some of the slow song phrases helped, some did not. The first, most popular tune I learned was "Jambalaya". I played it over and over until I learned the phonetics perfectly. I could sing it, but did not know what I was saying. I tried to translate it into Spanish to learn what they were saying that people loved, but to no avail. When I asked my friends to translate it into Spanish, some attempted, but their translation did not make much sense to me either! I didn't realize until much later that most of the words used in "Jambalaya" were Cajun words!

Expressing myself was becoming easier. However, I felt that as soon as I would say something to someone, I was answered with a machine gun-like barrage of words. I probably looked baffled, so a second and sometimes a third barrage of words would hit my ears, to which I frequently responded "please repeat slowly". Most of the time people would be very nice and repeat it accompanied with mimics and hand motions. I knew they were trying to be helpful, so I thanked them effusively, and they tried to help me more. Thus, my attitude earned me many friends.

Time was getting closer for me to report to Guggenheim, so I went to New York City. I was welcomed by Dr. Alexander Snyder and his lovely wife Helen, parents of the young Cornell University student, Joan Snyder, whom I spoke about earlier. They took me into their home until I could find my own place. They were very kind in helping me go through the ads in the paper to find a place within walking distance of Guggenheim's clinics.

Being on my own, my troubles in communication got worse. I had to guess what I was being asked or told. They all were very patient with me, but I felt dumb and stupid at times. I developed a strategy. I prepared and memorized a bunch of sentences in English using the phrases I learned in songs. I used them whenever I guessed it was appropriate, and that often worked very well for me.

On certain occasions, whenever I failed to understand what I was being told, I would find a way to channel my response to something I was comfortable with. At times my responses were like a news reporter interviewing a politician today. The reporter asks the politician a question, the politician seldom addresses the real question, they just jump in and say whatever they want to talk about and say it, with polite smiles, and try to lead the reporter to other topics where they are comfortable. The reporters appear to be pleased with what they thought they heard because frequently they cannot argue with a well prepared statement. Later on the reporters will tell you what ever they thought they heard.

Most foreign students have less problems understanding lectures or discussions of professional matters, than they do carrying on conversations, because they are familiar with the subject matter. The terminology is often simpler, because the words in the English terminology have the same origin or roots in Latin or Greek.

The school year at Guggenheim got progressively more manageable and fun. The Professors, as well as the clinical instructors were great, and the work load both in the classroom as well as seeing patients in the clinic were very gratifying. I liked working with children. I found American children to be great patients, well above their Peruvian counterparts, who I also liked, but who were more difficult to handle.

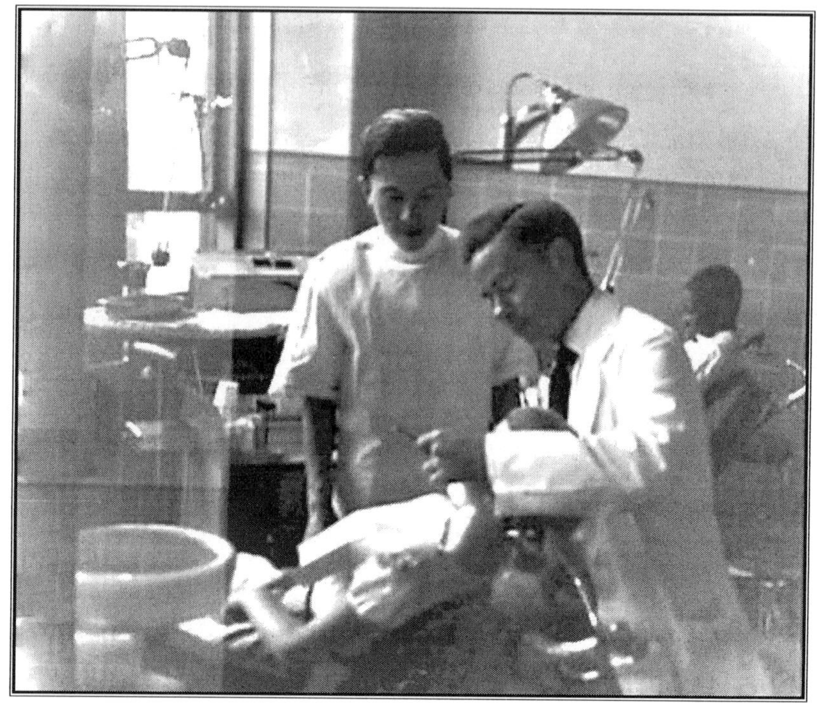

Clinical instructor checking Rolando's work at Guggenheim

Weekends and holidays were particularly fun and educational. The Museums, the Bronx Zoo, The Planetarium, and, needless to say, Broadway shows, Radio City Music Hall, and the Roxy Theater, made New York City the best place in the world to live and get a good education, I thought. I attribute my experiences living there to be the roots of my love for this country.

One unique and undeniably sweet experience I had was being invited by an American family from Pennsylvania for the Thanksgiving holiday celebration. I was not familiar with the Thanksgiving holiday. Thanks to an Organization called the Sonta House, which organized events for foreign students, two of us, a Brazilian fellow student and I, were invited for the 4 day week end. We were picked up by a Dutch family to spend the week end at their home on a farm in Pennsylvania. The house and the outbuildings which we toured were beautiful and immaculately kept, the people were very kind, the food so lavish, and just the whole experience was so touching, that I have never forgotten. On our departure, trying to express my appreciation, I told the family that they had been "wonderful ghosts". They smiled but I think they realized I meant "hosts". Thanksgiving is an American tradition that you can only appreciate if you are fortunate enough to live in this country. You can learn and understand the meaning of the true Thanks Giving celebration.

Even living in New York City, and in spite of my efforts to mingle more with Americans to learn English better, and learn the American way of life in general, I found myself surrounded by Latin Americans and speaking Spanish more often, especially after working hours.

We had over two weeks of vacation coming at Christmas time and I went to spend it in Boston visiting The Forsyth Dental Clinic for children and a couple of other institutions and being immersed in English. That was like jumping in deep water to learn to swim! Although I could communicate fairly well and deliver my message, it was quite difficult to understand what I was being told. It appeared to me people were less friendly in that part of the country than in other areas where I had been. I suppose it is understandable when dealing with strangers and people of other cultures. All and all I had a good experience observing Oral Surgery classes at Massachusetts General and learning about some research projects going on at Beth Israel Dental Clinic. Climate wise I had never experienced such cold weather in my whole life. I thought it was cold in New York, but at least in New York City there were so many places to visit and see, comfortably, even in the depth of winter. Not that Boston did not have similar places, perhaps, in the way of museums and other cultural venues, but getting around was far more difficult. I liked the subway system in New York City and the fun places to go. Upon my return, I was never so glad to be back in New York City. My Latin American friends added to the social warmth which I had gotten used to there.

One of the experiences that I had, while at Guggenheim, stuck with me long after I left New York. I had just learned to drive a jeep in Peru, but had not yet gotten my driver's license when I went to the States. While living in New York I thought that it was the most civilized place in the world to drive. The streets were mostly one way with clear traffic lights, and drivers keeping in their own lanes and not speeding and cutting in. What a difference from driving in Peru, where conditions were the complete opposite. I planned to get my license in New York, but I did not own a car.

Another Peruvian friend who was studying at Columbia University, a Brazilian student, and couple of other friends and I used to get together on weekends. We would usually go to a theater for a show, and then to dinner. We usually had only one check and divided it among ourselves according to what we had ordered, plus the tip. Once, at the end of the dinner, the bill came and it was over what we all could come up with. Somebody had ordered a bottle of wine, figuring that we had decided we could not afford it by the glass, but by buying a bottle and dividing it, we could come to a price that the majority had agreed would be okay. We all had some money at home. We never carried more than what we had assigned ourselves for the day (there were no credit cards then). I lived the closest to the restaurant, so we decided that I would drive my friend's car, with him, to my apartment to get the money. In less than 5 minutes I was stopped by a police car for speeding and going against the traffic. At first I did not think the policeman was very nice at all. My friend (car owner) and I were scared to death. We did not speak English very well. I spoke a little better than my friend, but my friend got absolutely worthless when he got nervous. His upper lip quivered, his hands shook, and he started almost shouting in Portuguese. I could notice the Policeman trying to suppress his smile when he turned away, went to his car, and in a rather pleasant way, he had me turn around and led me to the correct street to go towards my destination. We drove to my apartment and while my friend waited in the car, I got the money and we went back to the restaurant, where the rest of the group was anxiously waiting. As we rejoined the group, we calmly sat down and finished the wine. In looking around, we noticed that the eyes of the waiters were on us. One of the fellows that had been most uncomfortable, raised his hand and asked for the bill. The waiter presented us with the bill, and we could not help but notice that all eyes were still on us. We returned the bill with the amount indicated plus a generous tip. Their attitude immediately changed. They were all smiling, politely asking if anyone wanted more water or anything else. We returned the expressions of courtesy and left the restaurant. After that, anytime I got behind the wheel memories of that experience came back to my mind!

I graduated from Guggenheim in June of 1953 with a Certificate in Pediatric dentistry. My earlier plans were to return to practice my new specialty in Lima, but by then I was comfortable enough reading the newspapers and professional magazines to find a new world of opportunities available in the States and Worldwide. My circle of professional friends had expanded and through inquiries, I began to receive employment offers both from within the country and abroad.

While training at Guggenheim, I remember, rather vividly, receiving a phone call, (the clinic supervisors objected to any interruptions during clinic hours, and our dental assistants were instructed to screen the calls as to their necessity or urgency before interrupting the doctors or they just took messages). My dental assistant, Mrs. Black, a tall sophisticated adult lady, came to me and said "Dr. Bernui, you have a phone call from an important person in booth # 3 in the hallway, but I expect you to come back as soon as possible". I rushed to the phone booth and the lady at the other end of the phone started saying, "This is Lucy Bryan from 40 Wall Street"......before the lady could finish I interrupted and said "just a minute please". I rushed back to my cubical and told Mrs. Black that the call was not for me, but perhaps it was for the director of the clinic. It is WALL

STREET! Mrs. Black rushed back to the phone and came back to me waving her index finger said “It is for you and it sounds important”! At that point I had finished the treatment, but my patient needed another appointment in the Orthodontic department, for which I needed to complete a referral slip, so I said, “I’ll fill out the necessary forms in a few minutes.” I then rushed to the phone and the lady at the other end identified herself by saying “this is Ms. Lucy Bryan from the headquarters of Cerro De Pasco Corporation, a mining company operating in Peru. The director of our main Hospital, Chulec General, Dr. Robert Delafield is in New York City for a brief visit and would like to meet with you to discuss a professional opportunity for you in Peru”. The meeting had to be in a couple of days on a weekend when their offices were closed, but we made arrangements to meet at the Biltmore Hotel near Grand Central Station and she said she would call me with the details.

I returned to my cubical still with a puzzled look, but Mrs. Black brought me back to reality by saying, “Well, I am still waiting for the referral slip for Loraine Burkley, which form do you want?” (we had color coded forms for each department) I replied nervously in my poor English, please bring me the pink shit. Mrs. Black turned pink herself for a few seconds but she understood what I meant, so she brought me the pink “sheet”.

A little later, she came to me with a half-smile and took me by the arm to a quiet place and commanded me “ say sheeeeeeet” I repeated after her sheeeet two or three times, she had the different color forms in her hand, and said “ this the blue sheeeet, this is the yellow sheeeet and this the pink sheeeet, and not blue, yellow or any color SHIT, shit means what you may see or do in the bathroom......manure”.... and she walked away smiling. To this day I try not to use the word or use it continuously in its proper context.

The day came for the meeting with Dr. Delafield. He said he would come down from his room to the Lobby upon my arrival. So when I arrived at the hotel I phoned his room. Since there is usually a big crowd coming down exiting the elevators, he described himself briefly. He gave me the color of his suit and said that he would be wearing a red carnation in his coat lapel. To me that was not quite enough, because too many Americans would fit that description. I on the other hand, typically Latin looking, short, skinny, wearing a blue suit with a white shirt and red bow tie, would perhaps be much easier to spot. Voila! so it happened, a handsome reddish haired gentleman dressed as described by Ms. Bryan, with a beautiful tall lady on his arm were headed towards me before I could recognize him from the description. We had a cordial and productive meeting, during which, he offered me a position as chief of the dental services for the corporation, headquartered at Chulec General Hospital in La Oroya, Peru. In addition to my regular duties, he briefly described my additional duties as chief of the services at Cerro's other mining camp facilities.

After I was contacted by Cerro de Pasco, I had another overseas offer to work for a large oil company in Arabia. I had a chance to meet a dentist returning from there, and after his description on living in a compound, I decided that no matter how attractive financially and the opportunities to see Europe, Cerro's offer was better for me. Subsequently, I accepted the position and signed a four year contract with them.

After I accepted Cerro's offer, all I needed to do was some shopping for my family and friends, finish some last minute errands, and call the Company. So after a few weeks went by, I contacted Ms. Bryan, who was very efficient and helpful. She made all the necessary arrangements for my trip to La Oroya, Peru, including hotel accommodations in Lima before my trip up to the Andes, and my quarters at the Company hotel in La Oroya.

Smelter and refining plant at Cerro de Pasco mining camp, La Oroya, Peru

CHAPTER 19

WORKING FOR CERRO DE PASCO CORPORATION.

La Oroya, at over 13,000 feet above sea level is the lowest mining camp, and where the main ore processing smelters or plants were located. The hospital, staff housing and Chulec General Hospital, are located just a few minutes from each other by car.

The Cerro de Pasco Corporation was an American mining company which had it headquarters on Wall Street. It emerged as the brainchild of American investors in 1902, and was for half a century the dominant force in Peruvian mining. It was one of the biggest sources of income for the Peruvian Government. Cerro de Pasco was responsible for producing a third of the copper, two-thirds of the lead, and 60 percent of the silver and zinc as well as quantities of minor metals such as bismuth (of which it was the world's largest supplier), in the world. Furthermore, in the mid-1950s it gained control of a portion of its rival, SPCC. By the end of World War II Cerro de Pasco was the biggest employer in Peru after the government itself. Cerro also owned a network of haciendas on which it raised sheep to produce milk, butter, and meat for local consumption as well as wool and meat for export.

The mining operations were spread across a large geographical area, with a number of mines grouped in camps. Each camp had its own housing facilities, Clinics, Company stores and Hospitals. Non-company related businesses flourished and small towns formed in surrounding areas to the mining camps.

There were Company operated services for Company employees such as medical Emergency clinics near the mining operations. Cerro, also had some Hospitals in some of the major mining camps, but the large center of Operations was in La Oroya, where their main smelting and Refining was carried out. The main Mercantile Store was located there, as well as "Chulec General Hospital," the largest Company Hospital, and a large housing area with a Club, hotel, restaurant, train station, and other amenities in the immediate area.

The Hospital staff was composed of American, German, and Peruvian Physicians under the Direction of Dr. Robert Delafield, a well-known surgeon. Since I was hired as the Chief of Dental Services for the Company, one of my first jobs was to equip and staff a full service dental clinic at the Hospital. There were three other dentists already working at different camps, including the one in La Oroya. I was hired in New York City with a four year contract, and upon expiration of the term, I was to return to New York City.

The entire period was a very rewarding experience for me. The entire management team starting with Ms. Lucy Bryan in the Wall Street office in New York to the last Camp manager in Satellite Camps, were extremely kind, cooperative, and helpful to me. Therefore, I owe my appreciation and respect to all of them. Many of them had also become my patients and in time became good friends. Some are now lifelong friends and we still keep in touch. One couple in particular, Tom and Beverly Dahl, will be mentioned in this book many times, for we had adventures and memorable trips and other activities together, such as going to many remote and colorful areas of Peru and other nations.

It takes a little while to adjust to living at 13,500 feet above sea level, while doing any type of work, and once adjusted the Company encourages all workers to take some R & R or do some type of work at lower altitudes, preferably at sea level. Many of them took a two hour train ride to the nearby town of Huancayo at 9,000 feet altitude. Huancayo has a very good

Tourist Hotel, good restaurants, and a colorful Sunday outdoor market. Nearby villagers bring their goods, (textiles, ceramic goods, handmade Indian jewelry, vegetables and fruits of all kinds, etc.) to sell. They just take over the sidewalks and roadways to display their goods. Huancayo was also an access to the Amazon region by going through some historic Spanish cities to "Tingo Maria", a river port, so to speak, where river boats of all sizes starting with simple tree trunk dug outs, river rafts built to transport villagers and their goods to market places and larger transportation boats. The larger boats were available for large cargoes and to take passengers to the city of "Iquitos", the capital of "Loreto" the largest department of the 21 departments (states) that compose Peru.

Another close by destination was the town of Tarma, only one hour and 15 minutes from La Oroya. Tarma was a tranquil restful place, with a beautiful Tourist Hotel, about 3,000 feet lower altitude than La Oroya. For mining employees living in the town of Cerro de Pasco, the original main mining camp, it was an even shorter drive. Tarma was also another main entry point to the jungle or Amazon area by going through the the Chanchamayo Valley, a rich coffee growing area, near the towns of La Merced and Zatipo, a town known as the most German town outside Europe.

The Cerro de Pasco Corporation was a unique, world reknowned operation with offices in many countries. There were people of 28 different nationalities working in different types of jobs, but the majority of the labor force was Peruvian. With exception of the indigenous work force coming from nearby villages, employees formed "Clubs" to celebrate some festive occasions, or just for fun reunions. Some were relatively small, some others larger. One of the largest celebrations was Peruvian Independence Day, July 28, at that time it was a 2 day paid national holiday. Within the Company, there were special programs organized, such as; "Pachamancas", an outdoor pit barbecue, very similar to the Hawaiian Luau, as a daytime festivity and for an evening activity, a dinner dance was organized by

Peruvian wives at the "Inca Club" with professional bands playing Peruvian and other popular dance tunes.

The Americans had a beautiful outdoor program on July 4, presented by the "Ganadera" (Ranching) department, that included western rodeo activities, and a dinner dance at the Inca Club.

The third major celebration was the British group. All major mining Camps had similar social activities. The British group was composed of Canadians, Australians, New Zealanders, Irishmen, Scotsmen, and of course, Englishmen. The 4th group was known as the Europeans and encompassed people from all over Europe, i.e, Belgians, Germans, Italians, Dutch, Norwegians, Swiss, Yugoslavians, etc.

La Oroya in the 50s was the center of the mining operations where the ore from the mines was brought, mostly by rail, to be refined, processed, and made ready to be taken to the sea port for shipping. The staff was composed of a vast number of engineers with a variety of specialists and Laboratory scientific research degrees. Some of them had already been living there and working for the company for years, while some came with their entire family and had been promised renewed contracts. American style homes had been built and furnished for them, as it is done for the U.S. armed forces personnel. Most of us single personnel were housed in one of the two Company hotels. Meals were provided formal hotel style. The hotel lobby was a kind of gathering place, as was the Inca Club for those who enjoyed having some drinks after work and on weekends. There was also bowling, card games, music, etc. if you were staying in town. Soon people with similar interests were organizing their own activities. This is how I met a young active American guy who was almost fluent in Spanish. His name was Thomas Dahl and he asked me to just call him Tom, and I answered hesitantly to just call me Rolo, which was my nickname as a kid. (I used to not like being treated or called a kid.) He was from Seattle, had spent some time in Guatemala and experienced living during their revolutionary times. He was an accountant, but I believe deep in his heart he was an "Explorer". He had recently been married in Seattle, and hoped to have his wife join him soon. He did not particularly like social gatherings, nor dances, nor the hotel food. The Hotel was managed by a Belgian couple and had French and Belgian Chefs, and every meal during meal hours was formal. The chefs treated some American short order items with an obvious disdain, particularly hamburgers, hot dogs, and almost all sandwiches. The staff would prepare just about anything when asked ahead of time on non-rush hour, or meal times. This did not fit well with some hotel residents, while for the people living in the private housing area it was a treat to dine at the Hotel.

After my encounter with the police in New York, any time that I got behind the wheel, memories of that experience came back to my mind. So while I was in La Oroya, I only drove my car to work and back or to places within the company grounds, until I got my Peruvian driver's license. Until then I used my international driver's license which I had gotten in Miami with my Peruvian passport.

Some of my patients were engineers, who took me into several mines which were in actual operation. Some of the mines are quite spectacular. The shafts go from the surface in multiple directions. Some of them have rails like train tracks spread in different directions like a maze, where cars go for miles moving equipment, ore, supplies and rocks that have been excavated from the mines. These mine shafts go down thousands of feet, with elevators like those in city buildings. They have stops at lateral shafts on different levels. Sometimes you even see spectacular mine gas fires that have been burning for decades. You can also see fascinating Pyrite crystals that look like mountains of gold, a variety of Quartz formations hanging down, shining like gorgeous chandeliers. You can also hear the constant dripping of water, and the sounds of small currents of drainage water running along the sides of the trails. It was all very interesting.

Rolando in Rock Forest, near Cerro Mining camps, Junin

CHAPTER 20

ADVENTURES WITH TOM AND BEVERLY

Another young American, Donald Kirby, also hung around the club, and joined Tom and I in some activities, such as, bowling, golfing, etc. Eventually our group got larger and included a young Austrian, Manfred Aman, a Swiss fellow named Kurt Lieb and Sampat, an engineer from India. Most of the Peruvian fellows went to Lima to enjoy the big city life. Since most of them had been hired locally at the Lima office, their families and friends were probably from Lima or surrounding districts where their social lives were never interrupted. While those of us already familiar with Lima, frequently visited other places on weekends or traveled abroad on longer vacations. The Company often encouraged continuing education opportunities, with fully paid expenses if justified, or partially funded, according to the applicants explanation to the Company administrators. The Company General Manager's office offered greater incentives to those willing to sign a special contract that upon graduation, they would return to Peru to CdeP for a specified period, continue working in Peru and not seek positions outside Peru, for the benefit of the country. Peru had long suffered a "brain drain" because better financial opportunities would become available somewhere else in the world. CdeP wanted to help Peru by having Peruvians return to home after furthering their education.

Each one of us had pretty much planned our personal future. Our days off during the week and weekend activities were usually last minute decisions. Within my small group of friends we would make short term plans for weekends and vacation times.

Inspired by stories from coworkers about the diversity in climates, sceneries, fauna, flora, and ethnic variations in Peru, many Europeans, especially Germans and Americans, were interested in visiting the jungle, referred to locally as La Selva. La Oroya and Cerro were the two largest mining camps. The roads leading to both were probably the best roads of entry to this vast jungle area, and as far as travel is concerned, they were the best maintained because they had the most traffic going from Lima towards La Selva. Driving down to lower altitude towns or points of interest was easy in spite of the limited number of safe roads.

One of the roads from La Oroya passes through a 15,000 feet high pass in the Andes called Ticlio (It is the continental divide). Waters from the western slopes of the Andes go to the Pacific Ocean and waters from the eastern slopes of the mountains eventually go to the Atlantic Ocean. While the roads to Ticlio are steep in grade, the train tracks use a system known as "Switch backs". The Narrow Gage train tracks are laid in a zig-zag manner. The locomotive pulls the train on a steep climb to a suitable, level place, which will accommodate the total length of the train, (4 to 5 cars), the tracks are then switched to the rails going further up, so the engines reverse and push the entire train like "backing uphill" to another level place, where the process repeats by switching to upward tracks again.

The main road conditions are generally speaking, good. They are narrow with a multitude of curves, so a relatively slow speed must be maintained. Secondary roads are not reliable with rough surfaces, and there is an absence of road side help away from urban areas. So keeping your car in good condition and having good knowledge of the roads is essential.

There were several old archeological burial grounds with stone ruins around the camp and some caves that no one seemed to be interested in exploring. Tom's wife Beverly had recently arrived from the U.S. and was interested in joining the boys on whatever activities that we decided to try. Tom and Bev, were avid readers and soon they had lots of information about all the nearby areas, and we decided we would explore anything that appeared to be interesting, including caves and an interesting area of rock formations referred to as the "Rock Forest".

Tom on mountain overlooking the Cerro foundry, La Oroya, Peru 1957

Not far away from La Oroya we had spotted a large hole on the mountain side that no one knew what it was. Some speculated that it was possibly an abandoned mine entrance, others thought of it as just a geological cave. Tom, Beverly, Sam and I decided to check it out. So one day we hiked to the entrance and about 300 feet or so in, it got pretty dark. We had just decided to go back, when we heard Tom, calling us that he could see some light a short distance away. He was trying to get closer to the light when he realized that it appeared to be an animal. He yelled alarmingly and we all dropped everything and scrambled out of the cave tripping over things and running for safety! Sam said he could hear a loud hissing sound, but we never did find out what kind of animal it was. It could have been some kind of wild cat, or wolf or whatever kind of wild life lived in the area.

On one weekend, Tom, Beverly and I took one of those train trips to Huancayo, a popular tourist destination, as well as a rest stop for travelers to other old historic cities founded by the Spanish conquistadors in their search for gold. People from the countryside living as far away as a day's horseback trip, bring their goods to Huancayo, in the form of woven textiles (mainly llama, alpaca, sheep and vicuna wools) hand carved woods, gourds, ceramics, toys, handmade hats, scarves, blankets, etc., as well as vegetables and fruits for local consumers. They enjoy bargaining and marketers are very good at it. You might find some experienced marketers speaking some English. Most of them accept dollars, or even depending on the size of the market, there might be some Currency Exchangers around. Many large cities have Indian Markets, but many are open on Sundays only. In the country side, generally speaking, the vendors take over sidewalks and streets to spread and display their goods. It is very unregulated, but many tourists like it better that way.

Sunday street market, Huancayo, Peru

Today, Huancayo is also a gateway to La Selva, the origin and tributaries of the great Amazon River. It is also the point where you begin to find navigable rivers, which become the main means of transportation and commerce in the dense Peruvian and Brazilian jungles. There were no roads beyond the city of Pucalpa, but small hydroplanes, however rare, are available by private arrangements. The Peruvian Armed Forces use some of them. For us La Oroya residents, it was easy. One of the major Lima-Huancayo train stops was in La Oroya. It was also very convenient because you could catch a train to Huancayo on Friday afternoon and return on Monday morning on time to go to work. It was a pleasant trip to see new scenery, a more diverse group of ethnicities, cultures, foods, dances, local music, and of course the famous outdoor Indian market (American fair style).

The access road to La Selva continues southeast following the curvatures of the rivers except for areas where road construction is not too costly. It is practical for commerce in the small towns and settlements along the way. Following World War II, almost all Europeans were tired of the devastation and death tolls. Many of the immigrants just wanted to avoid cities of any size and Peru just offered many such opportunities. Although Peru offered everyone a warm welcome, the fiscally poor nation itself could not offer financial help that some other countries such as Brazil, and Argentina could. Argentina, the world's largest producer of cattle and grains (often considered the bread basket of the world during those days of war) would attract the lion's share of scientists and other highly skilled immigrants with work contracts and other incentives. Never the less, there were many of those, whose higher priorities were just peaceful environments and communion with nature, who opted for parcels of land on the Andean slopes entering the Selva. Some people had already learned of specific areas and example communities developed after World War II. One of those that I was somewhat familiar with was "Zatipo", a Selva jewel not too far away from La Oroya.

In earlier years, after World War II, and (prior to the 1950s) a small group of mainly German Immigrants started a small settlement known today as the town of Zatipo, it was a relatively isolated town, with no decent roads, or any modern means of access. This did not deter the new settlers. They had a plan for expansion, and there was fertile land and water available in all directions. The climate was divided into two seasons; rainy for 4 months or so, and dry for another 4 months or so, with 2 months or so of transition at the end of each season. The year around temperatures probably ranged between 70 to 90 degrees F. The town grew and prospered against all odds. Small but high quality coffee and tea plantations emerged, and a number of cottage industries began to develop. Getting their products to the market became the biggest obstacle. Trucks with daring drivers who would defy death; driving on narrow, dangerous, curvy, one lane roads, and narrow bridges over fast rivers with no safety rails, and no available help around to save them in case of disaster, were the only means of getting their goods to market. This became a constant challenge that merchants had to eventually overcome. Rumors of small chunks of isolated lost paradises, buried in the jungles, eventually lured us, and others working in nearby mines to explore them.

Tom was the most adventurous planner, and I had the newest and most reliable car. Beverly, was our meals planner and assisted Tom with the research of places to visit, and Sam, a native of India, gave us the impression of being an experienced bushman.

Rolando and Tom at mine entrance in Cerro

Rolando, Tom, Jenny, and Dick on a trip to Cuzco.

Before long, Tom came up with a plan to drive to San Ramon and La Merced, two towns on the way to the Jungle in the Chanchamayo valley alongside the river. The trip offered stunning views of trees of different colors, wild flowers, diverse fruit trees, short visible stretches of windy roads and waterfalls rapidly descending in altitude to eventually reach the Amazon River basin. People were friendly, hospitable, and helpful as they are in most of Peru.

Starting our trip after work on a Friday afternoon, our first stop was Tarma, just about an hour's drive from La Oroya, which had a beautiful Tourist Hotel with excellent dining facilities. The next day at daylight we started towards La Selva and at around 11:00 a.m., we came across a washed out piece of road, near a curve. We all got out of the car and worked diligently to repair just enough for the car to go through by pushing. Unfortunately, it appeared a useless effort. No road repair crews would be coming till Monday. Sam, an engineer, and Tom came up with a plan. The road before the break appeared to be well reinforced and firm, while the other side of the break, which was at a lower level, was soft and could be smoothed with little work. The driver would have to back up some to have room to gain speed and jump to the other side. To this day, I cannot figure out how I was talked into doing the driving! So, lo and behold I was up in the air unable to see where I was going to stop at the other side! But fortunately I landed and skidded for a few feet in front of Tom waving his arms for me to stop. While the others were getting in the car, I walked about 30 feet to the curve to see a prominently displayed wooden cross (meaning somebody must have left the road and died there). When I looked down, it appeared to be a vertical drop with no visible bottom. That is when we switched drivers...... I do not recall where we stayed in La Merced. Fortunately, we had an uneventful trip back to La Oroya.

On another trip Tom, Bev, Sam and I set out from La Oroya after lunch on Saturday, August 6, 1954 in the pick-up truck which we had bought by pooling our money. As per usual, there was a big last minute rush trying to get everything we had forgotten, or put off getting, until the last minute. I was still taking erythromycin for a sore throat. So I was privileged to ride up front all the way to Huanuco. The trip to Huanuco was uneventful except for a short rest stop in Cerro for a Coke etc. Just as we were arriving in Huanuco we had a flat tire, which only took us a few minutes to change. We paid to have the tire repaired, but they only patched the hole without removing the nail, so we were destined for further trouble before long.

The manager of the Tourist Hotel in Huanuco gave us two suites with views overlooking the plaza. We had a good dinner, took a short walk around town and turned in for the night. When the alarm sounded at 6am, it felt like we had just gone to bed because the beds were air foam and very comfortable.

A couple of hours after we left Huanuco, Tom saw a tire roll past us and commented that some poor guy was driving with a tire missing. Well, guess whose tire it was! We soon found out it was our tire. After we chased it down we looked in the glove compartment and there were the lug nuts that should have been holding the tire on the wheel. The person who repaired the tire had only secured it with two nuts!

After securing the tire on the wheel Tom drove the pickup all the way to Tingo Maria. We arrived about noon. We had a quick lunch and dashed downtown to a little Tourist Shop where Tom and I each bought a large colorful Bow & Arrows set, made in a little village, (Aguaytia) not too far up the Ucayali River. The Bow & Arrows were made for ceremonial purposes.

The reason for the hustle was because Victor Ponce, Tom's office assistant in Oroya, had agreed to drive the pickup back to La Oroya right after lunch and had to get started to avoid driving at night. We thought it would be a good idea if he took the bows and arrows with him so we didn't have to carry them to Iquitos, and back. It was a good choice. In the meantime, the battery in the truck gave up. Sam located a replacement and we sent Ponce on his way after acquiring a set of native Indian pottery, painted with a pitch based paint. It was quite unusual in that it does not wash or wear off.

We then had to find transportation to Pucallpa the next day. We were soon spotted by a couple of local guys who wanted $50 to take us there. We thought that was a bit expensive and told them to "go away". We finally found one that would take us there for $25. We gave him $10 down payment and told him to pick us up at the hotel at 5am sharp. Sound like a lot of confusion? It was. We then retired to the hotel for a cool lemonade and a shower.

The hotel manager tried to persuade us to stay a couple more days as he had a special deal to take us to Pucallpa along with several other people. We refused his offer as we had already made other arrangements. He told us not to worry, as our truck would probably not show up anyway. Nice fellow! We ignored him and went to dinner. Halfway through the meal I was called away to find a little "chunchi" standing there with our 200 Soles, and telling us that our truck to Pucallpa wouldn't be able to leave until 1p.m. (Guess who we thought was behind this?) We took our 200 Soles back and set out on our own to find other arrangements.

We walked up and down the street several times and were about to give up when one of the fellows we had talked to earlier in the day approached us and asked if we were still interested in going to Pucallpa tomorrow. We completed the arrangements and he said he would pick us up at 5:30am. He didn't even ask for a down payment for gasoline as the other big operators do. We did, however, insist that 5:30am was "hora exacta", not "hora Peruana". We set our alarm for 4:30am so we would have plenty of time to prepare oatmeal for breakfast.

As soon as the alarm sounded at 4:30 Tom began to get breakfast underway. As he was pouring the alcohol, (starter fluid) into the stove he spilled a little bit onto the table. He wiped it up with the hotel towel and lit the stove. As soon as the stove ignited, so did the table top where he spilled the alcohol. He grabbed the nearest table cloth or towel to beat out the flame and the towel ignited. Now he had a real mess. The stove, table and towel were all in flames. Bev was still lying in bed, but when she saw the whole hotel about to go up in flames, you wouldn't believe how fast she leaped out of bed. We put the fire out and vowed to be much more careful in the future. As soon as the water for the oatmeal began to boil, the truck arrived. It seems we made such an impression about the time we wanted to leave, that the driver couldn't sleep so he showed up early because he did not want to oversleep. Things became quite disorganized, but we managed to get everything packed and into the back of the truck and we left at 5:15, without breakfast!

It was pouring down rain when we left the hotel and it rained continuously until we reached the summit of the last range of mountains before descending into the Amazon jungle. We were sitting in the back of this open bed truck with no protection from the weather. We stopped at several little roadside restaurants along the way to eat breakfast and lunch and buy a can of soda. The meals were generally very good and cheap. We had eggs and coffee for breakfast, and soup or stew with rice and yucca for lunch and some other dishes common to the jungle, but unfamiliar to us gringos.

Bev's dinner the night before in Tingo Maria didn't agree with her. She had stomach problems all the way to Pucallpa. We had to stop on occasion for her to run off into the bushes. In general, though, the trip to Pucallpa was long and tiring. The road was in poor shape with lots of big deep ruts and plenty of dust. The weather got so warm that we all decided to sit in the back of the truck where it was cooler.

We arrived in Pucallpa about 6pm. We immediately found out that we had no room reservations at the requested hotel, so we settled on the second best, which turned out to be better than our first choice. The rooms were probably the cheapest we had experienced in Peru, 15 soles or 75 cents per night, per room. Since that averaged out to be about 35 cents per bed, we didn't spend a fortune in Pucallpa.

The first thing we did the next morning was to check with the Port Captain to see if there were any boats leaving for Iquitos in the next couple of days. Unfortunately, there were none and it was unlikely there would be any before the following Monday at the earliest. That wouldn't give us enough time to get to Iquitos, in time to catch our flight to Lima and get back to La Oroya on schedule. So we made reservations on a Military Air Transport plane to Iquitos the following Monday, August 15th, my birthday. It was a lucky thing we did because there weren't any boats anywhere on the river. The level of the river was too low and ships could easily run aground and get stuck for months. After getting that taken care of, we hired a canoe to take us up river to see some native and animal life. We left at about 10am and were supposed to be back in Pucallpa about 5pm. We traveled up river until about 3pm and still hadn't seen anything of importance. The pilot told us, if we could go another 2 hours we would stop at a little village where we could see “Chamas” (local Indians) for sure. We had a big discussion and decided to go for it. He also said we could go another half hour to the village of Masisea where we could get something to eat and even stay overnight there. If we didn’t want to stay overnight he would take us back to Pucallpa in the dark, which was not very appealing. Sam put up a big fight but was overruled because we had come so far already. We stopped at the little Chamas village about 5 pm. The Indians were very friendly, but we could not communicate directly because we didn’t know their language. They allowed us to take photos and were glad to show us samples of their work, tools, food, and just about everything they had. They wanted to sell us a fresh alligator skin for 50 cents, but it wasn’t even salted down yet. It was really fresh. He showed us the spear he used to kill it the night before. He was very proud of his accomplishment. The women all wore handmade clothing and their faces were colorfully painted, but no one wore a ring in their nose. Bev told Tom that she felt that the young girl thought I was “OK”.

Just a few minutes after we left the Chamas village we began to see the wildlife. Every few yards alligators were sliding into the river as we approached. We saw schools of fish feeding and breaking the surface of the water. There were flocks of parrots, canaries and parakeets flying back and forth across the river. It was really exciting because in every direction someone was pointing out something different to the rest us.

Just as the sun was setting, the village of Masisea appeared around the bend. There was no electricity in Masisea, but a couple of the stores had Coleman lanterns to supply light. After the boat was secured, Chino, the pilot, took us to this little thatched roof house where we got something to eat. The local people were all very friendly as were a couple of trappers who happened to be there at the time. When they finished eating we sat down. We had a good meal consisting of “chicken” soup, fried and highly spiced “chicken”, yucca, and some green vegetables that we had never seen before, bread, rice, fried bananas, coffee and a can of soda pop that we carried from Pucallpa. It was a very satisfying and good dinner. It was the first time Bev and Tom had ever tasted yucca prepared in this manner. And surprisingly, the fried bananas were delicious. Much different than the way they were served in the hotel in Oroya.

When we had finished dinner, Tom, Bev and I accompanied Chino up the road a short distance, maybe a couple of blocks, to a structure that supposedly could give us a place to stay overnight. The proprietor, an elderly lady said she would prepare the beds as soon as she finished eating dinner. Gee! We thought this wasn't going to be so bad after all. We walked to our rooms with our keys opened the doors, walked into our rooms and found ourselves looking at each other! There were no walls separating the rooms! It wasn't until later that we discovered the beds consisted of a bedstead with boards across with spaces in between and a blanket that we used to cover the boards we slept on. There was also mosquito netting to keep the bugs from bothering us. Of course, if a bug were unlucky enough to get inside the netting he could not get out. We spent quite a few minutes during the night pursuing insects. Fortunately, we doused ourselves thoroughly with insect repellant we had obtained from the hospital in Oroya before we left, so we didn't get too eaten up. Chino had never smelled citronella before and didn't know what it was. As we were approaching the place where we were to spend the night, Chino kept smelling Sam and saying "Que Fragante!" (How pretty you smell!). He explained to us that he smelled that on the boat and couldn't figure out what it was. He thought maybe we had accidentally spilled something. He even took the cover off the motor to see if something inside was causing the smell. He was quite pleased to find that it was only insect repellant that he was worrying about. We got a big laugh out of the way he explained it to us in all seriousness.

As we were getting settled for the night, Tom noticed that Bev had some kind of art work table cloth to cover the boards. Sam overheard the conversation and said that he had one too, but wasn't going to use it and asked Tom if he wanted to use it to put under his hip so that the bed didn't feel so hard. He accepted his offer, but used it as a blanket to cover himself. As it turned out, he was the only one who slept warmly that night. His cover was not a table cloth, but a small flannel blanket. Tom was not popular with the rest of us the next morning when we discovered that he had slept more comfortably than we did! But nearly every bone in our bodies ached from sleeping on non-padded boards. We didn't know boards could be that hard.

The funny part of the night was that we kept hearing animal noises and grunts outside the hotel. In the morning we discovered that some of the rooms only had 3 walls. It was the pigs down below in the yard making all the noise. We had to walk a plank, which was up on stilts, to get to the outhouse. Down below was where the pigs were doing their thing. Fortunately, no one had to use the "facilities" during the night. It seems that a couple of the pigs managed to get part way upstairs where we slept. Sam did not enjoy the night in Masisea.

We had breakfast in the same place as the night before, which was essentially the same food, except that we asked for eggs. It took them an awful long time to round up the eggs. We could only imagine what the problem was! After breakfast we walked down to the river, to discover that our boat had gone a half mile downstream to pick up a small cargo to take back to Pucallpa. The small cargo, turned out to be a full shipload of cedar planks. They had to rearrange the load to give us barely enough room to sit on top of the boards. We didn't embark until about 10:30 am, which equates to about 3 hours waiting around. Before we left they offered Bev a gift of a little baby pig which we could not accept. The trip downstream was uneventful and dull because we had to stay out in midstream because the boat was so heavily loaded. If we got too close to shore we might get stuck in the mud and remain there for quite a while.

The next morning, August 11, 1954, after we checked with the Captain of the Port and he said there was no news of any boats coming up from Iquitos. We set out to visit the Linguistic Institute, whose main base is on Lake Yarinacocha, 5 miles from Pucallpa. At that time, we didn't know how far it was, so we started walking as we had nothing else to do. We had only gone a half mile or so when a nice man in a Jeep drove up and offered us a lift. Sr. Palacios worked for the Development Bank of Peru (Banco de Fomento). It's a good thing he came along because it was getting kind of warm. He loaded the 4 of us into the back of the Jeep and took us out to Yarinacocha. He introduced us to a few of the people there and went on his way. One of the young men working on the seaplanes there was from Seattle. He was studying Theology at the University of Washington and was down here doing missionary work during the summer.

The Linguistics Institute headquarters was at the University of Oklahoma. These Evangelist Missionaries participate in missionary activities to preserve the local languages and translate the Bible into those languages in the Amazon rainforest, primarily in Peru, Ecuador, Brazil and Bolivia. It is a partner organization of the Wycliffe Bible Translators. The missionaries first step is to put the native languages into writing, then produce a primary reader in that language, then teach the sharpest or brightest individuals in the tribe to read and write. The next step is to bring 3 or 4 of the sharpest natives and their families, by plane, to Yarinacocha and give them a 4 month course in History, Geography, Spanish and the basics, such as Hygiene etc. The missionary remains with them constantly because he/she is the only person who understands their language.

They then return to their tribe with their missionary instructor and set up a school in the tribe to teach the others. The missionary remains with the tribe for 8 months. They are in radio contact with Yarinacocha daily. In the more dangerous places, such as the Ecuador border, where there are headhunters, they are forced to send out 2 women alone. The head shrinkers do not harm the women but will shrink a man's head at the first opportunity.

Yarinacocha always maintains a stand-by airplane in case of an emergency. Whenever possible the Institute flies the missionaries in to the tribes, but sometimes the tribes are in such a hard place to get to that they fly them in as near as they can and then they must travel by outboard up the river to the tribes. In some instances this may take 3 or 4 days from the nearest place where the plane can safely land. The Institute has 9 or 10 planes, little Grummans, big PBY's and several Piper Cubs and Cesnas. They are always handicapped by lack of funds. The medical department in Yarinacocha is quite lacking as is their printing department, but they do a wonderful job with what they have. We tried to ask the director about what their source of funding was, but he avoided the question.

It was obvious that somebody was paying for the jungle clearing they were doing in some nearby prospective oil fields. A devoted and strong Evangelist was donating most of his earnings to Evangelism. We speculated that he was the one who was paying for it.

He was doing a lot of development and road building in the Peruvian jungle in exchange for his concessions there. It seems to us that he was taking plenty of time, as if he was waiting to see what the oil exploration brings. The Tournavista settlement is about 34 miles south of Pucallpa.

Our visit to Yarinacocha was very interesting. One observation was the roofs on the staff buildings at Yarinacocha were metal, not thatch and some of the newer ones had sloping walls, projecting out at the top, so the sun did not hit squarely on the wall, keeping it cooler. We had lunch there, took a few pictures and departed on foot again. It was mid- afternoon now and the sun was much more intense than the morning. Fortunately, a pickup truck came by and gave us a ride back into town. Just prior to entering town we disembarked and visited with a German Naturalist, a Mr. Shunke. Tom and Bev purchased a bunch of butterflies from him that they hoped to make into a tray someday.

Still no boats from Iquitos, so we rented a dugout canoe for 15 cents and paddled across the Ucayali River for a picnic. It wasn't too difficult to paddle the canoe, but we stayed well out of the middle of the stream and the strong current. We found a nice spot, just a short distance downstream from Pucallpa. However, when Tom stepped out his foot, he was up to his knee in mud. It took a few minutes to get out of there, but we quickly found a more suitable place not far away. We set up our stove and heated a can of chili con carne. Just as we were beginning to eat, it started to rain. We ducked under some big leaves for shelter, but soon they got full and dumped water on us big time. We got completely drenched to the skin. The sun came out shortly and everything dried off quickly. We took a couple of pictures to show our miserable state. They are really funny.

Tom, Beverley, Rolando, and Sam after being soaked by rain during lunch stop at Ucayali River shore. Loreto, Peru.

The next day, Saturday, we spent looking for a tiger skin. Actually it's part of the leopard family, like a puma or cougar, but the natives refer to it as "Tigre". Tom and Bev had seen a couple previously in our wanderings, but the price was too high. Finally they purchased one for $3. They also purchased a couple of cute little green dwarf parrots for 75 cents each, which included the wooden cage. They named them "Pisco" and "Julio". They kept them in La Oroya until they left for home (the U.S.) and they gave them to someone else.

On Sunday, we were invited to accompany some people we met, on a power boat cruise down the Ucayali River a short distance. We accepted and had a nice time. We stopped to do some net fishing and did pretty well. We caught 300 - 400 fish and a little baby alligator that we threw back. As we proceeded downstream we hit a sandbar that capsized us and threw a couple fellows into the river. All we lost was a pair of shoes in the scuffle. Tom laughed at Bev and me because we were both trying to occupy the same spot on the seat. As we waded to shore the pilot of the boat shouted out to move fast because there might be piranhas in the water. I wasn't aware that I could sprint like that!

Fishing for Pirañhas

We stopped at a little village for lunch. The people were very friendly and gave us a half a dozen turtle eggs to take back to the hotel, plus a few ears of corn and a watermelon. They wanted to sell us a cute little monkey, but we couldn't imagine what we would do with a monkey in Oroya.

On Monday we boarded the plane to Iquitos. There was a lot of confusion because, as usual, they oversold more seats than they had room for. So everybody didn't get on. What a mess, and in the boiling hot sun too. Everyone was standing in the shade under the wings. They were fueling the plane from 45 gallon drums hoisted up onto the wing. While they were not paying attention, gasoline overflowed onto everyone below. Tom's camera bag got soaked, but the birds didn't suffer. It was a terrible and potentially hazardous situation. After finally boarding the plane, the flight to Iquitos was uneventful, a little rough in spots, but otherwise OK.

The Tourista Hotel in Iquitos was quite comfortable in spite of no air-conditioning. Upon our arrival we were treated to ice cold lemonade at the bar. The city itself was a bit of a disappointment however. The weather was considerably more humid than in Pucallpa. There were no Indians in native costumes or anything unusual. The Amazon River is over a mile wide there and everything seemed very civilized. There were very few boats for hire, so tourism was limited. Those that were available were very expensive so we promptly gave up on that idea.

We walked up and down practically every street in town. We got plenty of rest, as there was almost nothing to do. We read and played cards, etc. while sitting in front of the fan. We stayed in Iquitos a couple of days and then caught a flight to Lima. Tom had purchased a 9 ft. blow gun, so it was unusual to see him board the plane with a 9 ft. carry on. He laid it in the aisle, beside his seat. No one objected, so we just let it be. Due to the change in climate between Pucallpa and Iquitos he came down with a severe cold.

Tom and Bev spent 2 days in Lima at the Hotel Crillon, in the presidential suite, with a balcony, normally used by the president or other special dignitaries. I stayed in a standard room. It was quite a contrast from our accommodations in the Amazon! We went to a couple of movies and took care of other business, before driving back to La Oroya in my VW Bug, arriving at about 7pm. Tom had a difficult time holding onto that 9 foot blow gun for 6 hours with his arm out the window. Thus ended our Amazon Jungle Vacation.

As it always happens with vacations, time passes fast, and we had to return to work. However, before long it was time for us to starting planning for our next vacation. This time we thought we would travel out of Peru and visit the countries of Chile, and Argentina. During the evenings of the work week, we would gather around the hotel or the company social club, but mostly at Tom and Bev's hotel room to exchange ideas or just have leisurely activities, as well as tossing around ideas on what else to do.

Eventually, Tom and Bev, Sam and myself, four of us, decided to take the trip. Tom's father, Mr. Frank Dahl, Sr., who was visiting Tom from Seattle, Washington, joined us for the trip. From Lima we flew to Santiago, the modern capital city of Chile. We stayed at the "Carrera Hotel" which was known as the best hotel in the city, and where most foreign visitors stayed before traveling into the interior. Chile is famous for its ski resorts in the Andes Mountains, their seashore resort and gambling casino "Vina del Mar" near the seaport city of Valparaiso, and the beautiful lakes district in the southern part of the country, all the way to Patagonia (South Pole) in South America. We stayed at Puerto Varas, the farthest south city on the Chilean coast line, took a boat trip to one of the resort hotels near Argentina's tourist region, Bariloche. We were very impressed with the natural beauty of the region, the lakes, the forests, and the people were very nice and hospitable, but fortunately nothing extraordinary happened to us. We returned to Santiago safely by train, and flew to Lima, with a stopover at Bolivia's highest and most difficult international airport in the world, near Lake Titicaca. The whole trip was quite an experience and a fast moving trip for Tom's dad, who, in spite of his 70 plus years of age kept a good pace with all of us and told us that he had a great and enjoyable vacation. We returned to Lima, and Tom's dad returned to Seattle and the rest of us to La Oroya.

Each one of us had a larger circle of friends with whom we enjoyed other activities as well. Two other American couples living at the company Hotels participated with us in celebrating certain occasions and activities. Among those friends were George and Sally Beals and Richard and Jeanette Lowe. Both couples keep in contact with us. They are retired, the Lowe's live in the Boston area and the Beal's in Colorado. Sorry to say Sally and George and Jeanette have all passed away in recent years.

As far as I am concerned, I was blessed with a wide range of friends, age wise as well as marital status, and Nationality wise. There were four major categories: there was an American group, a Peruvian group, a European group, and a British group. Most whom were married with children and had priority in getting a Company house. All singles or married without children were housed in one of the two Company hotels. Most families hired housekeeping staff members to do the domestic work. The immediately emerging problem was communication. Like anywhere in the world, the people looking for this type of jobs are not exactly the most educated or motivated individuals. Their job skills are minimal, they hardly spoke proper Spanish, let alone foreign languages. With this problem in mind, the company offered fast courses in basic Spanish, referred to as "kitchen Spanish", to the non-Spanish speaking housewives who had to deal with this problem. As luck would have it, frequently, you might find experienced employees who may not have spoken a word of English, but are so experienced and efficient rendering their services that they seem to just read the minds of their employers. Both parties learn to love each other and work in harmony together. These are people who do not have problems getting hired and were considered valuable assets to any new employer, as families rotated at the end of their contract, which averages about every four years.

The social life after work is busy. Families like to entertain and frequently, the beneficiaries are people living in the Hotels. Although the food at the hotel was great, a home cooked meal at the bosses or other friend's houses was very much appreciated. The Peruvian cuisine is world renowned for its flavor and variety. Families having Peruvian cooks in their homes liked to show it off. The food at the Hotel is heavily European accented, which is often monotonous.

During the period of time I lived in La Oroya there were employees from 20 different nationalities. Cerro de Pasco had many offices of employment around the world.

There are four major club festival activities put on by the four groups mentioned earlier. The American group celebrated the 4th of July, featuring rodeos and other western type of activities during the day, and a gala dance in the evening. The European group displayed activities similar to the Octoberfest celebrations in this country. The Peruvian group featured Peruvian foods, drinks, music and dancing. The British group, represented by Irish, Scottish, Australian, Canadian and New Zealander; had activities and goodies served at the club or private homes.

Fourth of July Celebration, La Oroya Peru

Many American families who had children attending school in the U.S., would have the children coming to Peru for their three month vacation. As a dentist, I was very busy doing their dental work in time for them to go back to school. I was very privileged to be considered as a friend of their families, and I was included in many of their activities. Some of those children kept in occasional contact with me during the holidays, and I remember them fondly, as I do their parents, unfortunately some have already been called home by the Lord.

As time grew closer for Tom and Bev to return home, they were not going to renew their contract with Cerro, we decided to spend whatever remaining vacation time we had visiting more areas within Peru. One of the most attractive areas, particularly with Europeans is the "Callejon de Huaylas", where I grew up and it is also where some of the richest gold mines are located. The Santa River runs between the two chains of mountains, the white cordillera and the black cordillera. The white cordillera gradually turn west towards the black cordilleras, creating a canyon called the "Canon del Pato", where the river empties into a narrow desert area near the city of Chimbote, the anchovy fishing capital of the world. The snow melted water of the western slopes of the white cordilleras flows into the Santa River. This large amount of water runs on top of a narrow solid rock bed, creating an impressive waterfall into the sandy coast. Today those waters have been partially used for hydroelectric plants that generate electricity for a large area of the country. Only part of the river is used to generate electricity because the river fluctuations are not predictable. During the rainy season in the mountains, the rivers flow in enormous amounts, washing out farms and small towns in its course. In addition, natural disasters such as the disaster I witnessed on December 13, 1941, occur periodically. I found out later that the avalanche was caused when a huge piece of ice from a glacier fell into the lake below and broke the dam of the lake. The water and ice ran at an ever increasing speed towards the Santa River from an altitude of about 19,000 feet to the city of Huaraz at an altitude of 9,000 feet in the short distance of approximately 5 miles. The avalanche turned left following the course of the fast running waters of the Santa River, carrying granite boulders larger than entire houses, down through the Canon del Pato to the Pacific coast. In the aftermath, 70% of the city of Huaraz had been wiped out along with many small and large cities on its way. When Tom, Beverly and I visited the area, some of my relatives who had been spared by the avalanche, were living in the smaller farm houses we owned in farming areas, and where some of us stayed during farming activities.

After Tom and Bev left, the remainder of us who used to pal around together, gradually separated and engaged in different activities. Tom and Bev had been the nucleus of the group, and I in particular sorely missed them. I am sure the other friends missed them too.

CHAPTER 21

SOME OF MY ADVENTURES AND VENTURES

I continued to travel and embark on other adventures with other friends. Among them was a trip to the jungle to hunt wild boars, and another trip to hunt alligators. On the wild boar hunt, I had an interesting experience. When hunting boars, you always shoot the last one in the pack, because if you shoot one of the leaders or one in the middle, the others will attack you. We were following the path made by a pack of boars, when it crossed a river. I was tired so I told the others to go ahead without me, while I rested under a tree. I sat down and rested my gun across my lap and fell asleep. I was awakened by someone shaking my shoulder. I opened my eyes to see, not one of my friends, but a huge snake, probably about 12 feet long and six inches in diameter, crawling from the tree across my body toward the river! Fortunately, I didn't panic and remained as still as possible until it left me. If I had moved it might possibly have curled around me and squeezed me to death, as it was a constrictor. My friends returned without having been able to pick up the boars' trail and we returned home empty handed, but with a story to tell.

On another trip some friends and I decided to go alligator hunting in one of the rivers in the jungle. Alligators are hunted at night, because you can see their eyes shining in the water. The idea is to shoot them between the eyes. The wider the eyes are apart the bigger the alligator. So we rented a boat and went out into the river. We saw a lot of shining eyes and one of my friends shot one. We struggled to get it into the boat because it was a big one. Then we started back to shore because the boat was full. All of a sudden the alligator flipped its tail, it wasn't quite dead yet, and split the bottom of the boat open! We paddled as fast as we could with the boat sinking into the piranha infested water and reached the shore just before the boat sank. Unfortunately, the alligator sank with the boat and we couldn't recover it. So once again we returned home empty handed with just another story to tell.

Some of the ore that was mined by Cerro de Pasco was transported in large buckets from one mountain top over a canyon to the next mountain top to go to the smelter. The buckets were on heavy cables and the weight of the loaded bucket moved the empty bucket back to be loaded again. After seeing this, I thought it would be a great opportunity to take pictures of the canyon and surrounding mountains from a vantage point in one of the empty buckets. So one day I got my camera and rode in one of the buckets. Well, it was quite a ride. It was very cold and windy, I could hardly hold on to my camera. It was a very rough ride and I didn't get any good pictures. So it turned out to be another story to tell!

On one of my trips to visit my family in Callejon de Huaylas, my Uncle Roberto was riding with me in my Volkswagen. We came around a curve in the road and hit some big rocks that had been left there by a truck driver. We became airborne and went over the side of the mountain. Fortunately, we landed on a ledge on the nose of the car and flipped over. If the ledge hadn't been there we would have plunged hundreds of feet to our deaths. However, the car caught on fire! I was conscious but Uncle was not. I managed to drag him out of the car before either one of us was burned. After I put out the fire by throwing dirt on it, Uncle regained consciousness and we climbed up the cliff to the road and waited until a truck came by, picked us up and took us to the nearest town, where we were able to get a ride back home.

I came back to the U.S. a few times to take some advanced courses in Dentistry, one at Ohio State University School of Dentistry, and another one at the University of Michigan, in Ann Arbor, Michigan. When I went to take these courses, I flew to Detroit and bought a car to use while I was in the States and then drove it to Miami and sold it before flying back to Peru. I saved money that way because I didn't have to rent a car or take taxis.

When I returned to La Oroya, it appeared that everything was different, our friend Guido Rodriguez had also gone back home to Costa Rica, and our friend from India, Sam, a mining engineer, had been transferred to the Cerro camp, which was located about two hours away by train.

During my travels back and forth from Peru to the U.S., I noticed that postcards were very popular souvenirs for many visitors. There were no postcards available in Peru that I had seen. So on one of my trips back to the U.S. for training, I contacted a postcard company about making postcards from some of my photographs of Peru. They thought it was a good idea and so I contracted with them to print the postcards. They sent them to me and I distributed them to hotels, restaurants and tourist attractions, mostly in Lima. That turned into a booming business. There were some months when I made more money from the postcards than I made from my job with Cerro de Pasco! When I left Peru, I left a friend of mine in charge of the business. He was supposed to send me the proceeds from the business every month. He did for a few months and then less and less until I didn't hear from him anymore.

During my return for advanced training, I also had the opportunity to re-evaluate my future. Although, Cerro De Pasco Corp. had offered me a good future, and my experiences at work, and my relationship with my bosses and colleagues at Chulec General Hospital had been superb, I decided that in the long run, returning to the States at the end of my contract would be best. I hated the idea of leaving behind my patients, the people I had developed strong relationships with and my community at large. Little I knew, that every now and then in my future, I would experience the same feelings during my military reassignments, and of course more intensely upon my retirement from active duty from the U.S.A.F.

During the remainder of my time in La Oroya, I made some short weekend trips with some friends, primarily to lower altitude and warmer areas where the Company had some activities.

One trip that I was particularly impressed with was the Hydroelectric plant at Paucartambo. Mr. Walter Keenan, a brilliant young Engineer from New York City, who lived a few doors away from me at the company hotel, where I lived, was one of the principals in designing and putting the power plant into operation. The power plant was located in a new small Camp where the manager of operations was a Canadian American engineer whose last name was Remick. He and his family were my gracious hosts. It was an incredible facility that was designed to provide electricity not only for the Company operations, but for an extensive area of the country. From the opposite side of the mountain, you could see a huge, orange, almost vertical, pipeline carrying water at tremendous speed to power the generators, turbines or whatever force was involved in generating electricity.

One common denominator we all had is that our working life time in La Oroya was limited. Everyone had some type of financial plan for their future. Many Americans had either, individual, or group U.S. real estate investment plans, others in the stock market, and others in savings accounts. I was not knowledgeable enough to join any of them. I put whatever money I had left monthly in a savings account in an American Bank. I already had witnessed some unpleasant experiences dealing with Peruvian and other smaller national currencies. However, I had witnessed some spectacular gains in Peruvian real estate as well as in small industries. So I joined a small group of international co-workers from La Oroya who were investing in Lima. One of the Geologists from the company, Mr. Frank Cintron, was a close friend. He was an American citizen, I believe he was originally from Puerto Rico. He was a well-known figure and well connected in Peru, because he was the father of one of the most famous and beloved female bullfighters named "Conchita Cintron", who was known internationally as the all-time famous Peruvian horse riding bull fighter. At any rate, a group of geologists doing some drilling tests looking for oil on the outskirts of Lima, discovered a sizeable gusher of underground water in the middle of the desert. It was just north of Lima, and just next to Ancon, on one of the prettiest small coastal bays. It was a small fishing village and a summer refuge for the well to do. A plan to develop the land next to Ancon with abundant water to develop a resort with many amenities, including a golf course, would be a dream come true for the people from Lima. To make a long story short, the plans for the resort amenities; lots dedicated for governmental offices, and beautiful ocean side homes were drawn. I had invested in a beautiful residential lot and was an investor in the golf club. The potential was one for dreams. Unfortunately, political and economical changes began to take place, the building boom slowed down. The government had its eyes on our resort, because adjoining our project there was some government land. The Peruvian Navy decided to build a military facility supposedly for their exercises, and expropriated most of our water, causing investors to abandon the area and private building projects came to a halt. The price of the properties plummeted, and a series of convoluted regulations caused us to abandon it. We eventually lost our money by selling it just to pay the newly elevated tax assessments.

Another venture was born from my association with professional British and other international deep sea divers, who had discovered several sunken ships near Lima's seaport city of Callao. One ship in particular was only 30 to 40 feet below the ocean surface. The principal motivator was that the Insurance Company that owned it was willing to finance it by letting our group keep a big shipment of wine and other items that were aboard the ship. We had a special boat built in Callao for this purpose and a team of divers headed by a British diver, who I only remember him being referred to as Mr. Stone. He lived in Miraflores, a higher end residential neighborhood in Lima. The government red tape took so long, that some of the divers, who had full-time jobs working for companies like Cerro, had to return home. Mr. Stone, who knew other colleagues, traveled to Miami, and upon his return gave the good news of having successfully recruited a new team. One evening, several investing members visited Mr. Stone at his home. They had dinner, and rather late that evening the guests left, and Mr. Stone expressed that he was not feeling well. The family members attributed it to some wine served with dinner. He was taken to his bedroom by his daughter, who once he felt comfortable in bed, lit a cigarette for him upon his request. The following morning, Mr. Stone, who was known to be an early riser, had not come out for breakfast. His daughter, concerned for his tardiness, went to his bedroom and found him dead in the same semi seated position in bed, with a barely started cigarette still in his mouth. This time the project was killed by the slow and lengthy red tape, and untimely death of our project leader.

Last but not least was the purchase of a large urban city lot in one of Lima's most prestigious neighborhoods called Monterrico. Three of us were doctors working at Cerro's Chulec General Hospital in La Oroya, a Peruvian Orthopedist, a nationalized German ophthalmologist, and myself. We had discussed that one of our options beyond our life in La Oroya would be to practice our professions in Lima. We would be well ahead by purchasing a chunk of valuable land that after being subdivided into regular size city lots would give us a good financial foundation for building our homes. We purchased the land and here again we were faced with a series of red tape hurdles. The contracts with Cerro of the other two, had ended and they moved to Lima. They decided to buy or rent smaller houses to live in, when political unrest began. The ophthalmologist decided to return to Germany, and I was pretty much determined to come to the U.S. Monterrico was growing by leaps and bounds, neighbors surrounding our land were beginning to encroach onto our property. We had to hire a resident watchman who would live in a little existing shack, on the property and farm the land with produce in exchange for paying us rent. I was already living in the U.S. for a few years when the necessary paper work was finally approved.

By then the price of the land had really gone up, the two of us not living in Lima wanted to sell. The orthopedist did not agree, so we decided to subdivide it. When everything was in process for the sale we wanted to let the tenant go. The tenant had been advised by a lawyer, that we could not evict him, and in fact the land should be legally his, because he had been in possession for X number of years, and should be granted squatter's rights. Long story short, there were more headaches and mounting attorney's fees, until at long last the property was sold and we each received a good chunk of money, in Peruvian currency.

At that time I was in the process of being assigned overseas. Much to my family's delight we were being sent to the Pacific with headquarters in Hawaii. My wife Betty and I decided to make a quick trip to Lima to see my family and also sign the sale papers. We could not stay long because we had left the children with Betty's parents and we missed them too much.

While living in Lima, I had become well acquainted with the parents of one of my friends and classmates. His father, had lived in the United States for many years and made frequent trips there. So I asked him if he would agree to represent me during the final closing and deposit the proceeds in the bank and then after converting the Peruvian currency into dollars, to send the money to me. He agreed to handle this for us and we returned to Indiana. We returned from Peru with barely enough time to prepare for our move to Hawaii.

Once in Hawaii, adequate military housing was not available, so we needed to live on the local economy. We noticed that prices of houses were escalating rapidly there, and we did not have enough money for a down payment. We hoped desperately that the money from Peru would be arriving soon. In the meantime Peru had been experiencing financial difficulties because the government did not have Dollars, which was the only currency acceptable in international finances. The rate of exchange of Peruvian currency, the Sol, when Betty and I left Lima was 13.00 soles per dollar. By the time we got to Hawaii it was 27.00 soles to a dollar. The

Peruvian government had forbidden any sale of dollars by the banks. We started getting occasional remittances of a couple of hundred dollars now and then, purchased at 160.00 soles per dollar. To make matters worse, the Peruvian government confiscated every dollar deposited in the Banks. I understood that there were financial conflicts between the Peruvian and the American governments. Peru had been denied any loans from the U.S.A. Eventually I received less than $9,000.00, in small remittances from my representative, not even a fraction of my investment. Although, I was not only disappointed with the government, I was sad to learn that generally speaking the people I trusted, disappointed me, and I wished that with lessons learned I could just forget it like a bad dream and start my life again with a clean slate.

All in all, from the largest Camp like La Oroya, to the smallest facilities and centers of operation; from the scientific laboratories that conducted research, the polluted heating inferno of the smelters and foundries, or the isolated ore cable car operators to the cooks and housekeeping personnel at all the camps, my greatest admiration goes to all, regardless of their educational background, ethnicity or economic status. They work in different positions frequently in the most adverse conditions and locations; they should be very proud that they perform their jobs with high standards of ethics and their great accomplishments. Most of all I am grateful for the friends I made and the memories I have for having had the privilege and the opportunity to have been associated with them. For me, my experience at Cerro was an educational and life experience that I treasure.

CHAPTER 22

LEAVING MY HOME COUNTRY

I was very disappointed with the Peruvian government decisions of property ownership, monetary exchanging decisions, and some other few instances that I had observed during my years at Cerro. The most viable choice was to leave the country for a while or perhaps for good. The most appealing choice was to come to the USA. I already knew the way of life, and the risks that I would have to take. So I had to see what I had to do first, to live in the United States:

Prove that I could support myself or have a sponsor who would support me until I could

Seek legal entry to the USA with a permanent resident Visa.

Obtain license to practice Dentistry in the U.S.

Try to join the Military Service (Air Force or Navy)

Obtain license to practice in New York City or Los Angeles, California.

Make my final decision to stay in Peru or settle down somewhere else.

During my last trip to the U.S., while attending some graduate courses, that I mentioned earlier, I took time to do some research as to the choices I had as to what and where I would like to work, settle, and live. Of course, licensing to practice dentistry, was a big consideration. The professional practice laws were more restrictive and very different then from what they are today. Some states were so restrictive that they almost required you not only to be born in the state, but to have attended all your education in their particular state. Most states required American citizenship or a permanent visa and graduation from an American Dental School. So I decided to inquire from the institutional entities or get suggestions from Dental school officials for information and advice. I spent a lot of time in sending letters and application forms, etc., by airmail, because international surface postal services were very slow from Peru.

Because of some consideration to my graduate education in the U.S., a few States would allow me to engage in institutional positional practices, but in order to open a private practice office, I would have to take the state board examinations of any given state. That is when I decided to start everything with a clean slate.

Fortunately, when I came to the States, I still had the money that I had saved working for Cerro, paid in U.S. dollars and deposited in New York. I could use those funds to go back to dental school in order to get my U.S. degree and be licensed to practice where ever I would eventually decide to hang up my shingle.

I applied to almost all the Dental Schools in the country that were approved by the American Dental Association. I only received about 10 rather encouraging responses. I decided the response from Indiana University was the fairest in my opinion. They basically told me that if I felt confident enough, as my application papers suggested, then I should come to the dental school to take oral, written, and clinical examinations, as their own students had to do. Then in those courses I passed, I would be given credit, but I would have to repeat in all the courses I failed; which in turn would dictate whether I would have to attend two, three or four years of undergraduate studies. It was emphasized that regardless of passing all the exams, I would be required to perform two years of clinical practice at the school. I agreed, and came to Indiana University School of Dentistry, took the exams for a couple of weeks and was fortunate to pass almost sufficient enough courses as to be placed in the Junior Class.

I left Lima with one suitcase containing my clothing and a few items made of Peruvian Silver, intended as gifts for some friends in the U.S. My immediate family consisting of uncles, aunts and cousins, lived too far away from Lima to make the long trip to bid me farewell. We said our goodbyes on the phone, and shed some tears. We knew that we would not be seeing or speaking with each other for a long time because long distance phone conversations and mail exchanges were difficult at that time.

A couple of months previously I had made a trip back home to let them know about my plans for my future and my reasons. They could not understand why I would leave our country during uncertain times. I could only jokingly answer, because I am not "Don Quijote" material, I am a modern day "Sancho Panza".

A young friend of mine accompanied me to the Airport. My initial destination was to Columbus, Ohio to the home of Dr. William Lefkowitz, a former professor of mine with whom I had kept in touch since my days at Guggenheim in New York City. He was now a professor of Operative Dentistry and Research at The Ohio State University. Most of my friends thought that it was insane on my part to regress from being in a rather important position as Chief of Dental Services in a prestigious American Hospital, to become a lowly "foreign" student at an American Dental School.

I certainly was not searching for fortunes, money, or fame, my true reason was that I had just tasted and seen a way of life that was different to the one I had been living. I had been bitten by a bug, "the American Way of Life", as many casual visitors to this country may experience. I wanted to try it by myself. It was not an impulse, or overnight decision. I did a lot of soul searching. I would ask myself, who in my family would be hurt by my leaving the country? The answer was nobody. People that matter the most, like parents and siblings, I had none. I had been an orphan since an early age, I was single and had lived away from the family for years, self-supporting in later years. Professionally I had maxed out in the educational field in Peru, unless I traveled to the U.S. frequently. Socially, I had left my home area of Callejon de Huaylas, where I was born, raised and felt most connected. I had found out that due to the unstable political situation, most of my friends there had already gone abroad to avoid constantly worrying about mob uprisings, and either mob or government takeover of properties with no compensation, communist style takeovers or dictatorial regimes that left you uncertain about the future. I already had experienced uncertain times during my childhood. I needed to see how far I could go and develop on my own effort. I needed to develop any potentials I had by myself, for myself, or for my family if I had one, and in the long run for my community and my country wherever I definitely decided to stay and settle down.

I did not realize the magnitude of the disadvantages a foreigner in any country experiences if you are not proficient in the Country's language. Having seen the number of Europeans and Americans who came to Peru without speaking Spanish, who in a very short time, fared better financially than local Peruvians, and based on my success at Guggenheim in New York City, and later on in La Oroya, I felt that my future in America as I dreamed of it would be achievable. I had already accomplished, with hard work and God's help getting to where I was. Modest in many ways but with no regrets, I was very happy.

I applied for and received my permanent visa to enter the United States. Then from Lima I flew to Miami to go through immigration, and then I flew to Detroit, Michigan, where I purchased a car and drove to stay a few days with the Lefkowitz's. After my short stay in Columbus, Ohio, my deadline to report to Indiana University was just a couple of days away, so I expressed my gratitude to the Lefkowitz's for their hospitality, and drove to Indianapolis.

CHAPTER 23

LIFE AT INDIANA UNIVERSITY

At the Indiana University Medical Center campus in Indianapolis, there were two places where many students could find housing. One was the Student Union Building, where some of the Medical Center Junior Professors and a variety of medical, dental, Specialty Residents and undergraduate students lived. The other area was called Winona Village, a group of temporary war time structures. This housing accommodated students with families, or small groups of mostly foreign students of the same or compatible nationalities, who could rent a house equipped with kitchen, laundry and other basic necessities. I chose the Student Union Building, because it had all the necessary amenities and was walking distance to the Dental School. Not knowing how to cook anything, except make coffee or tea (instant), although now I am pretty good at cooking outdoors, (roasting, grilling, etc.), the cafeteria at the Union Building was a blessing.

After registering at the Student Union Building, I was assigned a room and a student guide took me to my room, and gave me a tour of the facilities, gave me a campus map showing the names of the buildings, the location of the schools on campus, the hospitals, laboratories, etc. and the relative distances to each, and a list of some of the scheduled activities for the week.

The following day I reported to the office of the Dean of the Dental School. After the welcome meeting, I was given a complete tour of the Dental School along with instructions for my future meetings with the chairmen of the different departments. I was also given instructions on where to buy all the necessary student equipment, books, required instruments, etc. I was also given a list of written clinical and laboratory tests that I needed to complete before Labor Day, in order to be officially enrolled into whichever class my grades determined I should be assigned. The whole process was supposed to take place in the months of July and August, but fortunately I was finished earlier and was notified that I would be enrolled in the Junior class starting in September of 1957.

All Junior class students are also offered to take Part 1 of the National Boards, which are recognized or given credit by many States of the country when applying for Licensure to practice in the given State. National Boards are composed of 2 Parts. Part 2 is given to the Senior students of the graduating class. Both, Part 1 and Part 2 are written exams. By themselves, they do not authorize or qualify anyone for practicing in the state, but they may be recognized as part of the state's licensure examinations. Although not officially mentioned, some states use licensures as a tool to prevent an overpopulation of dentists, attracted by their living conditions such as climate (i.e., California, Texas, Florida, etc.), and to avoid poorly prepared professionals to come to practice in their state. As I mentioned earlier, each state is different in their dental practice requirements, (e.g. some may even require proof of having attended higher education and dental education in their own state, others may also require proof of citizenship, etc.).

Although I was a permanent resident of the United States, I still had not applied for citizenship. The required time was 5 years of residency in the country. However, as a permanent resident I was eligible to be drafted or to join voluntarily into the armed forces. I opted to voluntarily join.

I presented my application to join the U.S. Air Force at a local draft board in the fall of 1958, with the thought that this would keep me from being drafted into the other branches of the Armed Forces.

I did not hear anything very soon because an international background check had not yet been completed. Once that was completed, I received notification that I had been approved and given a date for a physical examination. Shortly thereafter, I received my reporting date towards the end of June as well as a military serial number with a prefix. The prefix was DP (distinguished personnel), which I considered an honor. I still couldn't report for duty until graduation from Indiana University School of Dentistry.

Rolando in 1957.

CHAPTER 24

LOVE AND MARRIAGE

During my first year as a student at Indiana University, when I was having lunch at the cafeteria in the Student Union Building, I frequently noticed a young lady, but I never saw her anywhere else and no one I knew, knew who she was. Finally, in June of 1958, toward the end of my Junior year, I was with a student from the school of x-ray technology who knew who she was. He told me her name was Betty Malott, and she lived in the Student Cottages. He knew her because she was an x-ray student as well, but one year behind him. I jokingly commented to one of my friends that I was going to marry her one day! Well, I called her and asked her to go out with me. She was reluctant because she didn't know me, but she finally agreed to go with me just for a snack. After that, we started dating on a regular basis. Shortly, I had fallen deeply in love with her and had asked for her hand in marriage. She had accepted, so we were planning to get married soon after our graduation. Mine was scheduled for June 7th, and hers in August.

Prior to Thanksgiving in 1958, I had no indication on what to base my life beyond graduation from dental school, so rather than just waiting to hear from the U.S.A.F., I had made some alternative plans. I already had planned to live in California, so I applied to take the necessary examinations with the intent to start a dental practice and live there. In January, 1959, Betty and I decided that since I was graduating before she was and I was going to take the Boards in California, that we should get married before we graduated. She could finish her school requirements and take her two weeks of vacation and skip the graduation ceremony so she could accompany me to California. Early in the Spring I was notified by the U.S.A.F. that I had been accepted. With events happening so fast, and having a very busy schedule with fixed deadlines, Betty and I had to sit down and revise all of our plans accordingly.

Rolando's IU Dental School Senior Picture

Betty's high school senior picture.

As already planned, Betty went ahead with selecting her maid of honor, I asked a friend to be my best man at the wedding and invited two other friends to come along. Basically, it was family only at the reception, which was held at Betty's parents' house. All in all, it was a beautiful ceremony and reception, before Betty and I drove off to spend our honeymoon at a nice motel where my best man had reserved the "Honeymoon Suite".

In preparation for the wedding, Betty and I rented an apartment in a very nice, old neighborhood, where most of the houses were old mansions. Some of the owners had them converted into apartments. We found out about the place in conversations with another married classmate, Bob Coleman, who was renting an apartment there. This way, we already had a place to live for the rest of our school days. In March, we were excited to discover that Betty was expecting our first child. This didn't change our plans for the trip to California. Betty had never traveled anywhere except two trips to Florida when she was 9 and 10 years old.

Betty and Rolando's wedding.

CHAPTER 25

RUNNING OUT OF MONEY AND TRIP TO CALIFORNIA

I was to graduate in June and the Air Force had scheduled me to go to Basic Training immediately following graduation. My savings had been draining out faster than planned. While working for Cerro de Pasco, I entered a period of poor investments, as described previously in the book. I lost money in the "Salvage Business" the "Land investments" and the formation of the "Golf Club" business. But I managed to put some money aside for my education and to start my life in the U.S.A. Once again, I started to run out of money and having a family on the way, I started looking for means of earning some extra money. I did not foresee that our living expenses would escalate with both of us still being students.

Although I had the skills to generate additional income, being a full time student, the time necessary to satisfy my academic demands, did not leave much time for anything else. I did not have any student loans to rely upon, or even knew of their existence; my student out of state school tuition and related expenses took a big bite from my savings, so beyond paying our apartment rent we had to start cutting back to the bare necessities until I started getting some income from the Air Force. I always had a positive attitude and was pretty cocky based on nothing material. I had deep faith in God and as the Spanish saying goes, "A DIOS ROGANDO, PERO CON EL MAZO DANDO", which means "While Imploring to God, keep hitting the problem with a big club" and something miraculous would happen. In my case something completely unexpected did happen. Some of my professors who were engaged in private practice had seen my student work in the dental laboratory while I was under their supervision. They asked me if I would be interested in doing some occasional laboratory crown and bridge work for them. My answer was that I would be happy to do it within the little time I could carve out from school. I cheerfully accepted, first as a compliment, but inside myself I thought that it could bring in at least some food money. When asked for my fee, I answered that I could not possibly establish a fee for them and it would be O.K. by me to pay me whatever they felt it was worth. They were always very generous with me, and although I could not count on that money, it frequently paid for some occasional needed luxury breaks. By recommendation of some members of the research department in Dental Materials, chaired by Dr. Ralph Philips, I was hired to do some research on bonding porcelain onto metallic surfaces, such as, precious metals, meaning gold, semi-precious, meaning gold alloys with different percentages of gold content, and non-precious alloys meaning base metal alloys. This was a yearlong project under the chairman of Fixed Prosthodontics, Dr. John F. Johnston, and his Assistant Chairman, Dr. Roland Dykema.

To make my financial situation worse, I had requested that the Air Force delay my reporting date long enough to allow me to take the California State Boards, following my graduation from dental school. My request was granted, and moved to the first of October, 1959.

I was fortunate to receive three honor certificates and several honorable mentions at the indoor Awards Ceremony. Betty and other married student's wives received their P.H.T. (Pushing Hubby Thru) certificates. The next day we attended the outdoor Cap and Gown graduation ceremonies at the I.U. Bloomington Campus where literally thousands of students of all the different schools at I.U. receive their official certificates of graduation.

After I graduated I got a job working in the dental laboratory at the Dental School pouring models for everyone, until Betty finished her training.

I had a nearly 3 year old car, but in preparation for the long trip to California, I had my car fully serviced, including a new set of brakes as recommended by the service station.

In August we left Indianapolis and our first stop was in Hannibal, Missouri the home town of Mark Twain. Next we went to Denver, Colorado, where I had been invited to visit with a couple of families; one was Dr. Pablo Zubiate, a heart surgeon, his wife Ada and their family, and Mr. Willie Wurdack and wife Fritzi, a Swiss couple, that I had become friends with while working in La Oroya. Just before approaching the city of Denver, I started having some problems with the brakes locking up. While visiting I took my car to have the brakes checked and serviced. Our friends in Denver took us for a little tour of the surrounding areas including the "Red Rock Theatre", and of course for a Swiss couple, it also had to include a picnic trip to the foot hills of a snow capped mountain with a crystal lake below.

Rolando and Betty in Colorado in 1959

From Denver we drove to Salt Lake City to spend the night at a Motel. We arrived early and after settling down in our room I looked in the phone directory and found the name of a friend from La Oroya, who lived in the city. I called to confirm it was the family of Mr. and Mrs. Ted Wright to say hello and they invited us for dinner.

From Salt Lake City we drove to Reno, Nevada, where I wanted to show Betty the casinos. After we checked into the motel, she was very tired and wanted to lie down for a few minutes before going to the casino for dinner. Well, she fell asleep and didn't wake up until the next morning! So we had breakfast and went to the casino, which was still in full swing at 8 a.m. Betty was very excited when she hit the jackpot on a nickel slot machine, winning $35 dollars!

We then left Reno to go to the home of Dr. Craig Burns on the shores of Lake Almanor near Redding, California. Dr. Burns had been the chief Physician at Chulec General Hospital in La Oroya. Dr. and Mrs. Burns, their children, and I had become very good friends. Dr. Burns, a youthful, super physician with an adventurous and pioneering spirit to boot, was an avid rock hound, as well. He fit in very well with the mining engineers, who took him down into to the mines as they had taken me. You could see Dr. Burns down in the mines just as excited and comfortable with his little pick in one hand and a chunk of rock in the other, checking the world of gems, as you could see him in the hospital lab, looking into a microscope. When Dr. Burns left Peru, his total allowance of weight for household goods and baggage was taken by collections of rocks which later on would decorate the walls of his entire house, shelf after shelf. To the credit of the whole family, they built the entire lake house with very little help from contractors or mechanized equipment. I know it well because I spent a couple of weeks one summer helping to build part of the house. The house's center piece was a big fireplace built entirely with lava rock from the nearby Mt. Lassen lava field. He enjoyed the meat of wild animals and quinoa that he had discovered in Peru. He had quite an admirable knowledge of natural plant medicines and survival that I would later learn during my life in the Air Force.

Dr. Burns found employment at the Board of Public Health in Berkeley, California. He and his family lived in Berkeley during the school year in a home he had rented for the fall and winter. He offered the home for us to stay in while I took the California Dental Boards, since he and his family were not going to live there until the school year started. Berkeley was just across the San Francisco Bay from San Francisco where the Boards were to be given, so I took him up on his offer and we stayed there. We enjoyed going to the movies on the University Campus. Betty never forgot the audience there! It was then, the heart of the hippy movement. The movie we saw was the "Treasure of Sierra Madre", which was filmed before Betty was born! Betty and I enjoyed very much our visit, particularly the time spent at the Lake Almanor house.

After we arrived in San Francisco, we once again had problems with the brakes on the car. We took it to an auto repair shop where, once again, they told us they had fixed the problem.

One adventure that Betty had was on the first day of the Exams. Upon arrival at the Dental School in San Francisco for registration, I was given the forms that were to be checked off as I completed each required procedure. Among those was a button which I was told was necessary for me to wear at all times. Well, the day arrived for the exams and we went across the San Francisco-Oakland Bay Bridge into the city to the school. After arriving there, I realized that I had forgotten my button. I couldn't leave to go back to the house to get it, so I asked Betty if she could go get it. She didn't have much experience driving in a big city, but she said she would do it. At the registration the day before, we had met a young couple from Montana, who were also there for him to take the boards. The wife volunteered to go with Betty. They had an uneventful trip back to the house, but upon arrival Betty realized that I hadn't given her the key to the door. Well, they looked around for an open window and found one, on the second floor. Then the problem was how to get up to it. They went around to the back of the house looking for a ladder, but couldn't find one. However, one of the neighbors noticed them walking around and asked if she could help them with anything. The girls told her the story, and luckily she believed them and loaned them a ladder. Now, Betty was seven months pregnant, and her friend was afraid of heights! But, being the kind person she was, she went up the ladder and through the window and opened the front door. They got the button, returned the ladder and returned to the school just in time before I needed it!

After our visit with the Burns' and my State Board Exams, we drove north to Seattle to visit our friends, Tom and Beverly Dahl. As usual, they were very gracious hosts. They showed us the sites, and we got to visit Beverly's parents' beach house, and Tom's parents' house in Tacoma. They were all very hospitable and kind to us. Again we had problems with the brakes on the car. Tom took us to an auto repair shop, where, once again, they told us they had fixed the problem.

Betty and I were beginning to get short of time and Betty wanted to see some of Yellowstone National Park, entering from the north entrance, then proceed to see the Painted Desert, the Little Bighorn River, Mount Rushmore, the Corn Palace in South Dakota, and back home to Indianapolis.

As we got near the entrance to Yellowstone Park, we found out that there had been an earthquake and the Park was closed. We then decided that Gillette, Wyoming, which on our trip map appeared to be a large city with lots of conveniences, would be a good place to stop for the night. We could not see any place further east that would be a good place to stop.

We got to Gillette and drove around looking for a place to eat lunch and for accommodations to spend the night. We could not find anything until we came to a nice hotel building where they were still serving lunch. We stopped and went in and saw they still had a line for lunch because the dining room was full. We decided to join the line, and while waiting we noticed that the lobby was very nicely furnished and decorated, but it was full of saddles, saddle bags etc., reminiscent of the old wild-west days, which added to the atmosphere. We inquired if something special was going on, or, was this an everyday occurrence? That is when we met a very nice couple who had come to town from their ranch to buy supplies. They were further up in the line than we were, and they invited us to sit with them for lunch. They told us that the following day was the first day of hunting season, and there would probably be more people arriving the rest of the day. We immediately proceeded to find out if they still had room at the hotel, which they did, and we registered for the night.

The following day we left bright and early, hoping to get to see the Painted Desert and The Little Bighorn River. Unfortunately, the Painted Desert was flooded and it was raining so hard that we couldn't get out of the car to see the battleground at the Little Bighorn. The next stop was Mount Rushmore. We drove miles and miles of nothingness noticing road signs saying "Drive at your own risk". As the hours passed, fog and snow started to set in; and I am sure you already guessed it, when we got to the Mount Rushmore area, we could not see anything. There was a nice motel at the bottom of the foothills, so we decided to stop there. The people in charge were very nice and accommodating. We asked if there was a chance that the fog would lift later on so that we could be able to see the famous presidential faces, perhaps with some moon light. They said that the weather forecast was for the fog to continue for two more weeks! The next morning the fog was still thick, so we proceeded to have a leisurely breakfast, check out from the motel and drive up to the viewing area. We parked as close to the parking guard rail where people said it would be so close, that even with slight fog we should be able to see. We wasted almost two hours, because the fog was so thick that we couldn't even see the hood of the car!

We decided to leave and be on our way to Sioux Falls, South Dakota to see the famous "Corn Palace", which is advertised as being open 365 days a year. It was the week before the "Corn Festival" which attracts lots of visitors, so we thought that our timing was perfect for avoiding the crowds. When we arrived into the city we saw many attractive posters, advertising the Corn Festival Events, which further increased our excitement to visit it.

As we approached the building we could see the outside and noticed that it was not only beautiful, but unusual. We parked our car and walked to the entrance and we were shocked by the sign indicating that it was closed to the public to finish the work inside in preparation for the festival!

Our next planned stop was a southern suburb of Chicago where we had been invited to visit a young Peruvian couple living there, the Maneros, also acquaintances from La Oroya. On our way there, we started having some problems with the car brakes locking up again. It appeared that something was causing the wheels to heat up, and if we stopped for a while and allowed it to cool off, it was ok to continue driving. We had a nice dinner and visit with the Maneros, but we were running short on time to get back to Betty's parents' home in Indiana. We had to prepare for my trip to report for active duty training at Gunter A.F.B., Alabama. According to our AAA road maps Indianapolis was just a few hours drive from where we were, so with that thought in mind we started our trip the following morning. Not very long after we left, the car started acting up again. We were driving on state roads that had little traffic and few gas stations along the way. We stopped at a couple of gas stations to see if they could help us check the brakes and fix them, but since it was Sunday, some of them were closed and some didn't have a mechanic on duty. The next time that I felt the brakes begin to lock up I slowed down until we could see a gas station. By the time we found one, we were barely creeping and the brakes just froze up. I went in and explained my situation to the attendant. He told me that since it was Sunday, the mechanic wasn't there and there wasn't any place open where he could get parts, but he would see what he could do. Betty called her dad and explained the situation. Her dad offered to come up and see if he could tow us the rest of the way home. So that is what we decided to do. We were about a two hour drive from home. In the meantime, while we waited for Betty's dad to arrive, the gas station attendant had been able to at least get the wheels to turn. Mr. Malott hooked up my car to his with a chain. We decided it would be safer for Betty to ride with him and her mom. I rode in my car in order to keep it in neutral, and to keep my car aligned with his to prevent it from rear ending him, just using the hand emergency brakes. I never felt so helpless, ashamed, and humiliated in my life, just when I was trying to leave a good impression with my in-laws' entire family. After we got to Betty's parents' home, I felt relieved knowing that my wife and our first expected baby were safe. I prayed to God that they would remain the same during my assignment at Gunter Air Force Base in Alabama. Betty couldn't accompany me since the baby was due at the end of November and it was already October. I spent most of the night before I left worrying about Betty's well-being.

CHAPTER 26

BEGINNING MY MILITARY CAREER WITH BABY ON THE WAY

From Indianapolis I drove to Gunter A.F.B., Alabama, for Basic Military Training and officially started my military career. Upon completion I was to report for duty to Lackland, A.F.B. in Texas. The training at Gunter was hard for the physically unfit person, but, for me, it was exciting and lots of fun. Our instructors were strict, but among the very best. The day was filled with classroom classes and outdoor practices and exercises. It was still sunny at the end of our military activities. The base was beautiful, filled with impeccable yards surrounding the houses, and general areas with tropical foliage, flowering trees, and Pecan trees. It was my first experience with pecan nuts, which were largely wasted after dropping down from the tree branches. I began to rush to my quarters every evening to change into my civilian attire to go out and pick-up the Pecans on the ground, which had fallen from trees in the general areas. An occasional shaking of the tree branches would increase my collection of freshly gathered nuts.

The weekend before graduation we were allowed to leave the Base to go to the city of Montgomery. We had already heard the rumors of an exciting football game that was a bigger event locally than the national games. A group of us chose to go to this most heated football game of the season: Lanier vs Robert E. Lee High Schools. We were fortunate to find seats in small groups. Seats were hard to get because it appeared to us that the whole town would be going. Massive groups of young and old waved banners and flags for their favorite team, and carried umbrellas in case of rain. The band and cheer leading teams added to the atmosphere and excitement. The teams entered as their names were called on the loud speakers, one at a time. I was seated next to a young dentist from New Jersey, who was concentrating more on a comic book he was reading than watching the preliminary activities of the game. Behind us there was a family with an elderly, vivacious lady, who could easily have been in her eighties, waving her little flag and yelling for her team. The ceremonies began and as customary the band began playing the National Anthem. The excited audience stood up either saluting the flag or with their right hands on their heart. After the National Anthem the band started playing Dixie. I noticed that my friend, who had just sat down to continue reading his comic book, had suddenly been given a good wrap on the head with the elderly lady's umbrella! From behind I heard her telling him loudly, "You damned Yankee, we remain on our feet around here while Dixie is playing." My friend stood up in shock afraid of seeing if anybody else had heard the reprimand.

Following military procedures, I checked out of Gunter A.F.B., and with my travel orders in hand headed for Texas. Another fellow who was also going to Lackland, A.F.B. asked me if we could follow each other on our two day trip. Based on my recent past experiences, I readily agreed. Following military guidelines we were not to exceed 300 miles per day. Speed limits on the roads were posted at 45 to 60 miles per hour.

Every day after leaving Indianapolis, in the evening I called home to talk with my wife to catch up on the events of the day as well as to find out how the pregnancy was progressing. She had already been forbidden to take any trips of any kind six weeks before and six weeks after the baby was born.

After leaving Gunter A.F.B., on the way to San Antonio, my travel companion and I stopped for lunch, planned where it would be best to stop and call it a day. We decided that Baton Rouge, Louisiana would be the choice. After registering at a motel, I called Betty's parents' home. Her father answered, and proceeded to carry on a small conversation. I was worried about Betty because on our last conversation, she indicated that the baby might be born anytime. I was getting a little irritated with my father in law, so I interrupted him in mid-sentence and I asked him to tell me about Betty's condition. Of course he had been kidding me all along, and he said "Oh, is that why you're calling?" I could hear a laugh. "Well," he said, "she's O.K." I asked him if I could talk to her, and he said, "Well, she's not home." I asked when she would be back, he answered, "Probably in a couple of days." I said, "Can you tell me where she is?" Well, he said, "She's OK, I told you, she's at Franklin in the Hospital." "Is she in labor?" I asked. He replied, "No, the baby is already here. You guys have a cute little black haired girl!" (My mother in law, had always wanted a black haired baby girl). By then, I was just about emotionally drained, and I just hung up on him. The next day, my friend and I drove the rest of the way to our final destination.

The following morning, my friend and I dressed up in full uniform to report to our respective commanders. I reported to a highly decorated Colonel, who was in charge of the Dental Division at the Base. After the customary military formalities, he introduced me to CWO Lyle to guide me in "processing in".

During the processing steps, I had the opportunity to confide with CWO Lyle, that I had called my wife back home and that she had just delivered our first baby, and that I wanted to go home for a few days. The best way for me would be to fly home and back. CWO Lyle answered that if I had just started active duty, I probably would have no leave time accrued, so he suggested that probably a "well documented emergency leave request" would most likely be approved. At that time, air travel was expensive and scheduling for direct flights within the states were not often convenient or fast. So I asked if he knew of any means of financing the costs, because I did not have enough money to pay for it. CWO Lyle, smiled, and said, "I've seen worse situations, but we have to run it by the Colonel and I will try to expedite the paperwork immediately". We finished my processing in by getting me into temporary officers' quarters, where I would live until my wife could join me. My feeling of gratitude and admiration for the U.S.A.F. began to take deep roots in my heart. Within 24 hours I had all my papers and travel tickets confirmed, I called my in-laws house again to let Betty know I was coming to see her and our baby. The very next day I flew to Indianapolis, and spent one of the most enjoyable and memorable days in my life with my wife and our first born baby, Elena Leeann.

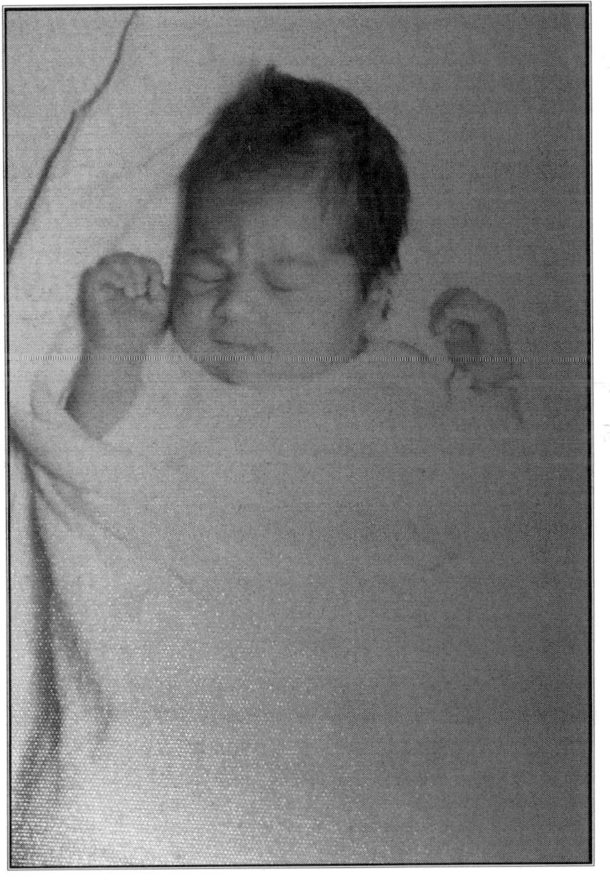

One day old Elena.

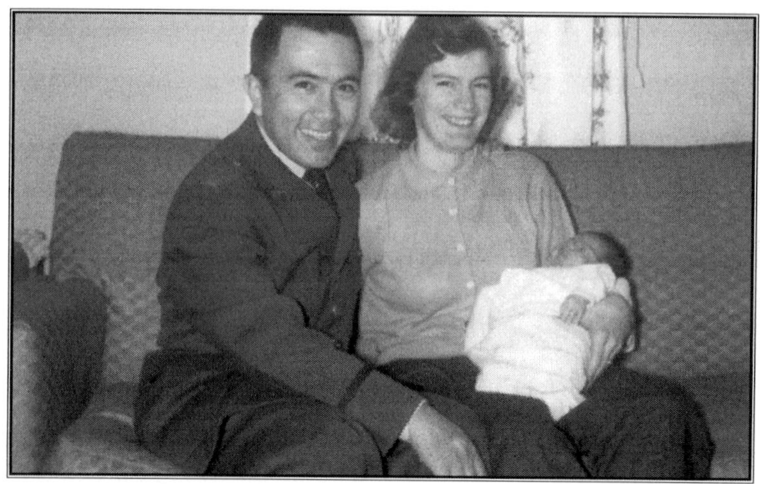

Rolando, Betty, and Elena the first time I saw her, November 1959.

CHAPTER 27

GROWING FAMILY AND MAN WITHOUT A COUNTRY

Betty and Elena couldn't travel until Elena was six weeks old, so I spent that time looking for a place for us to live. I found a nice little three bedroom, one bath house in a neighborhood called Lackland Terrace. It was all brick and had an eat-in kitchen, a living room, dining room combination and a carport with the laundry room on the other side of the carport. It cost $11,000.00. I signed a contract on the house and then I went shopping for furniture, because we didn't have any. So by the time that my family arrived, on December 31, 1959, I had everything ready for them.

Elena in front of Rolando and Betty's first house and car in San Antonio, Texas.

After I returned to Lackland from seeing our baby, I was ready to start my military career with the firm determination that I would do my best to serve in the U.S.A.F., and if possible, do well beyond what would ordinarily be expected of me.

And so it was, that I was assigned to the main dental clinic in General Dentistry, Dental Clinic # 4, also known on base as "the Amalgam line". It was called that because the majority of restorations placed at the clinic were silver amalgam, and Silicate restorations. The clinic also had a periodontist, an oral surgeon, an endodontist, an orthodontist, and a couple of dental hygienists. Any specialty type of services beyond the scope of general dentistry were referred to the specialty clinics at other locations within the base.

In addition to the procedures being recorded in the patients chart, the administrative personnel kept a record of the number of procedures completed by individual dental officers. The chief of the clinic, usually a seasoned dentist, would randomly check on the quality of restorative services being provided. This was one of the factors that the clinic commander would use for evaluating and grading each individual dental officer. It did not take long for the commander to identify some slackers or poor quality dentists to whom he would occasionally offer fatherly-like counseling. Likewise, some commanders would discretely offer some relaxation time off or other incentive reward to those who rendered better services to their patients.

My military pay frequently was not enough to cover all my family's basic needs. On a couple of occasions I had asked my commander for permission to work outside the base on Saturdays when not needed for my regular military duties. To do so, I had to take the particular state board exams to be licensed to practice. So it was an added barrier or difficulty, but if I had the permission to do it, I would be willing to get prepared for them. And that is exactly what I did, and that is how I became licensed in five States.

Betty and I had been expecting our next child and in 1960, the Lord blessed us with an early Christmas Gift, Our first boy to carry on the Bernui name. Betty and I decided to name him Michael Rolando.

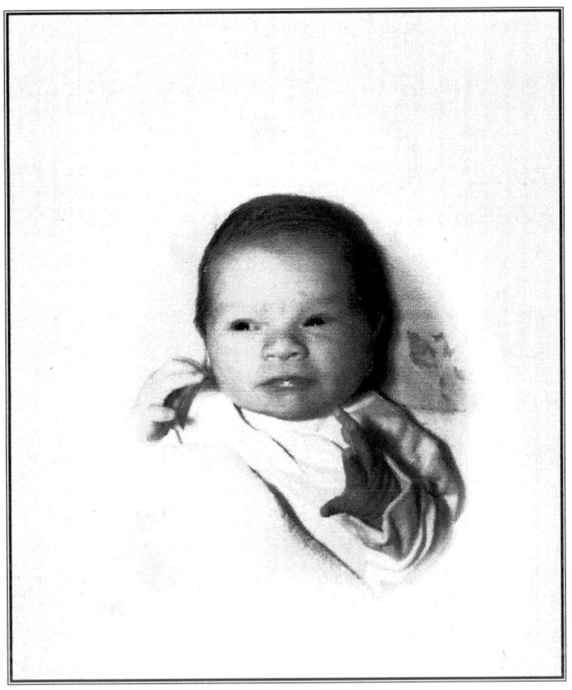

Newborn Michael

There are occasions in everyone's life that you never forget. This was a second time for Betty and me. We now had two beautiful children, a girl and a boy, a Hoosier and a Texan, both with a Peruvian flavor!

Shortly after Michael's birth, I was invited by one of the institutions aware of my academic accomplishments in Peru to present a paper on Dentistry at a forthcoming international dental meeting to be held in Lima. I was stationed at Lackland Air Force Base in San Antonio, Texas at that time. After applying and receiving permission from my Dental Commander, I started preparations to travel. I sent my Peruvian passport to the Peruvian consulate in Houston, Texas to obtain a visa, indicating the reason for my trip. Within a few days I received a phone call from the Peruvian embassy asking me to explain to them my present status in the U.S. A.F. I was asked if I had permission from the Peruvian government to join the United States Air Force, to which I answered that I had not. I explained that I had not applied yet for citizenship status, but I intended to do so of my own free will. I was not aware that I needed to request anybody's permission, since this was my own personal choice. The Peruvian official making the call, sarcastically stated that they also did not need anybody's permission to deny me permission to return to Peru, and therefore they were not going to return my passport. From that point on I was a man without a country. My Peruvian citizenship had been taken away, and I was not a citizen of the United States of America. Since I didn't have a passport I could not go to Lima to present the paper. I had been looking forward to taking Betty and the children to meet my family and friends, but the trip had to be postponed to a later time, after I became an American citizen.

Rolando, Betty, Elena, Mary Beth, Michael 1962

CHAPTER 28

MEETING AND TREATING THE ASTRONAUTS

Most of the doctors in the general, medical or dental professions join the armed forces for two, or three years, just enough time for them to improve on their practice skills and production speed. A few doctors, whose commanders felt worth keeping, were encouraged to consider staying in the service and making it a career. Financial incentives were not a consideration for the majority of doctors, because the Military Service pay scales could not compete favorably with civilian practice opportunities.

After two years at the General Dentistry clinic, I was assigned to the Dental Clinic at Wilford Hall U.S.A.F. Hospital. The clinic Commander was Col. Al Monhac, an outstanding Oral Surgeon, a former POW, and a survivor of the infamous Japanese "Bataan Death March" during World War II. This was the clinic where all Oral Surgery Specialty students would come after their Academic training to do their Residency training. In addition, it had a General Dentist, who was me, in charge of rendering services to hospital personnel and patients that needed conscious sedation, or general anesthesia, as determined by their physicians.

In addition to the Oral Surgery Residency students and me, there were also two other rotating interns from other specialty clinics that were in the General Practice Residency Program.

This also was the clinic that processed, evaluated, and treated the dental needs of the chosen candidates for special programs, such as NASA. Since I was the ranking General Dentist in the clinic, I had the honor and privilege to process in the first SEVEN MERCURY ASTRONAUTS, from which my commander, Col. Mohnac, assigned me as Col. John Glenn Jr.'s dentist. All of Col. Glenn's treatment was performed by me at the Oral Surgery Clinic, under the supervision of Col. Kenneth Rudd, chairman of the Department of Prosthodontics and Dental Laboratory Services. The laboratory technician who worked with me was Tech. Sergeant Carlos Gutierrez. I was truly honored to be able to call John Glenn and Scott Carpenter, and Gus Grissom friends. Personal conversations with Col. Glenn, and his unusually friendly personality and friendly suggestions, would heavily influence my decision to stay in the military.

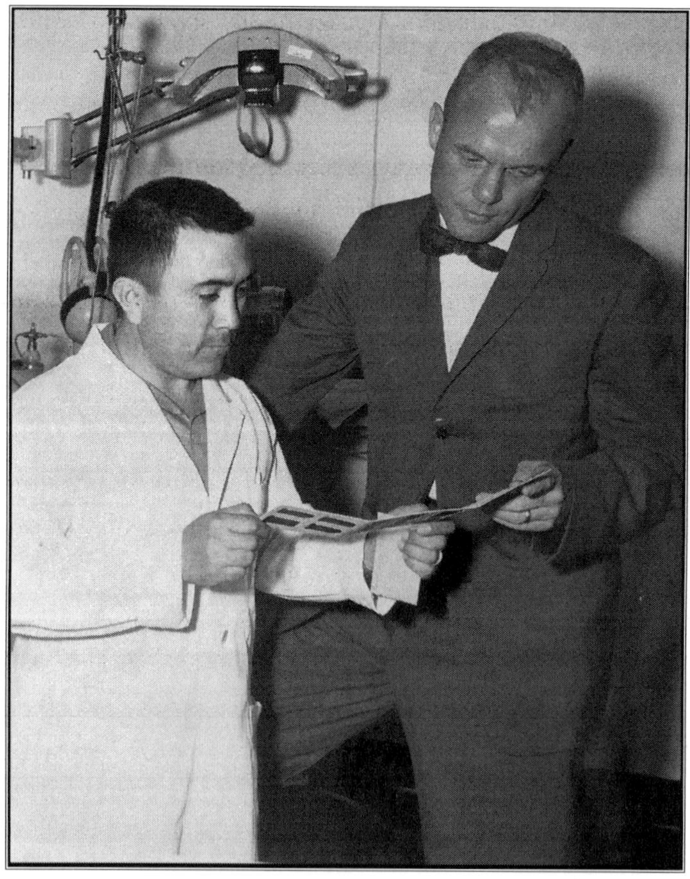

Captain Rolando Bernui and Colonel John Glenn, Astronaut

When we found out that our third child was on the way, we realized that our little home was not going to be big enough for all of us. I was fascinated by the way houses were built in the U.S. so, frequently, I would stop on the way home and watch how the homes that were under construction in our neighborhood were being built. I soon met the owner of the construction company, who was on the job supervising the workers. His name was Col. Davenport, he was retired military. One day when I was watching, he said "you like my homes so much, why don't you buy one from me?" I said, "I don't think I can afford one of your homes". He asked me if I had a house and I told him that I just lived down the street. So he said, "I can take a look at your house to see how much I think it's worth and it could work out that you can trade your house for one of mine". So he came to the house and appraised it, then he took us to see a lot that he had two streets over from where we lived. He said he could build a house on that lot for $16,000.00 and we could trade our house with him and have just a small amount more than the mortgage we already had. So we agreed and he sent his designer to see us, so that we could pick out all of the colors, type of tile, brick, wallpaper, etc., for the new house. We moved in June of 1962, just in time, because in July, we had another answer to our prayers, a baby girl, who we named Mary Beth. I had told Betty that I would like to have six children, and this baby would put us half way there, and perhaps we should start thinking of where we would like to live. We were beginning to like San Antonio, but also wanted to consider other cities like Dallas, Houston and the Corpus Christi area, because of the beaches. But we had not completely ruled out Indianapolis. After all that is where Betty's family and many friends lived.

A Dental Prosthodontic Study Club had been founded by Col. Ben Dunn, Chief of Prosthodontics at Wilford Hall, USAF Hospital, Col. Kenneth Rudd, Col. Allen Brewer, Chief of the Dental Research Division at Brooks AFB, Col. Earl Feldman, and Col. T.K. Jones, all of whom were Prosthodontists The main purpose of the study club was to provide the

Prosthodontics Residency students a forum where they could give their training presentations on matters of interest within the specialty, promote research ideas and get experience in giving public presentations. It was mandatory for all first and second year Prosthodontic residents. Other dental officers who were actively treating prosthodontic patients and interested general dentists like myself were allowed to attend by invitation with approval of the chairman of the study club. Col. Sam Hoskins, Col. David Detamore and Col. Timothy O'Leary from the Department of Periodontics were also frequently invited to presentations of guest speakers or residency student presenters on topics that peeked their interest. I was honored to be invited to attend all of the meetings. After all, my main interest in dentistry was to restore patients' mouths to their best dental health.

The Air Force offered me specialty training in Prosthodontics, which was only given to Officers with Regular status. So with the encouragement of Col. Mohnac, I submitted my application for career status, known at that time as "Regular" status. What that means is that if you are not "Regular", you may be vulnerable to "RIF". RIF stands for Reduction in Force. Every now and then, the government may call for a RIF. Some airmen, who made the decision to remain on temporary active duty till the minimum time of service (20 active years) in order to receive their retirement benefits, including their pension, could be discharged before the twenty years. Therefore, they could have served for 18 or 19 years and then not receive the retirement benefits. The RIF does not affect career officers.

I was sent to Randolph AFB to take the required in-depth qualification exams, including physicals, to determine whether I would be accepted or not. In the meantime, while waiting for the results many other life changing things happened.

About this time, I was called by my commanding officer to report to Wilford Hall USAF Hospital to translate for a VIP patient from a Latin American country, who only spoke Spanish, and didn't understand the translator they had sent. I spent the next two days translating for a General

Velasco, who was having a complete physical examination. Later, I was called to go back to the hospital because the General wanted to talk to me. He greeted me warmly, shook my hand and told me he really appreciated my help because the other translator they had before me didn't speak Spanish the way it was spoken in Peru. He then asked me where I was from because my Spanish was so good. I told him that I was born and raised in Peru. He looked at his aide, who was another General, and said, "These Americans have everything. They probably have a Chinese translator for a person from China, and a Greek translator for a person from Greece, and now they have a Peruvian translator for a Peruvian!" He then told his aide to give me his card and told me that if I came to Peru to give him a call, so that perhaps we could get together at the Military Club in Lima. So I kept the card and thought no more about it.

By this time I had applied for citizenship, and was prepared to take the necessary exams that all candidates for citizenship are required to take and pass. It was an emotional time for me, to review my humble past and realize with how much I had been blessed and what I had already been able to achieve. Full citizenship would be a crowning event on which to start my new life. At the official ceremony of the oath of citizenship, the Judge administering the oath said, "By the authority vested in me, I now grant you all the rights and privileges of citizenship of the Great Republic of Texas and of the United States of America".

When Col. Glenn learned from my commander that I had just received my citizenship, he sent me a letter of congratulations. This was the first of three letters that I received from him.

"Best regards to my friend 'Rolo' Bernui, and sincere appreciation for all the help. –John Glenn, Jr.

Shortly after the first letter, I received a large printed picture of his rocket and space capsule on the launch pad with the following inscription:

"With best regards to my friend 'Rolo' Bernui, with sincere appreciation for all the help". Signed, John H. Glenn, Jr. The second letter was to congratulate me on my retirement from the Air Force. The third letter was to give me permission to use his name in this book. It is as follows:

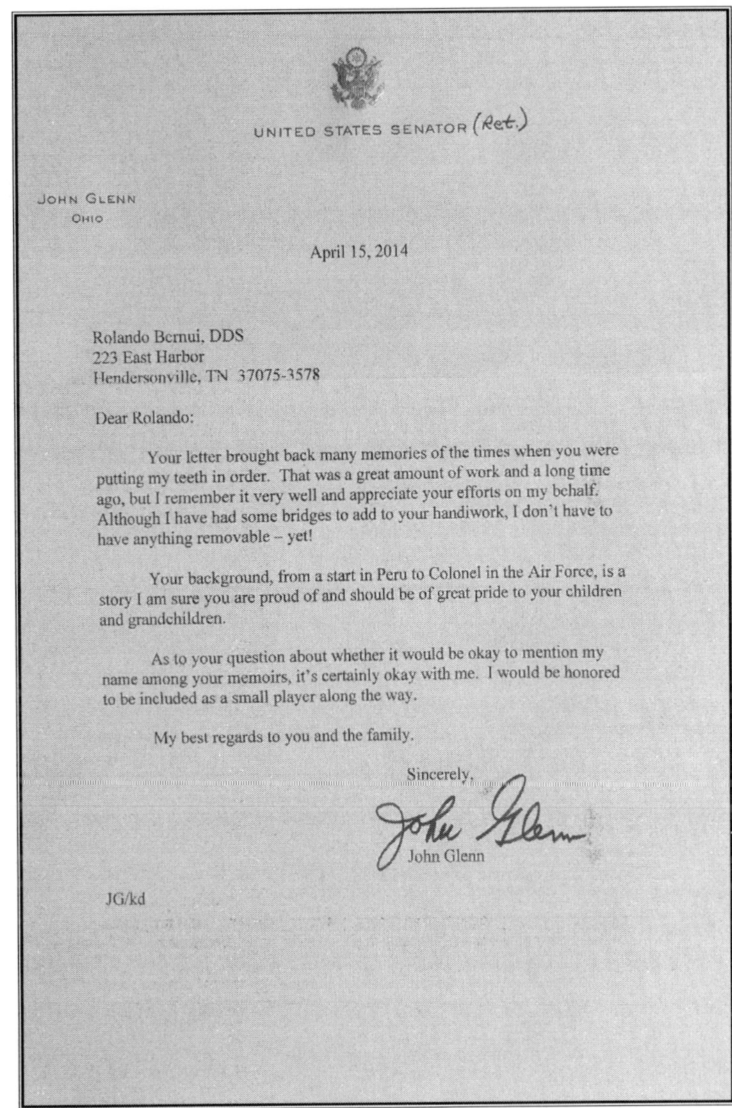

UNITED STATES SENATOR (Ret.)

JOHN GLENN
OHIO

April 15, 2014

Rolando Bernui, DDS
223 East Harbor
Hendersonville, TN 37075-3578

Dear Rolando:

Your letter brought back many memories of the times when you were putting my teeth in order. That was a great amount of work and a long time ago, but I remember it very well and appreciate your efforts on my behalf. Although I have had some bridges to add to your handiwork, I don't have to have anything removable – yet!

Your background, from a start in Peru to Colonel in the Air Force, is a story I am sure you are proud of and should be of great pride to your children and grandchildren.

As to your question about whether it would be okay to mention my name among your memoirs, it's certainly okay with me. I would be honored to be included as a small player along the way.

My best regards to you and the family.

Sincerely,

John Glenn

John Glenn

JG/kd

Letter to Rolando from John Glenn.

John Glenn's cordial and jovial attitude, in addition to the patriotic fervor he displayed was something that would inspire anyone who got to know him closely. He was always a humble and unassuming gentleman and he inspired me to want to make a career of the Air Force.

I personally had an outstanding offer from Indiana University School of Dentistry offering me a teaching position in the Department of Prosthodontics under Dr. John F. Johnston, upon my separation from the Service. I exchanged a couple of letters with Dean Maynard Hine, at I.U., who, in addition to a teaching position, also offered me specialty training at no cost and time off allowed from teaching duties.

After a couple of weeks, Col. Mohnac who was my commander and was aware of my situation called me into his office and informed me that I had been accepted for career status and he was confident that I would also get selected for Specialty training. I was torn by having to make an immediate decision. After discussing it with my wife, and with heartfelt prayers, we decided to cast our lot with U.S. Air Force.

The following day I called the Dental School and spoke with Dean Hine to inform him of my situation and my decision. He listened silently, and calmly told me.... "I just want you to reflect on the following: While the Government offers might look like a dream, the Government can also take it away without asking for anyone's permission. Should you change your mind, give me a call. Otherwise, here at your alma matter, we all wish you good luck." He hung up his phone, and I silently wept while saying a prayer to my God before hanging up the receiver at my end.

The following years were exciting and very busy. The U.S.A.F. specialty studies program consisted of two years at a civilian institution, or one year at a civilian institution followed by a two year Residency at a U.S.A.F. teaching facility. The main requirement was that each candidate had to apply and get accepted at an ADA approved school program, before the Air Force would pay the necessary tuition fees. I applied to the University of Pennsylvania, Graduate School of Medicine because it had a perfect combination of Periodontics and Prosthodontics. After completing the requirements on either or both specialty fields, I would be qualified to take either one or both boards, and be a specialist in two separate fields.

My position at the hospital kept me extremely busy. The little time left I spent with the family. On a couple of occasions Col. Glenn would come to the hospital on official business. Being the kind of gentleman he is, he would always take the time to stop by and say hello at the office. On a couple of occasions he invited us, Col. and Mrs. Rudd and Col. and Mrs. Hoskins to dinner in town. He also came to our home for lunch and dinner a couple of times.

CHAPTER 29

TAKING MY FAMILY TO PERU

Now that I was a citizen, I applied for a passport and in January of 1963, Betty, Elena, Michael and I went for a trip to Peru. The baby, Mary Beth stayed with my in-laws in Indiana. My relatives had been very anxious to meet my American family and I had been anxious for Betty to meet them and to see where I had grown up. We spent a few days in Lima where we stayed with the Ghersi family and at the Crillon Hotel.

While staying at the hotel, I remembered that I had the card that General Velasco had given me when I was his translator. So I decided to give him a call. The person who answered the phone was very curt and asked me, who I was and where did I get the phone number I had. I told him and he said the General wasn't available at that time, but if I gave him my phone number and where I was staying he would call me back later. The next day when we returned to the hotel from sightseeing, I had a message to call this number. So I called, and the person who answered told me that the General was not available, but he wanted to know what I was doing there and what plans I had during my visit and how long I was staying. I told him that I was planning to take a taxi up to Callejon de Huaylas to visit my family but there were no cars available until Monday, so I would be in Lima until then. I told him I didn't know how long I was staying. He told me he would be in touch with me before Monday. The next day, he called me and told me there would be a military plane for me and my family to take us up to Callejon de Huaylas on Tuesday. He gave me instructions on what time and where to report for the flight. It was then that I began to wonder who General Velasco was, that he had that much power. It turned out that he was the Commander of the Armed Forces! And later, in 1968, he staged a coup d'état, and became President of Peru!

We reported to the airport, got our instructions, and boarded the plane. It was a very interesting flight on an old B-29 airplane that had been a bomber in World War II and was converted to carry passengers. After boarding we were told that the cabin wasn't pressurized and we were each given cotton balls to put in our ears and a tube to hold under our noses for oxygen. The seats were benches along the sides of the plane. When we were descending for our landing, I told Betty, "There's the airport!" She looked out the window and saw only a grassy pasture with one small building on one side. She said, "Where?" I said, "There where you see those people standing, one of them is my Uncle Roberto". We landed safely, much to Betty's relief! The pilot asked when we would be returning to Lima. I told him that I wasn't sure, so he told me to call a day or two before we were ready to return and he would fly up to pick us up and take us back to Lima. So I told him I would do that.

We were greeted by Uncle Roberto, Polo, and Senorita Luz Consuelo Mendez, a close friend of the family, also known as Aunt Luz. They took us to Uncle Samuel's home in Carhuaz where Betty met Aunt Haydee and some other cousins. While we were in Callejon de Huaylas, we visited many places that I had told Betty about, including the farm in Pariahuanca, Aco and Huaraz. While we were in Pariahuanca, Uncle Roberto wanted to show us the properties that belonged to the family. The only way to get to them was on horseback. So, early one morning we left Elena and Michael in the care of Aunt Luz and the servants, and set out on our trip.

Betty and Uncle Robert exploring the farm.

Betty with Uncle Samuel Obregon in Carhuaz, Peru, 1963

Betty had very little experience riding horses, but this was a trip that she has never forgotten. Right out of the corral, we started up a mountainside that was so steep that people had carved steps for the horses and people to ascend. We got up to a certain point where there was a narrow trail where it was straight up on one side and straight down, thousands of feet, on the other side and of course no guard rails. Every so often there was a wider place on the trail so that if there was anyone coming the other way we could pass each other. This came in handy when a train of donkeys carrying cargo came down and passed us. I had ridden these trails and others like them many times, but it was a new experience for Betty. As we went along Uncle would point out boundaries of our different properties. We came to a place very high up where a whole valley was spread below us and we could hear the roar of the river far below. This was the continental divide. Then we arrived at a place where Uncle pointed out some boundaries and then said, "That's it, now we will turn around and go back." The trail at that point was narrow and Betty asked, "Where are we going to turn around? It's too narrow here." I replied, "We're going to turn around right here". She said, "If we're going to turn around here, I'm getting off of this horse until it has turned". I told her, "Just stay on the horse, it knows what it's doing better than you do". She did and the horse turned around without any trouble. Then we returned to Pariahuanca the same way we had come.

After staying another night in Pariahuanca, we went to Huaraz to stay in the family house there. While there, I gave Betty a tour of the area that had been destroyed by the avalanche when I was a boy. We also visited Yungay, a town that had just recently been mostly destroyed by another avalanche. We left Huaraz, and returned to Carhuaz where Betty and the children rode my horse, Tantaleon. While we were there we went to another family house where my dental equipment had been stored. The room that had been designated as mine was empty. All of my equipment and belongings had disappeared except for one broken instrument and a plaque with my name on it. We were very disappointed to see that.

Betty with Elena, Michael on Tantaleon

A few days before we were going to return to Lima, I was reflecting on my phone call to General Velasco and the arrangements he had made for me and my family. Since everything about it was so mysterious, I didn't know what I might be getting into. So I decided it might be safer to just take a taxi back to Lima, instead of calling for another plane. So after leaving Carhuaz, we returned to Lima by taxi so Betty got to see the countryside of Peru. We stayed in Lima for a few more days and visited with many of my friends there. We then returned to Indianapolis to pick up Mary Beth and return by train to San Antonio.

CHAPTER 30

ILLNESS AND TRAGEDY

About a month after our return, we learned that we were expecting our fourth child in September. Soon after, we received a phone call from Peru letting us know that Uncle Roberto had been in a truck accident on his way to Lima, and they were sending him to us in order to get medical treatment. About that time Mary Beth became ill with an ear infection. She was treated with antibiotics, and was fine for about two weeks and then the ear infection recurred. This went on every two weeks for a couple of months. Each time the infections were worse and harder to treat. Her ears were lanced (myringotomy) each time and the antibiotics caused her to have gastrointestinal problems. She was admitted to the hospital at one point where they irrigated her ears several times a day and the infection seemed to have disappeared only to return two weeks later.

The ENT specialist advised us that the infections were caused by her adenoids being enlarged and the only way to cure her was to remove them. Our pediatrician advised against the surgery because she was only 10 months old. After one more ear infection, the ENT doctor stated to my wife that the infection was spreading to her mastoids and could then go to her brain. He said that unless those adenoids were removed, she would continue with the problem indefinitely.

Upon his recommendation, Mary Beth was admitted to the hospital overnight and the surgery would be performed early the next morning, June 15, 1963. As planned, she was taken to surgery around 7:30 a.m. At about

10:00 a.m. we were notified, that an artery had been severed and Mary Beth had lost so much blood that she had gone into shock, and although she was breathing, she was unconscious. She remained in the same state for three days. So on June 18, 1963, after our pediatrician explained that she had suffered irreversible brain damage and would never regain consciousness, and after asking my permission, she was taken off of life support and allowed to peacefully expire. She was almost eleven months old. Anger and disappointment followed for a while, but the love of our two older children, their activities, and the support of other dental wives, carried us through. The senior dental officers wives were very uniquely organized, and cohesive, and very supportive for anyone needing help. They seemed to make it their business to find out who needs help and what kind.

In the meantime, Uncle Roberto was living with us and receiving medical treatment. He had a severe wound infection from the truck accident, he needed to have prostate surgery, he needed treatment for an ear infection and an eye infection, and he needed dental treatment. I consulted with physicians at the Air Force hospital about how to get treatment for him since he had no money and neither did I. One of the physicians knew someone at the Santa Rosa Catholic Hospital in San Antonio. I took him there and they agreed to treat him free of charge since he was a priest. He had been wearing hearing aids that didn't work very well for several years. During his treatment, the ENT doctor discovered that the hearing loss was caused by fluid in his ears. They put tubes in his ears to drain the fluid and he could hear without hearing aids for the first time in many years. He was amazed by all of the sounds. He had never heard an airplane fly over or a telephone ring.

Uncle Roberto, Dick, Mary Beth, Betty, Michael, and Elena, Easter, 1963

CHAPTER 31

THE CUBAN MISSILE CRISIS AND DISASTER TRAINING

The following years were exciting and very busy. In October, the Cuban missile crisis was in full progress and everyone in the Air Force thought we were in for a nuclear war. President Kennedy had taken a hard stand, but the Russians kept pushing. We lived in a civilian neighborhood that was 95% or more military personnel. We had been informed of possible events and advised to stock up on food supplies, and water in particular, to last at least two weeks. There were no basements in most of the houses. Some decided to build themselves cement block bunkers and everyone got themselves armed with handguns and other heavier arms. We took the necessary precautions as well. We had our survival plans ready and continued to work as usual. Everyone seemed to have some type of radio or news update. We had our dinners in front of our TV to watch the news. The rumor was that San Antonio would be one of the primary targets because it was the home of five military bases. It was a very frightening period of time which lasted about two weeks and ended when the Russians turned their missile bearing ships around before they entered Cuban waters.

Shortly after that, at the hospital, some of us were summoned to attend mass casualty disaster exercises. The most shocking and sobering exercise was one at Camp Bullis. At the top of one hill, in a flat area, bleachers had been constructed similar to those at a baseball field. Behind the last top row of seats were posts with high powered speakers mounted on them. At the pitcher's mound was a microphone stand for the narrator and at some distance behind the narrator the hill dropped towards a treed valley, a creek and the beginning of other hills beyond. At a short distance behind the bleachers, the hill dropped more rapidly than at the front or the sides. The access road to our hilltop came from one of the sides and was used by the troops who made the preparations for the training event. The group of medics, as we were called, was composed of physicians, dentists, nurses and enlisted personnel. We were transported from our bases by military buses, all dressed in fatigues and boots. By 0600 we were all seated on the bleachers. The military commander of the exercise stepped up to the microphone and announced that today we were going to experience, realistically, what would happen in a surprise attack with an atomic bomb, what we might see and what we would need to do. We were there only to visually observe and learn, by watching the experienced people do what needed to be done. We were not to interact with anyone no matter the temptation. Then as he pointed to the distance he said, as you can see there are some military installations with surrounding populated areas. These are supposed to have been targeted by the enemy…Suddenly, we saw two airplanes speed silently above us and they dropped something that made two small flashes. A deafening sonic boom followed just a few seconds later, long after the planes had disappeared. Soon we saw the all familiar mushroom cloud rising and as it began to settle we were instructed to descend the hill slowly from different directions until we reached the bottom. Then we were to follow the trails to the camp which had been set up at the center of a meadow like area. We all saw different things and some of us took notes about what we were experiencing for later discussions. Most of us saw grotesque injuries. Everything from a person literally pierced through with a tree branch, human limbs hanging from trees and charred body parts, to people with less severe wounds and uninjured people just wandering around cluelessly or crying for help, etc. The U.S. Army should be credited for having prepared the most realistic moulages and the personnel should receive Oscars for their acting. Some observers were so deeply moved that there were many tearful eyes, and some were nervously shaking. Most of us who had paid attention to the preparedness lectures were able to control our emotions. I returned home physically and mentally exhausted at about 5:00 PM.

CHAPTER 32

MY EXPERIENCE AT MEDINA AIR FORCE BASE

Sometime after the exercise at Camp Bullis, I was transferred from the hospital dental clinic to the dispensary at nearby Medina Air Force Base. Medina was thought to be a nuclear weapons disposal facility. The main structure there was a gigantic, solid concrete bowl-like structure that was used for disassembly of weapons and parts disposal by incineration. Although it was considered a new facility, it had already been in operation for a few years. Medina was also the headquarters for the Officers Candidate Training School (OCS). It had a small medical dispensary which was under my command. There was a junior physician, two nurses and a dental assistant. My duties were the dental treatment of the OCS trainees in order to place them in class 1 dental health condition, ready for deployment worldwide. The dispensary was built with painted concrete walls and cement slab floors. The majority of the dental procedures were relatively minor because all of the candidates had to be in good physical and dental condition in order to be selected to qualify for OCS training. They had also already been thoroughly indoctrinated as to what conduct is expected from an Officer. (An Officer and a Gentleman).

My dental assistant was experienced and well trained militarily and professionally. Her name was Technical Sergeant Taylor. On September 22, 1963, our first patient was seated by 0730 and we were ready to start by anesthetizing him. As I approached the dental chair where the patient was seated, I said, "Good morning O.C. Smith". He replied, "Good morning, sir," without turning his head or making eye contact. He was perfectly dressed and seated correctly as if he were standing at attention for personal review. Sergeant Taylor was standing with the anesthetic syringe uncovered, when we heard the sound of an unusually loud explosion. I immediately looked out the window expecting to see the trail left in the air by a supersonic airplane, since sonic booms were a common occurrence for us. I turned my eyes toward Sergeant Taylor, who was still holding the syringe, shaking and with big tears coming down her cheeks. Before I could say a word, she pointed to a big crack in the concrete wall which I had not even noticed when I had gone to the window to see the plane that I thought had caused the sound. From our operatory we had a view of the massive disposal structure, which now had a mushroom like cloud rising from it. I couldn't hear T/Sgt. Taylor very well, but I needed to have her to reappoint the patient. We didn't have enough time to complete a procedure because each patient's schedule only allowed them 45 minutes to an hour maximum to be away from their unit. When we turned around to inform the patient, the chair was empty and we had no idea as to when the patient may have left! We then received orders to remain indoors until ordered otherwise. We continued looking outside for any activity and noticed an Army helicopter approaching. All of my experiences at the Camp Bullis exercise started flowing into my head, so much so, that I could swear that I could hear the helicopter pilot's Geiger counter report checking on detected radiation fallout…15 minus Zero, 10 minus Zero, five minus Zero…I was quickly trying to figure out how far away from the possible fallout we might be. I desperately wanted to get in touch with Betty to let her know that I was O.K. and to keep herself and the children indoors. Unfortunately, the phone lines were down and I could not hear very well. Early in the afternoon we received the "All Clear" message and all non-essential personnel were allowed to go home. The following day, the first order of business was the assessment of personal injuries and structural damage to the buildings. To my knowledge there were no major personnel injuries and my hearing was improving. Further evaluations revealed that I had had my tympanic membranes ruptured. There was no conservative means to repair the damage other than to allow time for natural healing, so I proceeded as advised. That is probably when my hearing loss started.

It was rather weird to hear the reports on the news as to the direction that the destructive sound wave had followed. No immediate logical explanations were given about how buildings near the epicenter of the accident were almost untouched, while the Greyhound Bus Station in downtown San Antonio, 30 miles away, had all of its windows blown out.

As time passed Betty and I spent some leisurely times on the Gulf Coast. We enjoyed the beaches in Corpus Christi and Rockport and we went to Six Flags Over Texas in Dallas. We also visited NASA Headquarters in Houston, Austin and the Dude ranches near San Antonio. We went to Nuevo Laredo, Mexico a couple of times to see the bull fights. One of our favorite events in San Antonio was the "Fiesta Week" which included day and night parades, a River Parade and an excellent show presented on the banks of the River.

The best thing that happened to us in 1963, was the birth of our fourth child, on September 30, another beautiful baby boy to carry our last name, Anthony Robert, Tony for short. God had blessed us with another beautiful child. Betty went into labor on the same day that I took my exams for regular Air Force status, so once again I missed the birth of one of our children!

Tony's First Birthday, 1964

As time passed, Tony would surprise us unexpectedly with a blood curdling scream for no apparent reason. Most of the time it came from out of the blue and we became hesitant to take him with us when we went out. Fortunately as he got older the episodes became fewer and farther between. One time we went to Rockport, Texas for a weekend. We had accommodations at a very nice waterfront motel and restaurant, The SeaGun Inn, that was well known for having the best fresh seafood on the Gulf. Our two older children were always well behaved, and had such excellent table manners for their ages that we never hesitated to take them out to eat with us anywhere. We had dinner reservations in the main dining room one evening and we all dressed up for a sunset dinner. The dining room was full of people who appeared to be attending a formal event. The atmosphere was rather quiet and we were all hungry. After we had ordered and were waiting for our meal, Tony suddenly let out his horrible blood curdling scream. Betty calmly reached over and lifted him out of his high chair, where upon he just smiled. We were very embarrassed to look, but we felt that all eyes were probably on us. Betty laid him across her lap where it looked as if she had hidden him. Fortunately he remained very quiet for the rest of the dinner.

On November 22, 1963, President John F. Kennedy was visiting Dallas. Betty was watching the television when Walter Cronkite, interrupted the scheduled program to announce the shocking news that the President had been shot and was being transported to the hospital for evaluation. It appeared to me that everyone was following the developments that followed. At the end of the work day I rushed home to join Betty and Uncle Roberto, who had been sadly watching the developing news on television. The next day there was nothing on television or radio except classical music and reruns of what had happened in Dallas. It was a very sad period of time for the whole nation.

CHAPTER 33

LEAVING SAN ANTONIO AND LIVING IN PHILADELPHIA

After Tony was born, we had to begin to plan for the next phase of my career in the Air Force. I was accepted into the specialty training program, which included one year in graduate school at the University of Pennsylvania followed by a two year residency program at Malcolm Grow USAF Medical Center at Andrews AFB, Maryland.

In the meantime we learned that we were expecting our fifth child, who was due in September of 1964. I was to report to school in Philadelphia in August. Betty and the children couldn't come with me until the baby was born and was six weeks old. I hired a lady who had babysat for us several times, Mrs. Smith, to come and stay with Betty and the children, after I left, until after the baby was born. On September 12, 1964, we were blessed with the birth of another son Joseph Richard.

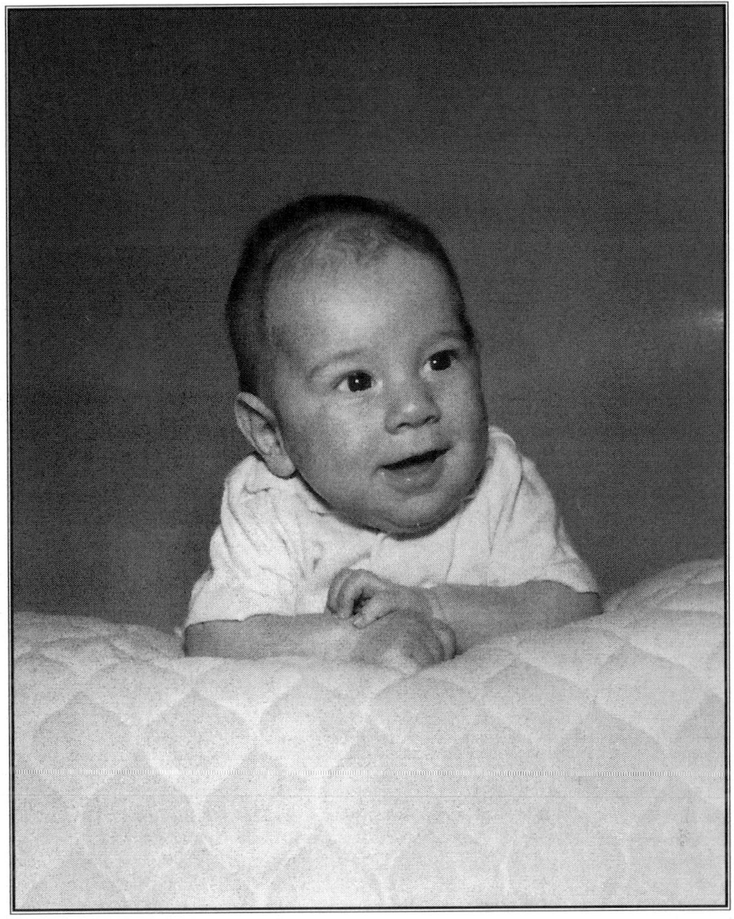

Joey at two months old.

Two weeks after Joey was born, Mrs. Smith left and Betty was on her own to recover from childbirth and to supervise the move from San Antonio to Philadelphia. Once again, the Air Force Dental Wives came to her rescue. Nan Mohnac, Norma Dirlam, Pat Hoskins, and Pat Triffon helped her in any way they could, including getting on the airplane with her and telling the flight attendant to be sure and help her when she changed planes in Houston! Elena was 4, Michael was 3, Tony was 1 and

Joey was 6 weeks old at the time. They flew to Indianapolis where they stayed with Betty's parents until I found a house to rent and our household goods arrived in Philadelphia.

In the meantime, I got in touch with a former Air Force colleague, Dr. Larry Friedman, who was from Philadelphia. He had returned home to attend specialty training at the University of Pennsylvania and he generously offered to let me stay at his house for a couple of days until I could find a house to rent. He was very familiar with the city and its surrounding neighborhoods. I couldn't find anything anywhere near the school, so we went to Drexel Hill, where we found a double that we could rent that was only a 35 minute drive from the School of Dentistry.

I called Betty and let her know about the house I had found and made plans for her and the children to join me soon. They waited in Indiana until our household goods arrived from San Antonio and then they flew to Philadelphia.

They arrived in Philadelphia in November. The first evening we were there, Betty was preparing dinner for us when the oven caught on fire. I hadn't returned from school yet. The house was a duplex, so she ran next door and asked the neighbor, whom she had never met before, if he had any baking soda because our oven was on fire! She knew not to put water on a grease fire and had learned that you should throw baking soda on the fire instead. The neighbor, Ed Winters, came over and put out the fire. We learned that the landlord had bought the stove from a dump and wouldn't replace it. After that we never used that oven again. I did a lot of grilling that year, even in the snow!

After the family arrived I was shocked that the children didn't act as warm to me as I had expected. They smiled and looked happy to see me, but they appeared cautious and held onto Betty as if they were afraid to let loose of her. So I proceeded cautiously, but I was anxious to hold them close to my heart without being forceful. I didn't like my schedule at school at all, because it required me to be there so early in the morning that I usually left before they were awake and then three times a week I would get home so late that they had already gone to bed.

The weather soon began to turn colder. The children had never experienced cold weather, much less seen snow, and they had always been outdoor children.

When school started Elena seemed to adapt very nicely. Only one bad experience scared us tremendously. Elena had gotten in the wrong line to walk home and ended up alone in a strange neighborhood. Fortunately, a mother whose child had been walking with Elena, noticed that she looked lost. She asked Elena where she lived, and Elena said she didn't know, but she knew her phone number. Betty had made sure that she knew that, and the lady called and told her that Elena was with her and gave her the address where she was. We only had one car and Betty couldn't get in touch with me, so she asked the neighbor to watch the other children and she walked to the place where Elena was and brought her home.

Michael was always a little adventurer. He had a little friend who lived in the house behind ours, his name was Anthony. They played together every day. One weekend when I was home and had taken a break from studying, Michael and I went for a walk. He told me he wanted to show me the train tracks. I didn't know that there were any train tracks nearby. Anyway, he led me to a cliff near our neighborhood, where we looked down on railroad tracks! Suddenly he said, "Duck Daddy, the cops might see us". I was shocked but I ducked and then I told him I thought we should go back home. When I told Betty what had happened she was shocked to hear about it. After that she told Michael he couldn't leave our yard anymore.

CHAPTER 34

MOVING TO MARYLAND AND ANOTHER TRAGEDY AVERTED

I had already received my Air Force travel orders to report to Andrews AFB in Maryland, near Washington, D.C. immediately after my graduation from the Graduate School of Medicine at the University of Pennsylvania. We were told that there was no base housing available for us, so we were directed to search for a place on our own, keeping in mind the housing allowance established by the government. When we drove down to Maryland in April, we couldn't find anything suitable close to the base, so we ended up buying a newly finished house in a new development called Rosaryville Estates near Upper Marlboro, Maryland. We were close to Highway 301, but the nearest gas station and small country grocery store were about 10 or 15 minutes away. It was a new community with less than one hundred houses and we were the first family to move into the neighborhood. The house was a split foyer design, on a sloping corner lot and had a walkout basement. The driveway from the main street had a direct entrance to the kitchen on the first floor. It had a living room, dining room, three bedrooms, eat in kitchen and two bathrooms on the first level. The basement had a large recreation room with a fireplace and a laundry room. That house cost $20,000.00.

After we left Philadelphia in May, we drove to Andrews AFB and stayed overnight at the base Visiting Officers Quarters. We had notified the telephone company that we wanted to have our phone connected, but they couldn't get it done until the following Monday. The next day, we met the moving truck at the new house and they proceeded to unload our furniture and household goods. Since we had moved from a larger house in San Antonio to a smaller house in Philadelphia, we had not unpacked some of the boxes since we left Texas. The mover's contract included putting the boxes in the rooms they were supposed to be in and unpacking all of them. So they started unpacking things and just setting them on the floor. When we saw that, we told them to stop unpacking and told them we would do it in a more orderly manner. We took the children down to the rec room and surrounded them with toys so they could play while we started putting things away in the kitchen. Elena, who was 5 at the time, liked to play with her younger brothers and used to command them with a motherly like authority. We asked her to let us know if any of them were not behaving or needed anything while they were playing.

We were getting things organized so that we could prepare lunch. After a couple of hours, Elena came up and excitingly told us that Joey, who was 8 months old, had a "pill" stuck up his nose! Betty and I rushed downstairs to find that one of the items that the movers had taken out of a box and placed on the floor, was an emergency medicine kit that had been on a high shelf in a closet in the rental house. Apparently, Tony, who was 19 months old, had opened the kit and the bottles of medicine and poured them out on the floor. Joey had picked them up and was eating them and had stuck one capsule up his nose!

Of course, at that point we didn't know if either one of them had eaten any of them. They included some sedatives and some antibiotics. I started picking them up and putting them back in the bottles so that I could count them to see if any were missing. Betty was holding Joey in her arms and suddenly he just went limp! She told me he had passed out, so I took him and told her I was going to take him to the hospital at Andrews. I got to the back step and he stopped breathing. I shouted for Betty to come up there and then I told her to get the other children and the pill bottles in the station wagon, while I started CPR. (CPR was new at that time and miraculously, I had just had a training class on how to administer it. Thank God!)

Since we had no phone, no neighbors and the nearest payphone was at least 15 minutes away, I told Betty to drive to the Hospital at Andrews as fast as she could. (Remember Betty is from Indiana, Home of the 500!) I was nearly desperate but I controlled my emotions and did what I had been trained to do. CPR procedures were not as sophisticated then as they are today. I laid Joey on his back in a proper position on the back seat of the station wagon and started mouth to mouth breathing. I was monitoring his pulse and his breathing constantly. About halfway to Andrews, I felt no pulse so I started external heart massage, or compressions, as it is called now, and mouth to mouth.

When we arrived at the base, Betty had to stop at the gate, where she told the guard what was happening and asked for directions to the emergency room. As soon as we arrived at the emergency entrance, I jumped out carrying Joey and continued breathing for him until two medics came out to meet us and took over. I walked alongside of them and gave a third medic a description of what had happened so that he could relate it to the E.R. doctor in charge, who was not available immediately. As in all emergencies, the rescue procedures in the military were executed very quickly and were well done by the available, well trained personnel.

By the time the doctor arrived in the emergency room, the NCOIC, had already inserted a stomach pump tube and extracted a total of 30 pills and capsules! Obviously, some had already been digested and were working in his system. The doctor ordered them to give him an injection of a stimulant to get his heart started. They inserted an IV into a vein in his scalp and started him on oxygen. I had the medicine kit in my pocket, it was new and the contents were properly labeled, including the number of pills in each bottle. Some of the pills that had been removed from the stomach were still identifiable and were counted. Joey was still unconscious and

I went out to the car where Betty was waiting with the children to give her an update on what was happening. We decided that I would stay at the hospital with Joey and Betty would take the children back to the house for the night. When she arrived at the house it was dark and every door in the house was open. She said it was very scary, but, she did what she had to do and got everyone fed and in bed for the night.

In the meantime, I stayed by Joey's side all night. At around 4:00 am, he started to regain consciousness. What a relief! When the doctors arrived I briefed them on what had happened. I stood back while they examined him, wondering what was going on and what comments they were making as they occasionally, and in a discrete manner, looked towards me. I myself wondered how Betty and I could have prevented this from happening.

The Pediatrician in charge reviewed with me step by step the procedures they had performed and informed me that it appeared that there was no evidence of damage and no visible injuries had been sustained. But, we needed to keep a very close eye on him in order to notice any changes in his behavior for the following few days. So, we did just that and Joey recovered completely. It was really a miracle that we were able to save his life. If one of us had been gone we couldn't have gotten him to the hospital in time. If I hadn't known how to administer CPR he would have died before we could have gotten help. We just thank God that he lived!

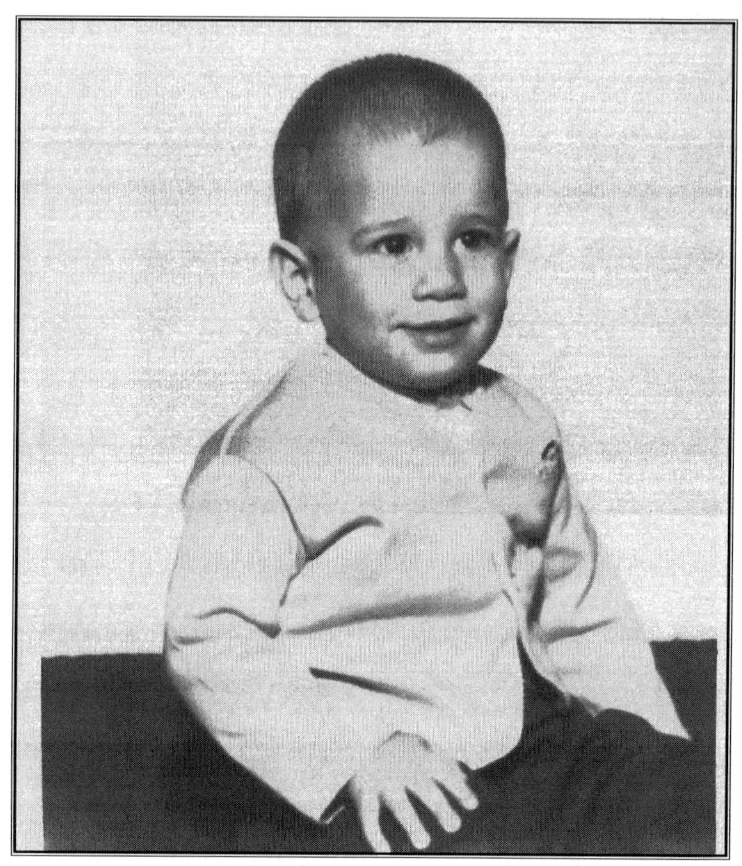

Joey at nine months old

CHAPTER 35

MEETING MILT HEIN

So, we settled down and I started my residency program. It was a very intense program and I was gone every day and some evenings. New families started to move into the other houses and we greeted them all as they moved into the neighborhood. The houses were built slowly, maybe two or three at a time by the same builder. Mr. Milton Hein, with whom we developed a strong friendship during the following months, was the foreman on the job. Mr. Hein, "Milt", as everyone in the neighborhood called him, was a very knowledgeable person in all aspects of the construction business. He was congenial with everyone who worked for him and with all of the homeowners. He kept his boss out of trouble when some of the homeowners became irate because they were having some problems with their homes. He tried to calm them down by talking to them and tried to do something to appease them by fixing whatever problem they were having. This frequently involved coming back after working hours or on weekends. You would assume this would be recognized and appreciated by the builder since these actions would increase the builder's profits. However, Milt's employer didn't appreciate him and treated him badly in the end.

Milt was about my age and sometimes he would see me doing some work around our new house and would take the time to give me some helpful hints on "how to" by giving me a quick demo. He was an all-around accomplished builder, not only in theory, but in practice. I had never seen anyone take a nail with his bare fingers, push it into a piece of wood in the wanted position and with one stroke of the hammer, drive it all the way into the wood where you could barely see the nail's head! I'm sure he could read on my face that I was saying to myself, "Where did it go?" When he noticed my look of amazement, he didn't say anything, he just smiled and proceeded to drive a couple more nails before leaving. As time went by we met the rest of his family, his wife, Marge, and seven beautiful children. Milt was originally from Iowa, but had moved to Maryland after marrying Marge and being discharged from the Marine Corps. After his employer skipped town without paying him for several months, he was very angry and wondered how he was going to support his family. He was a family man of great integrity and was a superb craftsman. I lost touch with him when we were transferred to Hawaii, but I looked him up when we returned to Maryland and were planning to build our house. He asked me if I remembered the builder that he was working for when we left the area. I said, yes, and he proceeded to tell me what the man had done to him. His employer came to him one day and out of the blue he said, "I know I owe you in excess of $27,000 dollars, but I am not going to pay you. I'm leaving for Florida tonight and what are you going to do about it"? Milt who was six feet tall, very muscular and strong, turned red with anger and asked him if he was joking. Milt said he felt his adrenalin rising and for a fleeting moment he felt like killing the guy. But, though still angry, he turned his head and thought about his wife and seven children and what they would do without him if he was sent to jail, and turned around and left. He had planned to use that money to buy some land and build a house for the family. I asked him if he had considered taking legal action against the guy, but Milt said that he didn't want to put more energy, time, and money into that because he had little faith in the legal system. He added that he trusted only one Judge, who we all have to face one day, and He is not in this world. He had many sad but colorful stories of survival and the story has a happy ending. He started his own construction company, Mil-Mar Construction.

It became one of the premier construction companies in Maryland by building well built homes with outstanding floor plans.

In time, Milt achieved most of his dreams. He became one of the biggest and best builders in Southern Maryland. He built a beautiful home for his family, grew his own vegetables and raised his own beef. He would describe some delicious food he had eaten in such a way that it made you want to go out and eat what he had described. He would always say, "It was some kind of good!" Since his death a few years ago, his children have kept his dream alive by continuing to build outstanding homes.

CHAPTER 36

RESIDENCY PROGRAM

I started my residency in July of 1965. The program was to be headed by Col. Allen Brewer, who I knew from the Prosthodontic study club at Lackland. He had been transferred from Brooks AFB to Wiesbaden AFB in Germany and was supposed to come to Andrews AFB as chairman of the department of Prosthodontics at Malcolm Grow USAF Hospital and chief of the Prosthetic Residency program. I was excited to hear that he would be in charge of my residency program, because he shared the same theories on Prosthodontics that I had been trained in by my mentor at the University of Pennsylvania, Dr. Morton Amsterdam. Unfortunately, as so often happens in the military, plans changed and Col. Brewer was assigned to Bolling AFB in Washington, D.C. They had just finished building a state of the art Dental Clinic there. Col. Brewer had not yet arrived when I arrived. Since he was not there, my program supervisor was the clinic commander, Col. Frank Ketchum. As a newly assigned resident I was to report to my assigned clinic and start seeing patients. It so happened that Col. Ketchum requested his annual leave shortly after I arrived. In the interim, the chairman of the Department of Prosthodontics was to be my supervisor.

Now, the specialty of Prosthodontics has two major branches. One is called Fixed Prosthodontics and deals mostly with permanently installed prosthetic devices, such as crowns and bridges. The other branch is called Removable Prosthodontics and deals primarily with complete dentures and removable partial dentures. To pass the specialty boards and be qualified as a Board Certified Prosthodontist, you need to pass the written examinations on both parts. However, for the clinical part of the board examinations, you are required to take the practical tests on a patient for the branch that you have chosen to practice. All applicants for Prosthodontic specialty training must specify the branch for which they are applying. Col. Brewer, Col. Rudd and Gen. Dunn, who had been promoted and was then the top commander of the USAF Dental Corp at the Pentagon Surgeon General's office in Washington, D.C., were all well aware that I had specified Fixed as my specialty. However, the chief of the Removable Prosthodontics Department, was in temporary charge of the Fixed branch as well. He personally didn't believe that any teeth should be replaced by anything other than removable prostheses while on active duty. Professionally, we had opposing views, and militarily he outranked me. The first day that I reported to him for duty, he made it very clear that he was not going to allow me to practice anything except removable dentures and removable partial dentures. In fact, he told me to "forget everything fancy" I had learned at the University of Pennsylvania! But, professionally, he could not dictate to me how to treat my patients.

He proceeded to make life very difficult for me. One day, one of the children was sick and needed to go to the doctor. Betty needed me to help her, so I asked my supervisor for permission to take two hours off that morning so I could meet her at the pediatrician's office at the hospital. He refused my request. By that time I was fed up with him and the whole program, which was nothing like anything I had been promised. So, I left the clinic and met Betty at the hospital. When I returned to the clinic, my supervisor confronted me and told me I had been derelict in my duty and that he was going to report me to the Dental Clinic commander, Col. Ketchum. I proceeded to tell him what I thought of him and the program. Well, it turned out that Col. Ketchum was still out of town and wouldn't be back for two weeks, so the supervisor ordered me to report to the Area

Dental Laboratory for duty until I received further orders. In the meantime, I had talked to Betty and asked her how she felt about leaving the Air Force and going into private practice somewhere. She told me to do what I needed to do. So I submitted my resignation from the Air Force to the office of the Hospital Commander, Gen. Archie Hoffman.

I didn't hear anything from anyone for two weeks. Then when Col. Ketchum returned, I was ordered to report to his office. When I arrived the Colonel had some papers on his desk. They were a transcript of everything I had said to my supervisor, word for word. He handed them to me and told me to read them. He then asked me if the report was correct. I said, "Yes Sir, this is correct and I have submitted my resignation to Gen. Hoffman". He told me not to be hasty in my decisions and he would see what he could do about the situation in which I found myself. He ordered me to report back to the Prosthodontic department until further notice.

A few months later, my supervisor was reassigned to Clark AFB in the Philippines. Lt. Col. William Akerley and Maj. Ronald Blackman were put in charge of the residency program with a few lectures by Col. Brewer at Bolling. I never did hear anything about the resignation papers I had submitted.

The second year of my program was much better. The hospital commander held a small graduation ceremony where he awarded each resident with certificates of completion of the program. This completed my specialty academic training program. Now I needed to successfully pass the Board Certification Examinations in order to become a full-fledged Board Certified specialist. The two parts of the examination were each given at different locations in two different calendar years. This meant at least another two or more years of specialty practice to enhance clinical experience and preparation in order to qualify to take the specialty board exam and become a DIPLOMATE in Prosthodontics, while simultaneously fulfilling my regular duties as a dental officer, including being available for worldwide reassignments.

Before the end of my residency, much to our delight, we were notified that we were going to be reassigned to Hickam AFB, Hawaii, which would provide me a more proper environment for concentration and the practice of my specialty.

Maj. Rolando Bernui with residency completion certificate

CHAPTER 37

OVERSEAS: HAWAII BOUND

In early August of 1967, Betty, our four children and I boarded the plane that would take us to Honolulu, Hawaii. I was to be assigned to Hickam AFB for an estimated three year tour of duty. All branches of the military were represented there. The Air Force, Army, Navy, Marine Corp and Coast Guard were all under the Joint Pacific Armed Forces Command headquarters located at Camp Smith Marine Base. The Commander in Chief of the Pacific (CINCPAC) was Navy Admiral John McCain. The Commander in Chief of the Pacific Air Force (CINCPACAF), was General Nazzaro.

When we arrived at the airport, which had an open air terminal, we were greeted by the sweet smell of flowers, Hawaiian music, and free pineapple juice! We learned later that the flowers that smelled so sweet were on the Plumeria trees. Anywhere that you saw a Plumeria tree, the air around it smelled wonderful.

All new Air Force arrivals in Hawaii had an appointed sponsor, who was to help get you and your family settled at your new assignment. Ours was Lt. Col. Dale Rank, who after welcoming us at the airport took us to the Kalakauan Hotel on Kalakaua Avenue in the heart of Waikiki. One of the first things that he told us was that the only places to live on base were in sub-standard housing. The Vietnam War was raging and Hawaii was one of the busiest places in the Pacific area. Therefore, those of us assigned there for a long tour of duty, had to find places to live off base in communities that were convenient to our duty stations.

There were no rental places available, so we had to buy a house. We contacted a realtor, who took us around to several different communities, during the week I had off before I had to report for duty. At the end of that week we still had not found a house that we liked, so I started going with the realtor after work during the week. One day the realtor was showing me a house in Aiea, when I saw a newly constructed house that looked nice and it had an open house sign on it. I asked her if we could stop and look at it, and she said, "That house is out of your price range." I really liked the looks of that house, so after she dropped me off at my car, I went back to look at the house on my own. The realtor there, Jesse de la Cruz, gave me a tour of the house and the more I saw the more I liked it. However, the price of the house was $35,000 dollars. We couldn't qualify for a mortgage for that much money, and the money we were expecting from the sale of the land in Peru for a down payment hadn't come yet. Jesse, however, had options for unconventional financing. There was an option called an agreement of sale, where the builder would finance the house for three years with no down payment. At the end of three years, if you still couldn't get your own financing, the builder got the house back. Jesse told me that the prices of homes in Hawaii were appreciating by leaps and bounds and he was sure that in three years the house would have appreciated so much that we wouldn't have any trouble getting a mortgage. I left, feeling very encouraged.

I went back to Waikiki to get Betty and the children to take them to see the house. They all loved it! It had three bedrooms, two baths, kitchen with a breakfast bar, dining room and living room. There was a laundry room that was enclosed, but the tops of the outside walls were screened in. This led from the kitchen to the carport, which was called a garage, even though it didn't have a door on the front of it. Because the house was almost at the top of a mountain it had a fabulous view of Pearl Harbor and the surrounding mountains and it was brand new.

We signed the contract as soon as possible. The next thing we needed to do right away was to enroll Elena and Michael in school. There was a Catholic school, St. Elizabeth's, in Aiea just down the mountain from our new home. The school had openings in second grade for Elena, but none for Michael in first grade. We were told that they could put Michael on the waiting list, and after the first week of school if there were some no shows, he would be admitted. So Elena started school before we had moved into our house. Since we only had one car, I drove her to school on my way to the base every morning and picked her up after school for a few weeks. After the first week of school Michael was admitted, so that all worked out.

When we left for Hawaii, we were not allowed to take any furniture with us because of the cost of moving it. We were allowed 3,000 pounds of household goods. All furniture, large kitchen appliances and carpets were to be provided by the military. So our furniture was stored in a warehouse in Washington, D.C.

Our household goods didn't arrive until six weeks after we did, so we stayed at the Kalakauan "on the Beach" for seven weeks. Fortunately, the hotel there had kitchenettes in the rooms, so we were able to cook some of our meals there.

We met Joan and Bill Kuebker, who became lifelong friends, there, when they arrived a few days after we did with their three children, Craig, Candy and David. Bill was also a Prosthodontist and was assigned to Hickam as well. We all had fun getting acquainted with each other and the surrounding areas. They bought a house in an older neighborhood, which was closer to the base.

Most of the houses in Hawaii are built with single wall construction. That means one side of the boards are the outside of the house and the other side of those boards are the inside walls of the house.

We had some interesting experiences after we moved into our house. One time when we were moving in Betty was hanging pictures on the living room wall while I was doing some work outside. I had just leaned up against the wall for a moment, when I felt something poke me in the back. It was the nail that Betty had just put inside for hanging a picture! After that we used shorter nails!

None of us had ever heard of geckos, and Joan had quite an experience with one. After they had moved into their house, she was doing the laundry outside on their patio, where the laundry area was located, when a gecko suddenly dropped down off of a tree and ran into the house. Joan didn't know what it was, but she knew she didn't want it running loose in the house. So she got her vacuum cleaner and vacuumed the gecko up into it! After she told us this story, Betty realized that the skeletons that looked like baby alligators she had found when she was cleaning the tops of our kitchen cabinets, were actually gecko skeletons.

One day when Betty was driving the children to school, Joey told her, "Mommy there's a frog in the car". She just laughed and told him "No, there's no frog in the car," but he insisted that there was and told her it was on the back of her seat. She looked over her shoulder and sure enough there was not a frog, but a gecko there! Well, Betty is deathly afraid of mice, spiders and other such creatures, now including geckos. So she drove as quietly as possible so as not to disturb the gecko, until finally they arrived at school. She jumped out of the car and got the children out also. Then she saw our neighbor boy, Keala, and told him she would give him a quarter if he would get that lizard out of the car. (At that time she didn't know it was called a gecko). Keala was happy to get a quarter, so he removed the gecko and Betty was able to return home.

While all of this was going on, I had reported for duty to the dental clinic, which was located in the Dispensary at Hickam. The main military hospital facility for the Islands was Tripler General Hospital, which was located on a mountainside overlooking the city of Honolulu. It was a huge

Army hospital equipped and manned to offer all specialty services to all of the military service personnel and their dependents who were stationed in Hawaii. In addition to treating local military patients, they were equipped to provide whatever services were needed by some of the Vietnam casualties who were flown to Hawaii. All of the military branches of service had their own local facilities for dental care, but all medical services beyond emergency care, were rendered at Tripler.

Our dental clinic was very busy, but it was well equipped and staffed. We all enjoyed the beautiful scenery and pleasant weather during off duty hours and weekends.

The local dental societies were very friendly and frequently invited us to participate in some of their professional and social activities. Few, if any, of the doctors assigned to Hawaii went home to spend their vacation times. On the contrary, many family members from the mainland took advantage of the opportunity to come to visit us.

In May of 1968, just nine months after we had moved to Hawaii, we were notified that the warehouse where our furniture was stored, had been burned down. This happened in April during the riots that took place after the assassination of Dr. Martin Luther King, Jr. That came as quite a shock to us. We were saddened at the loss of some precious mementos that we had lost; irreplaceable memorabilia, such as, John Glenn's letter of congratulation on my citizenship, and other autographed notes from astronauts Gus Grissom and Scott Carpenter. We learned that the inventory we had was not very accurate, complete, or descriptive. How do you remember what was in a medium size box, or what year you purchased a piece of furniture and how much it cost? We didn't dwell on it because we couldn't do anything about it until we returned to the mainland after my tour of duty in Hawaii was over.

CHAPTER 38

LIVING IN HAWAII

There were many activities to choose from for the children. When we lived in Maryland, there was a horseback riding school near where we lived. Elena and Michael had heard about it from some of their friends and wanted to take riding lessons. When we inquired they told us that the children were too young. So after we were settled in our house in Aiea, they were delighted to find out that riding lessons were available at nearby Camp Smith Marine Corps Station. Betty took them up there and enrolled them for lessons. Later on, she took lessons also. Elena took Hula lessons and she and Michael took Ukelele lessons as well.

After a few trips to the beach we realized that our children needed to learn how to swim. We learned from neighbors that a couple who lived down the street from us were Red Cross certified swimming instructors and gave swimming lessons in the pool at their home. So we enrolled all of them for lessons. That was one of the best things we ever did for them. They all became excellent swimmers and still are to this day.

During the second year that we lived in the house it had appreciated in value so much that we were able to get a mortgage and have enough money to have a pool built in our backyard. After my three, near-drowning experiences, I was reluctant to get into water that was over my head. Betty told me that if having our own pool helped me get over my fear of water that it would be worth it. And it was, because I became a good swimmer again.

Bernui family ready for a luau in Hawaii, 1969

Joe, Elena, Tony, Michael by the pool at the Hawaii house, 1969

Children in Hawaii

When Michael was in the third grade he learned that he was old enough to be an altar boy at church. He announced to us that he wanted to do that. Altar boy practice was at 7:00 am on Saturday mornings. There was also a 6:00 am Mass every day. The altar boy teams rotated through the Mass schedule so every six weeks they had to be at church at 5:30 am. We thought that he wouldn't last very long if he had to get up that early, so we agreed to let him do it. On the first Saturday practice, he was up before anyone else, dressed and ready to go without anyone waking him up. He continued with this pattern until we left Hawaii. In fact, he was named altar boy of the year the last year we were there, even though he was only a seventh grader and that honor was usually reserved for an eighth grader.

One time, Michael was giving Joey a ride on the handlebars of his bike, when they hit a curb and both went flying. Joey hit his head which caused a big cut in his scalp which bled profusely. Michael came in the back door, white as a sheet, carrying Joey who was crying. They both had blood all over them. Betty took them to the bathroom to wash off the blood so she could see what kind of wounds they had. Michael just had minor scrapes but, Joey kept asking, "Am I going to die? I want my Daddy!" Betty assured him that he was not going to die, but he still kept asking for me. Betty tried to call me at the clinic to let me know what had happened, but, she couldn't locate me. I had been called to Tripler to consult on the case of a V.I.P. patient. There are times when a military member's specific whereabouts are not for public information. By the time I got home, Betty had already taken care of the situation by taking Joey to the dispensary and having his wound sutured.

All of our children were very interested in pets. They really wanted a dog. Betty said that whenever Joey was out of diapers we could consider it. So when that time came we talked to the children about the work involved in taking care of a pet. We told them that there would be additional expenses such as, pet food and veterinarian fees, not to mention training time. They all agreed that this is what they wanted to do. So we looked in the local paper and found an ad for a black, part German Shephard dog. We went to see him and we bought him. Michael, who was the most attached to the puppy stepped in and without complaining, led the others with the chores, including formal training with an instructor. We named him Prince and as he grew it was apparent that he was more German Shephard than anything else. One of his ears stood straight up while his other ear was partially lopsided. It was also apparent that taking care of a pet was a lot more demanding than we had thought. He was becoming a great watch dog and we began to worry that he might be dangerous to strangers, but to children in particular. He used to chase birds, rabbits and anything that moved. In Hawaii there is a breed of toads called buffo toads. We had been warned about them because they were poisonous and could be a danger to children. One Saturday morning we awakened to the sound of an animal screaming. We looked outside and saw Prince take off running as fast as he could around the neighborhood. One of our neighbors called to tell us that they had seen him and he appeared to be foaming from the mouth. I stepped out of the house just as he ran back into the garage and collapsed in convulsions. I had seen cases of dog poisoning in Peru and at least at that moment I was pretty sure that Prince had been poisoned. We rushed him to the veterinarian, but it was too late and he died. The veterinarian explained to me that the Buffo toad has a poison sac under its neck and when an enemy bites him, he gets a mouth full of poison. He said that this poison is fast acting and perhaps more lethal than strychnine. I felt some relief finding out that it was a poisonous toad that had killed our dog and not a cold hearted human being. Nevertheless, I was very sad and angry watching my children mourn the death of their pet. The only way we could console them was to promise them that we would get another pet. The children were keeping their eyes on ads in the paper for dogs for sale. We had been advised to consider a "Lab" because they are supposedly ideal to be around children. The following week we heard that one of our neighbors had a Boxer that had given birth to 13 puppies that were half Golden Retriever. It didn't take long before they had sold 12 of them. Michael was playing outside when the owner of the Boxer started a conversation with him. She had heard about our dog dying. She brought a puppy and put it in his arms telling him that he could have it if he wanted it and it would only cost $15.00. It was a female puppy that looked more like a Boxer than a Golden Retriever. We didn't particularly want a female dog because of their propensity to multiply. Michael came home with this puppy in his arms and asked Betty if we could keep it. When she saw the expression in his eyes, there was no way that she, or any normal parent could say no. So we bought the puppy and named her Katie. When we took her to the vet to see about having her spayed, he told us that she would be a better pet if we let her have one litter of puppies before she had the surgery.

Well, Katie turned out to be a lot more work, especially for young children, than we had expected. For one thing her bowel movements were bigger than a cow's! She soon learned how to sneak out of our fenced in yard and the first time she was in heat she got together with a neighbor's German Shephard and became pregnant. A few months later, much to our children's delight, she presented us with 9 puppies. It began to appear that we should hire janitorial services for them alone!

One evening our neighbor ladies, who were ardent pet lovers, knocked on our door. They had big smiles on their faces, and proceeded to tell us that they had a gift for Katie. They had just returned from having dinner at the Officer's Club and they had a large box in their hands. They proceeded to tell us that when they were going through the buffet line, when they got to the steamship round of beef, they asked the Chef what they did with the bone when all of the meat was gone. He told them that they just threw it away. They said that they looked at each other and commented that Katie would sure love to have it. The Chef asked, "Who is Katie?" They replied, "Mother of nine," and went to their table to enjoy their dinner. Just as they were leaving, the Chef rushed over to them and handed them this big box of bones, and said, "take this home to Katherine," and left. They couldn't wait to get home and bring it to us. Katie enjoyed those bones, which still had a lot of meat on them, for several days.

The children loved those puppies, but we knew that there was no way that we could keep them. I asked the vet if he knew anyone that we could give them to. He advised me to sell them rather than give them away. His reasoning was that if a person doesn't pay something for a puppy, they might not treat them well, because there is no value to them. So we put an ad in the paper to sell them for ten dollars each. When the last one was about to be sold, Betty couldn't find it or Michael. As I went to find them, Michael met me with the puppy under his arm and a ten dollar bill in his hand. He said he wanted to buy the puppy from me. To this day that is probably one of the saddest days in my life. I will never forget the expression of sadness on my son's face when I told him that we weren't selling the puppies for the money. We were selling them because we couldn't afford to keep them, so he agreed to sell the puppy. Fortunately, our involvement in lots of activities locally and our trips abroad, helped us to forget those difficult times. Unfortunately, when we left Hawaii, we had to leave Katie there.

When Tony was in the first grade he came home from school one day and announced that he was going to take piano lessons. Betty said, "Oh, you are, where are you going to take them?" He said, "Sister Jean told me she would give me lessons at school". So Betty said, "But we don't have a piano at home for you to practice on". He said, "Oh, Sister said that I could practice after school on the school piano". When Betty told me about this, we discussed it and decided that if he was so interested in learning to play the piano that he had made all of the arrangements by himself, that we should buy a piano. So we bought one, which came with 6 free lessons. We decided that since we now had a piano, it would be a good time for the other children to take lessons, too.

When we told this story to our friends, Bob and Sue Lockyer, Bob was a dentist at the clinic at Hickam, Sue told us that she had been a piano teacher back home in Seattle. Betty told her we were looking for a piano teacher who would come to our home and give the lessons there, and asked her if she would be willing to do that. She said she would and so all of the children took piano lessons for a year or so. This was the beginning of their interest in music.

One of the activities they enjoyed the most was the horseback riding lessons that they were taking. One day while Betty was watching them at their lesson, she kept feeling a fly on her leg. She kept trying to brush it away, but, it didn't go away. When she looked down to see the "fly" she saw a gecko there. She was so startled that she took her purse and hit her leg so hard that the gecko disappeared! She was embarrassed to explain to the other moms who were there, what had happened! But, then they all had a good laugh.

After Elena and Michael had been taking lessons for about a year, Betty decided that she would like to take riding lesson, too. She asked Sue Lockyer if she would like to go with her. Sue said she would like that, so they both took lessons. One day one of the horses, whose name was Honey, bit Sue on the behind, Sue turned around, shook her finger at Honey and said, "Don't you ever do that again."

Rolando in new Datsun 240Z, 1969

CHAPTER 39

BLUE EAGLE FLIGHTS AND ANOTHER DISASTER IN PERU

Many of my patients were crew members of the Blue Eagle Squadron. In those days, during the Cold War with the Soviet Union, there were planes in the air 24 hours a day, seven days a week, which carried orders about what action was to be taken in case there was an attack on Washington, D.C. and the President wasn't able to give the orders. The Blue Eagle Squadron was one of those groups of planes. Each plane was required to have medical personnel aboard. One day I was asked if I would like to be put on the list of personnel available for those flights. Of course I agreed, because I knew that the flights carried V.I.P.'s with them who had to be in different locations in Asia. They would fly to Taiwan, Thailand, Viet Nam and other locations in order to stay in the air for 24 hours. When they reached their destination they had 48 hours to rest before they had to take off again. During those 48 hours they were allowed to shop or take tours, as long as they were able to be reached and be at the air field within 15 minutes in case of an emergency. I went on several of those flights. That's where I learned that there were furniture factories in Taipei and Bangkok that could make any kind of furniture you wanted as long as you gave them a picture of it. I told Betty about it and we decided that we could take the insurance money we had received for our destroyed furniture and have a house full of furniture made to take back to the mainland with us. We decided that we preferred to have teak furniture from Taipei rather than rosewood furniture from Bangkok. So we scoured furniture catalogs and came up with a list and pictures of what we wanted. Each of the children chose, with a little guidance, the kind of furniture they wanted for their bedrooms. So I took the pictures to the Ricardo Lynn Furniture factory in Taiwan and ordered a whole house full of furniture. They built it and shipped it to Hawaii. It so happened that was the year the government decided to pay to move furniture back to the mainland for everyone! So we didn't have to pay the moving expenses when we were transferred.

One of the exciting experiences I had on one of those trips, happened in Taipei. When we left the plane we were told exactly what time we had to return. I went shopping and lost track of time. Suddenly, I realized what time it was and I only had a short period of time to make it back to the airfield. I knew that they would leave on time whether I was there or not. I got a taxi and told the driver I was in a big hurry. When I got to the airfield, the plane was already on the runway. I jumped into a jeep and one of the airmen drove me out to the plane. They pulled me up, with all of my packages, into the plane through a door in the floor of the cockpit! That was a close call. After that I made sure that I always got back to the plane on time.

In 1970, there was another disaster that happened in Huaraz. It was an earthquake that destroyed almost all of the buildings in the Callejon de Hauylas. At that time one of my former patients was the White House physician. He remembered that I was from Peru and he called me and invited me to fly to Peru on Air Force One with the First Lady, Pat Nixon, who was taking aid to the area. I was also to be a guide and a translator. Of course I accepted the invitation. I flew to a Marine Base in California, where Air Force One picked me up.

After arriving in Lima, we flew by helicopter to Callejon de Huaylas. As we flew over the affected area, we could see the devastation. It looked like the pictures I had seen of Europe during World War II. All of the houses and buildings looked like they had been bombed.

After we landed near Huaraz, I immediately started looking for my family. There were no houses where theirs had been. Finally, after asking many people if they knew them and if so did they know where they might be, they found me. They told me that they had nowhere to stay and that the people in charge of distributing tents and food would not give them anything. They were told that they had money and the aid was for those who didn't have any! Well, money doesn't do any good if there is nothing to buy, so I went with them where things were being distributed and told those in charge that this was my family and they needed tents and food. So they were given what they needed. In the meantime, no one had any idea where my Uncle Roberto was. So I continued to look for him. On the second day that I was there, on the front page of the newspaper was a picture of him in front of what had been the Cathedral in Huaraz. So I went there and found him. He was not injured and had been given food and shelter. None of my family members had been killed or injured except a distant cousin.

CHAPTER 40

OUR TRAVELS IN ASIA

One of the advantages of being stationed in the middle of the Pacific Ocean was that it created opportunities for us to visit places that many of us could not otherwise afford to go. This is how we took advantage of those opportunities. We saved our money and vacation time so that we could go on Space Available flights. The key was to have our traveling papers ready at all times just waiting for opportunities to arise. The first trip we took was to Expo 70, the World's Fair that was held in Osaka, Japan. We acquired permission for the children to take time out of school in order to go. We first went to Tokyo where we visited the Kokusai Theater, the Japanese version of Radio City Music Hall in New York. Another place we visited near Tokyo was Yomiuri Lando. We were told that it was the Japanese version of "Disneyland". It was very nice, but couldn't be compared to "Disneyland". It was more like Six Flags.

We were staying at Tachikawa Air Force Base that was nearby. While there, we went to the Base Exchange, which was huge, to do some souvenir shopping. We were walking around looking at what was available, holding tightly to the children's hands, when suddenly we realized that Joey was missing! I thought Betty had him and she thought I had him. We were looking around, desperately trying to see where he was, when we saw a tall Air Force sergeant with a little boy on his shoulders coming toward us. The little boy was Joey, the sergeant had put him on his shoulders so he could look for us and sure enough he spotted us. What a relief, from then on we always checked to see who had which child before we started out.

One of the tours we took was to a Shinto Shrine. Outside of the entrance, there was a small raised pool where everyone was supposed to purify their bodies by washing their hands and mouths with the water before entering the Shrine. It looked like a very unhealthy thing to do because after rinsing their mouths they spit the water back into the pool! When we turned around after watching what the people were doing, we saw Joey, inside, following the priest, who was performing the formal ceremonial ritual. Joey was clapping his hands and bowing every time the priest did!

We left Tokyo to go to the World's Fair. There were so many people coming to visit that there were no hotel rooms available in Osaka, so we had reserved a room at a private home in Kyoto. There we slept on mats on the floor and traveled by train to Osaka every day to attend the Fair. One day when we were returning to Kyoto, the train was very crowded and there was a family standing next to our seats. The mother was pregnant and was holding a small child. So I got up and offered her my seat. Well, her husband promptly sat down in it and didn't even offer to hold the child! That's how I learned how Japanese men treat their wives!

While we were at the Fair, our family became instant celebrities. There were many Japanese school groups visiting the Fair and when they spotted our "blonde" children, they would come up to us and ask if they could take pictures of them with their groups. They then would practice speaking the little English they knew with them and asked for their autographs! It was a sweet experience for all of us.

We often wish that our children had been a little bit older at these times, so that they could enjoy those memories during their adulthood. Memories are often like sandcastles on the beach that appear to wash away a little at a time with the tide of life. But we have no regrets about all of the trips we took.

The next trip we took was to Thailand, Taiwan and Hong Kong. On the way to our first stop in Thailand, we had a brief stopover at Tahn Son Nhut AFB, in Vietnam. The plane was an American airliner leased by the government to transport military members and their dependents to their new assignments in the Pacific, so they were dropping off some soldiers there. As we took off we could see the spotter planes dropping smoke bombs to mark the places that were to be bombed. It was an exciting and scary experience, especially for Betty.

In Thailand, we took a tour to a place called the Rose Garden, where we rode on Elephants and saw the Thai version of a bullfight. It was two bulls on long leashes butting heads with each other. We also took a boat tour on the Chao Phraya River to see a floating market. Along the way we saw how they floated the teak logs from the forest to the lumber yards. The logs were placed in the water by elephants and then taken out of the water the same way after they reached their destination. We also observed life along the river banks. We saw people bathing, using the bathroom, washing clothes and gathering drinking water from the river.

After leaving Thailand, we flew to Taipei, Taiwan. There we did some shopping and sightseeing.

Then we flew to Hong Kong on a commercial, civilian airline operated by Japanese Airlines. That is when Tony discovered sashimi and sushi, which he still loves today. We stayed at the Hong Kong Hilton and took the ferry boat over to Kowloon, where we visited Kowloon Tailors. There you could buy tailor made clothing, custom made shoes, watches, jewelry, etc. When you shop in Hong Kong, they treat you like royalty. They serve you any kind of drink you can image, seat you in very nice chairs, and cater to your every need. The clerks were fascinated with our children and the children were fascinated with them. One of the clerks offered to give us a personal tour of Hong Kong. So the next day, he took us to Tiger Balm Gardens, where there were carvings and statues of all kinds of animals, people and graphic scenes of torture. It was built by a Chinese multi-millionaire, who invented Tiger Balm, an ointment that relieves muscle aches and pains. Then we went to lunch at a floating restaurant, which really was floating, not attached to land at all. To get there you were taken in a small rowboat called a sampan. The restaurant was on a "Junk". "Junks" are basically Chinese houseboats. There are hundreds of them in the water between Kowloon and Hong Kong. The next day our guide took us to the border of Taiwan and mainland China. There we saw what is typically characterized in the US as a Chinese man. He had a long white beard and mustache and was wearing a round hat, dressed in a robe with sandals on his feet. Of course we started taking pictures of him, after which he told us how much we owed him for taking the pictures! That was our first experience with people who hang around tourist attractions and expect to be paid when tourists take their picture.

After leaving Hong Kong, we took a commercial flight to Okinawa where we were to get on a Space A flight back home. When we arrived in Okinawa I reported to the base to put our names on the list for a flight to Hickam. I was told that many of the flights were full because we were withdrawing troops from Vietnam. We ended up staying there for five days before we got a flight on a plane that was taking a jet engine back to the Mainland to be repaired. Our family and one other couple were on the plane with this huge engine in the middle. We were seated on jump seats along the sides of the plane. Our luggage was stowed under the engine. It wasn't a very comfortable flight, but it got us home. When we deplaned we were all very hungry and I heard Michael say "Let's get some good old American food, let's get Pizza"!

My assignment to Hickam was to have been for three years, but in 1970, when I was to be reassigned we were notified that no one was being reassigned because of lack of funds to move us. When we found out that we were going to be staying for another year we were very happy, because we loved living there. Betty's parents and siblings had come to visit us that summer, and had a very nice vacation with us. Her brother, Garry, went with me to take a lawnmower to be repaired and when he talked to the owner about what was wrong with it, the owner was so impressed with his knowledge he offered him a job! Of course he couldn't take the job because he was only sixteen and still in high school.

After we found out that we were not moving, we decided to try to take a Space A trip to Australia and New Zealand. The Air Force was responsible for transporting the military members who were stationed at the South Pole to their destinations in the Spring and back home in the Fall. So there were empty planes going there in the Fall, that stopped over in New Zealand and Australia. We were fortunate to get on one of those flights. On the way we stopped for refueling on Midway Island and American Samoa before arriving in New Zealand. Our plan was to spend a week there and then catch the next flight to Australia. We arrived in Christ Church where we stayed overnight and then we started our tour. We left Christ Church by bus to go to Mt. Cook, where we stayed overnight.

Elena at Mt. Cook, New Zealand. 1971

The next morning we signed up for a tour of a glacier. We had to rent hiking boots in order to be able to walk on the glacier. When we arrived at the place where the walk was to begin, the guide there told us that Tony and Joey were too young to go on the walk. So Elena, Michael and I started out to walk on the glacier, while Betty and the boys went for a hike up the mountain with another guide. After we had been walking for a little while, we came to a rift in the glacier. The guide explained to us that we would have to jump over the rift and if we didn't make it over, there would be nothing he could do to save us! An older European woman, who was in the group asked him why he couldn't just throw us the rope he was carrying and pull us back up if we fell. He explained that it was too far down for a rope to reach and there was a river under the glacier that would swiftly carry us way. He said that our body would not be found until the summer when it reached the lake. What a shock! I was so glad that Betty, Tony and Joey were not with us! After that we all made sure we jumped over those rifts as far as we could. In the meantime, while Betty and the boys were climbing up the mountain trail, they heard a loud noise in the distance. They asked the guide what that was and he told them that it was an avalanche! We apparently had signed up for a rather dangerous tour. But it was an experience that none of us have ever forgotten.

The day after that we went on a horseback trip up into the mountains. The horseback riding lessons that Betty, Elena and Michael had been taking at Camp Smith really paid off, because the trail was not easy. We stopped in a scenic area to rest and while we were resting we looked around to see Joey walking under one of the horses. He had no idea that it was a dangerous thing to do! We are still glad that we went on that trail ride, the scenery was beautiful.

The next day we boarded another bus to go to Queenstown where we stayed in a hotel on Lake Wakatipu. This is a huge lake that has tides. The legend is that there is a sleeping giant at the bottom of the lake and his breathing is what causes the tides to rise and fall. The day after we arrived we went by boat to visit a sheep station about an hour from Queenstown. It was a very interesting place that was written up in National Geographic magazine a few months after we had been there. The owner, Mr. Lucas, who was known as "Popeye", was very nice and took an interest in showing our children around personally. He told us that we should have stayed at his place instead of a hotel. We told him that in his brochure, it specified that no children under twelve were allowed. He said he would have made an exception for us!

Popeye Lucas with Elena, Michael, Tony, and Joe in Sheep Station, Queens Town, New Zealand

They gave us an exhibition of how the sheep dogs rounded up the sheep and how they could separate one sheep out of the whole herd for sheering. Then Mr. Lucas took our children and showed them what he called a hermit sheep. That is a sheep that has avoided being rounded up for several years and has very thick wool. After the exhibition, they gave us tea and scones before we returned to our hotel. It was a very enjoyable tour.

The next day we got on a plane to fly to Rotorua on the North Island. It is completely different from the South Island. When we departed from the plane the air smelled like rotten eggs. The whole area is very volcanic. There are boiling streams and waterfalls and hot geysers and if you see a pothole in the street with water in it, the water is hot. The next day we took a tour of the town. We saw a Maori Village where they demonstrated how the women would prepare their meat and vegetables in pots in the morning and put them in a neighborhood pit, which would be covered all day. In the evening they would collect their pots and take home their cooked meal. It was cooked by the steam from the ground. When we were in the city the guide told us that heating the houses was very inexpensive because all they had to do was stick a pipe in the ground and distribute the steam through radiators throughout the house. I don't know if that was true, but it made a good story.

From Rotorua we took a bus to Wellington, the capital of New Zealand. Before we departed we went to the Tourist Bureau to make hotel reservations. The travel agent there recommended a hotel called the People's Palace since there were so many of us. We arrived around 8:00 pm and had to find a place to eat. After we ate we checked in to the hotel. The clerk showed us to our room and informed us that the bathrooms were down the hall, women on one hall and men on another hall. We thought that was kind of strange, but we were only going to be there one night so we decided to tough it out, since it was too late to look for another place. The next morning we went to the dining room for breakfast, which is included in all hotels in New Zealand and Australia. The menu was very hearty, including eggs, ham, oatmeal, toast, etc. We were surprised to hear a band playing at the other end of the large dining room. When we looked to see what was going on we noticed that all of the band members had on uniforms. That is when we realized that the People's Palace was a Salvation Army hotel! That's why the bathrooms were on separate halls. One hall had rooms for men and the other hall had rooms for women. Since we were a family we were in the middle between the halls in a large room with eight beds and a lavatory!

After touring Wellington, we took a ship back to Christ Church, where we were to get our flight to Australia. We found a small family owned motel for an overnight stay. The next day we went to the airport to wait for our flight. After waiting for a few hours, we were told that our flight had been canceled because our plane had equipment problems and had to wait for a part to come from California. We were told that it would be two days before they could get the part and we were to check in then to find out when we would be departing. It took a whole week before we finally were able to fly to Sydney. During that week we stayed at the same motel that we thought was only going to be overnight. The couple who owned it had two children, a boy and a girl, who were about the same ages of our children. They turned out to be very nice and the children played together when we weren't sightseeing. Their children asked our children if they knew how to play "knots and crosses" and of course they said they didn't. So they got out a piece of paper and made a drawing which turned out to be "Tic-Tac-Toe"! What they were really saying was "Naughts and Crosses". They had a good time. The owners offered to let us use their washer and dryer, which was really nice because Betty had been washing underwear by hand and letting it dry overnight for each day. So we had enough clean clothes to last for the rest of the trip.

When we finally got our flight to Australia we only had one more week of vacation left. We stayed in Sydney for a few days and saw the Sydney Opera House from the water on our way to the Sydney Zoo. The Opera House was still under construction so we couldn't go into it. We reported to the American Consulate to see the Air Force Attache and let them know we were there. The Colonel in charge there asked what we were planning to do during the rest of our trip. We told him we were planning to take a bus from Sydney to the capital, Canberra, because we wanted to see some of the Outback. He warned us that it would be too dangerous to do that because the buses were not very reliable and if the bus broke down there might not be any help arriving for a few days. So he offered to fly us there and back on one of the military planes that flew every day. So we took him up on his offer.

Canberra is an interesting place. It's laid out like Washington, D.C. with numbered streets going east and west, lettered streets going north and south and diagonal streets with names of Australian states. However, it has no suburbs, when you got to the end of a street there was nothing there except scrubby land. So it was as though you were in the city and then you were in the middle of nowhere! We spent one day there and flew back to Sydney, where we caught our flight back home. So we weren't able to see much of Australia, but what we did see was very interesting.

Michael in Canberra, Australia

CHAPTER 41

AN OFFER I COULD REFUSE AND ANOTHER I COULDN'T

In 1971, when we thought we would be reassigned to the mainland, my commanding officer, Colonel James Decker, called me into his office. He told me that he had received a call from Headquarters telling him that I had been chosen to be the new White House dentist. So instead of moving somewhere else, I would be reassigned to Washington, D.C. I was shocked and flattered. At that time, one of my patients was the General, who was Commander in Chief of the Pacific Air Forces. When I told him that I was going to be reassigned right away to Washington as the White House dentist, he asked me if I really wanted to leave Hawaii or if I would like to stay another year. I told him I would like to stay in Hawaii, but I had already been told that I was leaving soon. He said that he could arrange for me to stay another year if I wanted to stay. I told him that I would like to ask my wife what she thought. He said to let him know what we decided. So when I got home that evening, I asked Betty if she would like to stay in Hawaii another year. She said she would love to stay as long as possible. I didn't tell her about the fact that they wanted me to be the White House dentist. When I went to the base the next day I notified the General that we would like to stay if possible. He said he would take care of it.

A few days later we were at a party and Mrs. Decker, my Commander's wife, asked Betty if she was excited about moving to Washington for me to be the White House dentist. Betty, not knowing anything about it, apparently looked surprised, because Mrs. Decker apologized and said "Oh, I'm sorry I guess I let the cat out of the bag. I wasn't supposed to say anything about it, just forget I said anything." Betty said okay and didn't say anything more about it until we returned home that evening. She asked me about it, so I told her the whole story. Then she asked me if I was sure that this was something I should turn down for the sake of my career. I told her that this was what I wanted to do. So we stayed another year.

After our return from Australia in November of 1971, it was time to start preparing to return to the Mainland. We decided to visit some of the places in Hawaii that we had not yet seen. We visited Maui, Kauai, and the Big Island. All were beautiful and different in their own way, but, we still preferred Oahu, where we had the best of both worlds, the cosmopolitan atmosphere of Honolulu and Waikiki and the rural areas of the North Shore and the Windward side of the Island.

We were to leave in June and in May, Betty's sister, Sherry, came to visit us to stay until our return home. We enjoyed having her with us and she was a big help while we packed up to leave.

We decided to fly to Los Angeles, rent a car and tour the Southwest on our way home. First we visited Las Vegas, then we toured the Hoover Dam and visited our friends, Howard and Betty Grounds on their huge ranch in Kingman, Arizona. We had met them at our hotel in Lima the first time I took Betty to Peru. We stayed overnight with them and enjoyed a western style cookout. The children rode a Brahma steer that they had in the corral and took a Jeep tour of their ranch. It was a wonderful experience that we all remember to this day.

After we left Kingman, we drove to the Grand Canyon National Park. On the way there we visited an Indian Reservation where we saw the ancient Indian Cliff Dwellings. After that we drove to Phoenix, where we got our flight to Indiana.

As a Board Certified Prosthodontist, my assignments were limited to large Air Force facilities which had Medical Centers. Although, since I had already been stationed at Andrews AFB during my residency program, I would have preferred to go to California, Texas or Mississippi. However, the Air Force powers that be decided that they wanted me to be involved in the new Prosthodontic Residency Program at Andrews AFB, Maryland. The old facilities at Andrews had reached maximum capacity and they were expanding the facility. Since the expansion was not yet completed, they reassigned me to nearby Bolling AFB in Washington, D.C. This facility was part of the Malcom Grow Medical Center and had a brand new Dental Clinic Building, which was better suited for the Dental Internship and Prosthodontic Residency programs.

After learning where I would be working, Betty and I left the children with her parents in Indiana and flew to Washington to look for a house. The fact that Betty's brother, Garry, went with us made the trip a lot more interesting!

While we lived in Hawaii the children wanted us to buy a horse. We knew that wasn't practical because we had nowhere to keep one and it would have been prohibitively expensive to ship one to the mainland when we were transferred. So we promised them that when we returned to the mainland we would buy them a horse. That made our search for a place to live more complicated. We had heard that Virginia was horse country, so we started looking there. We found that houses were much more expensive there than they were in Maryland, so we started looking there. We looked in the Upper Marlboro area where we had lived before but couldn't find anything that could fit our needs. Our priorities were, first, good educational facilities, then a comfortable house at an affordable price and zoned to accept a couple of horses. In our search we came across a brand new development, near a new country club with all kinds of amenities, including a golf course, swimming pool and nearby riding stables, which was only about 12 miles from Bolling AFB.

There were two very good high schools nearby, LaReine Catholic School for girls and Bishop McNamara for boys. There were also two Catholic elementary schools nearby, since none of the children were in high school yet. We signed a contract to buy a house that was under construction in that subdivision. Elena was in 8th grade, Michael, in 7th grade, Tony in 5th grade and Joey in 4th grade. Betty called the Archdiocese of Washington to find out which parish we lived in so that we could enroll the children for the coming school year. They told us that we were in St. Mary's Parish, so she called there and was told that they couldn't take the two younger children because those classes were already filled. So she called St. Columba, the other nearby school and spoke to the Priest there, Father Dewan. He said they could take all four of them as long as we registered in their Parish.

Everything they told us about our new neighborhood was true except there were no stables nearby! We didn't learn that until after we had moved into the house. Since we had already moved in we had no choice but to start looking for stables. We found a place owned by a young couple, Mr. and Mrs. Fields, which was about 25 minutes away and then we started looking for a horse. After answering an ad in the paper about a horse for sale, we found "Jack", he was very gentle and had been taught to shake hands. So we bought him and boarded him there and Elena and Michael started taking riding lessons from Mrs. Fields once a week. Unfortunately, we lost Jack when he was struck by lightning in the field, when a sudden storm came up. Everyone was heartbroken again. So we then bought another horse. His name was "Whiskey".

While driving home from work one afternoon, I noticed a group of children playing soccer in a field near our house. So I stopped to inquire about it. It turned out to be a small, local sports club called the Fort Washington Recreation Club and they were just starting practice for the fall season. I went home and asked the children if they would be interested in playing soccer on teams and they all said they would like to do that. I went back to the field and spoke to the Director, Mr. Townes, about enrolling them. He said they could play but they needed coaches and asked me if I would be able to coach a team. I agreed to coach Tony's and Joey's team. That is how we all became involved in soccer and we still are to this day!

Betty heard about a program called "Wendy Ward" at the Montgomery Ward store nearby. She asked Elena if she would be interested in enrolling there. This was a program that taught young teenage girls etiquette, how to walk, how to apply make-up, how to dress, and manners in general. At the end of the six week program they had a Beauty Pageant. Elena won a prize, but I don't remember what it was. However, her biggest prize was in her personal growth in becoming an impeccable dresser and groomer. She became the consultant and advisor on that subject for the entire family.

Elena at the completion of the Wendy Ward modeling course, 1973

CHAPTER 42

ANOTHER HEALTH SCARE

Everything was going great, I liked the work I was doing, the children liked their school and Betty was happy helping us all with our daily activities. Then in December Joey developed what appeared to be a cold or flu. One afternoon when he got up from a nap, he called Betty, crying that he couldn't stand up. She took him to the Doctor. It turned out that he was diagnosed with Scarlet Fever and had to be hospitalized. It was another rather sad and painful period of our lives, seeing him in pain, losing weight and seeing him sad and worried about what was going to happen to him.

Betty was by his bedside every day and she knew that he was interested in football. It was the time of year for the playoffs, so she started turning the TV on to watch the games. She didn't know much about football so she started asking Joey about the rules, player's positions, penalties, etc. This really perked Joey up. He was happier and feeling better, still in the hospital, but not well yet. Christmas was approaching and Betty asked Joey what he would like to have for Christmas. He said the only thing he wanted was a puppy! All of the children and I had wanted a new dog, but, after our experiences with pets in Hawaii, Betty had been resisting getting one. However, after seeing what Joey was going through, and wanting to do something to make him feel better, she relented and we started looking for a puppy.

We answered an ad in the paper about some German Shephard puppies for sale. We made an appointment to see the puppies and found an entire litter. The biggest one of them was dominating all of the others. The owners said they were all pure bred German Shephard, but the mother and father were not registered, so that was why they were selling them for twenty-five dollars. So we bought the biggest one and took him home. Although Joey was still in the hospital, his fever had gone down, after three weeks there; and they allowed us to bring him home for Christmas. When we brought out the puppy, his eyes lit up and he was so happy, we both cried. The children all had a say in what we were going to name him. There were many suggestions, but we finally all agreed on Charlie. We made a place for him in our laundry room, with papers on the floor and his feeding bowl and water bowl there. The week after Christmas Joey was finally released from the hospital and we all went back to our normal activities.

Charlie began to grow and rapidly develop the facial characteristics of a true German Shephard. One of his ears would not stay up, but would frequently flop down. It looked funny! The whole family just loved him and he was a constant companion to the children. As he grew older he became the children's protector and was a great watch dog. Michael, who was Prince's trainer in Hawaii, became Charlie's main handler. Whenever we were all at work or school, Betty would put him in the laundry room and close the door so that he couldn't get out when she had to leave the house. One day when she returned home she found Charlie in the family room. She assumed that she hadn't latched the door properly. So the next time she left she made sure that the door was shut tight. When she returned he was out again! None of us could imagine how he had gotten out. The next day Betty closed him in the laundry room, but didn't leave the house. She just watched the laundry room door and after a few minutes she could see the door knob turning and out came Charlie. He had learned how to stand up on his hind legs, put his paws on the knob and turn it until his weight pushed the door open! That's when we knew that we had a very smart dog! There are so many stories about Charlie that I can't put them all in this book. We all loved him and he lived to be 13 years old.

The complete Bernui family with Charlie and Whiskey. Fort Washington, Maryland, 1973

At work, I was super busy with a long list of patients to see, involved with the General Dentistry Internship and the Prosthodontic Residency training programs. The chief of the department of Prosthodontics was Col. Sam Adkisson, a gentle, southern type gentleman, who was in charge of the Removable Prosthetics teaching program. Much like a miracle, a recent graduate in Prosthodontics from USC had joined the Air Force and was assigned to our facility. When I first met this new Prosthodontist, he looked like a teenager. I told my commander, Col. Fritz, that I hoped that he did not expect me to "babysit" as well. He smiled and answered that I had been asking for help and now I had some and I should not complain. I spent my first few weeks glued to my new colleague both in the clinic and Dental Laboratory finding ways that I could help him to ease my work load.

Shortly thereafter, I found myself learning from him more precise Laboratory methods in fabricating crowns and bridges. He spent hours doing his Lab work, with me sitting near him, fabricating restorations while listening to the song "Ventura Highway", his favorite tune, and chewing on California raisins. As time went on, my wife and I became closer friends with Dr. David Eggleston and his wife Laraine, and their cutest little daughter Jamie. In spite of geographical distances, my family and I are blessed with their friendship to this date. Dr. Eggleston is an outstanding Prosthodontist who has served our country honorably at the highest professional level and has served our Specialty in Dentistry up to the highest position as President of the American College of Prosthodontists. He is still serving the profession as Professor at the University Of Southern California School of Dentistry, as well as maintaining a private practice in Newport Beach, California. His wife, Laraine, a talented ceramist is busy with grandchildrens' activities from their two equally talented children, who all honor us by being our friends.

There are many others with whom we have lost touch, but who we still remember fondly.

There are many civilian friends who we never would have met if we had not been in the military

.Rolando and Betty at Venezuelan Embassy reception.

CHAPTER 43

BUILDING THE FORT WASHINGTON HOUSE AND STARTING A BAND

All of us were busy with work, school and extra- curricular activities. Betty seemed to be glued to the car seat all the time, carpooling the children to and from school and all of their other activities. Driving them to their riding lessons took a lot of time and they weren't able to ride as much as they would have liked. In order to make our daily activities simpler, with less driving around, I started looking for some land nearby with enough acreage to build a bigger house where each child could have their own bedroom, build a barn and have enough space to exercise the horses and ride them. Fortunately, there was a four acre tract of land nearby, that we had seen when we originally were looking for a house. We had called the number on the sign to no avail. I decided to try calling again and got an answer this time. No one had bought it in those four years because it didn't have any road frontage except for an unpaved, steep, 12 foot easement. That was the only access to the property. The owners were willing to sell it at a reasonable price, but we had to find out if we could actually build on it. After lengthy research and innumerable trips to the Prince George's County administration offices, we were told the necessary steps we would have to take in order to build a house there. It was completely undeveloped raw land. No water, no sewer, no electricity, no gas, in other words, no utilities at all. All of the utility access lines stopped two lots up the road.

The first thing we needed to find out was where to begin. The people at the county suggested that the first thing we should do was to see if the land would perk, so that we could have a septic system. They told us who to call to schedule the test. The way they test the soil is to drill a hole near the building site, pour water in it and time how long it took for the water to be absorbed. Betty was present when the test was done. While drilling on the second or third site an abundant loose, black material started coming up. Betty jokingly laughed and said, "It looks like we struck oil!" The engineer smiled and said, "No, just Marlboro clay, no sense even trying to perk test this site because that doesn't absorb water". In conclusion, there was no chance of building a house on the property, unless we brought in utility lines.

There was no way that I would give up on my dream project! My dream plan was to build five houses, one for us and one for each of our children as they became adults. We would still have room for a barn and a riding trail around the property. There would also be a swimming pool and tennis courts in the center of the compound.

So we proceeded to file the necessary applications to have all of the utility lines extended to the property. This seemed to be an endless, expensive and time consuming series of tasks. However, we continued to plan and consider our family's future beyond high school and even college. We thought that this would be our home for the rest of our days. The long process was not easy, but, we finally had all the utilities extended to the property. We had fulfilled all of the requirements that land developers have to follow in order to build a subdivision! It was a registered subdivision so we had to come up with a name for it. We chose, "Sol de Oro", which was the name of the Peruvian currency before it was devalued and its metal content was changed and was not made of gold anymore.

Fort Washington House, 1983

Twenty fourth wedding anniversary vow renewal at home Mass with Fr. Bob Nagel and Fr. Jeff Larouer

We finally had a large and comfortable house finished. Each of the children chose the paint color, wallpaper and carpet color for their rooms. Betty did much of the painting and wallpapering. In fact the whole family was involved in building the house. The furniture we had made in Taiwan fit into each room very well, and we all moved in, two months before Elena left to go to college.

Elena chose to go to Old Dominion University in Norfolk, Virginia to become a Dental Hygienist. It was a difficult program to get into, but she took all of the tests and was selected to enter the program. We all missed her very much. It was too far away for her to come home on the weekends, so we only saw her during the holidays, spring break and during the summer.

Michael was a senior in high school when Elena started to college. During the summer before she left, he got together a group of his friends, who played musical instruments, to play "Chicago" music, just for fun. "Chicago" was a very popular music group at that time. Michael played the drums, Rob Eisele played the trumpet, Paul Cunningham played the guitar and sang, Kyle Johnson played the saxophone and sang, Walt played the keyboard, Jimmy Flynn played the guitar, and Chris Cubbage played the trombone. Paul also provided the PA system. They met once a week and had a good time all summer and in the fall after school started. Tony sometimes filled in for Walt on the keyboard and sang and Joey played guitar sometimes.

During the Fall semester the Spanish teacher, who was the Sponsor of the Spanish Club, told the Spanish class that they were going to sponsor a school dance to raise money so that the class could have a field trip to a Spanish restaurant in Washington, D.C. She asked if anyone knew of an inexpensive band they could hire to play at the dance. Michael raised his hand and told her that he had a band! She asked him how much his band charged to play. Of course, never having played anywhere before, he didn't know. So they negotiated a price, if they took in more than a certain amount of money, they would get $200.00 if they took in less they would get $100.00. They had two months to learn enough songs to play for a whole evening! This was quite a challenge! They would listen to records of the songs they wanted to play and each of them would learn their part by practicing individually on the days between practices. They needed a female vocalist so Paul's sister, Rose started singing with them. They all sang background vocals. They also needed a lead guitar player, so Jimmy suggested his friend Phil.

The week before the big performance, Michael asked the principal of the school if they could have a dress rehearsal, so that they could learn how to set up their equipment. He agreed, so they all gathered at the school gym to practice. Everyone knew their parts except Walt, the keyboard player. He had missed several practices and left practice early frequently, saying he already knew his part and didn't need to practice. Well, Michael fired him and he took his keyboard and went home! Tony knew all of the keyboard parts, but we didn't have a keyboard. Michael came to us, told us about Walt, and asked if we could buy a keyboard. We asked who would be playing it. He said Tony would be playing it. So Betty went with him to a music store and they bought a keyboard!

The evening of the dance arrived, they had no idea how many people would show up. It turned out that many of the other students thought it was going to be a bust and came to laugh at them. They had a big turnout and nobody laughed. They were really good and after the first few songs the girls were standing in front of the stage screaming and dancing! We stood in the back of the gym with tears in our eyes because we were so proud of them.

After that, Michael contacted the agent who represented several bands who played for proms and other dances, and asked her to book their band. She came to listen to them and agreed to get them some gigs. Before they played anywhere they had to have a name for the band. After much discussion, they decided on "Ignition" because they were going to "turn people on"! They started playing at junior high dances, store openings and other small events. Eventually, they played for proms and started making some money. Then, graduation arrived and most of them went away to school and had to be replaced. They held auditions and replaced missing members. Michael went to school at Loyola College in Baltimore and was able to come home on weekends to practice and play. "Ignition" became one of the most popular bands in the DC area and they went on to play for 13 years. Michael played with them until his third year in medical school.

Rolando and Betty at annual picnic, July 1983

After Elena graduated from college, she became the manager and sound engineer for them. When they started playing in clubs, Betty and I went to hear them as often as we could. Many times people were lined up around the block to get in to hear them. I had not heard them practicing very often, so one time when we were at a club listening to them play, I was surprised to hear Joey play the lead guitar part in the song "Freebird" by "Lynard Skynard". I was amazed at his skill! It was an exciting time for all of us! They played in Baltimore, Philadelphia and all around the DC area. They even played in Peru once!

As I mentioned, Michael went to Loyola College in Baltimore as a pre-med student. There he met Greg Cannella, they became roommates and best friends and both went on to medical school at the Philadelphia College of Osteopathic Medicine. They then did their Internships in York, Pennsylvania and their Residencies in Family Practice at Franklin Square Hospital in Baltimore. They decided that they wanted to practice together somewhere other than the Baltimore-Washington area. They ended up moving to the Nashville, Tennessee area.

"Ignition", 1984

CHAPTER 44

MORE ABOUT MY MILITARY CAREER

As I mentioned earlier, I joined the U.S. Air Force right after my graduation from dental school, in June of 1959. I will never regret one day of my career in the military. Yes, there were some trying times, just as there are in all of our daily lives. But they were soon forgotten unless someone specifically brings them to my attention. Even so, if I offended anyone you can rest assured that it was not my intention, and I am sorry. I grant the same forgiveness to anyone who might have felt jealous or cast aspersions on me. After all, we are still a military family and I am proud to have served alongside many patriotic brothers and sisters, regardless of rank or branch of service, who joined unconditionally and put their lives on the line.

I would like to recognize some of the outstanding line officers and enlisted men who imparted on me the fighting side of the Air Force, such as the fighter pilots at Hickam Air Force Base and the crews of the Blue Eagle Squadron. There was Col. Paul Greenwade, Col. Charles Leigon, Col. Fred Keish, Col. Alfred Lynn, Maj. Mulick, Sgt. Atwell, Sgt. Kelly just to name a few.

On the professional dental practice side of my military career, I was successful well beyond my own expectations. After receiving my specialty training and being assigned to Hickam AFB, Hawaii, I returned to the mainland in order to take the written part of my specialty Board Examinations in Chicago. A year later I returned again to take the second part of the exams in Indianapolis. By passing those exams, I became a Board Certified

Specialist in Prosthodontics. That made me eligible to be assigned only to the largest military facilities, such as Air Force Medical Centers.

I had a great rapport with all of my military patients, regardless of rank. Many of them have become lifelong friends with whom we still keep in touch, even today.

We also still keep in touch with many of the dentists with whom I served, and their wives. Among them Jim and Norma Dirlam, Lois Solinski, whose husband Ted passed away recently, Joy Archambault, whose husband "Arch" passed away several years ago, Ed and Ellie Herbold, Sam Adkisson, Bill Binzer, Don and Rosemarie Butz, Mercedes Willarson, whose husband Kenny passed away several years ago, and David and Laraine Eggleston, who live in California. There are many others with whom we have lost touch, but who we still remember fondly. Jim and Norma Dirlam, Don Butz, and Bill Binzer have passed away in recent years.

There are many civilian friends who we never would have met if we had not been in the military.

After we had moved into our new home and Elena and Michael had gone off to college, I started thinking about what would be next for us. I had known that some of the medical officers moonlighted at local hospitals when they weren't on duty, so I looked into how I could do that too. We needed some extra money for the children's college and high school expenses. There were also rumors that I would be transferred in the next two years. The possibility of an overseas assignment was very possible. I was excited that I could be assigned to a base in Europe because we had never been there. But, when I thought about it further, I knew it would have a negative impact on the family. We would have to leave the children in the States since they would all be in college soon. I didn't want to do that, so I considered all of the options and I requested permission to practice part time with a local dentist, Dr. Steven Lynn. The hospital commander,

Gen. Vandenbos, gave me permission to do so and I started moonlighting on Saturdays.

When the Dental Clinic Commander, heard about what I was doing, he came to me one day and told me that he was suspending all of my privileges as a Colonel and that I was not allowed to leave the clinic, except for lunch every day and I was not to continue practicing off base! I immediately left the clinic and went to the Judge Advocates Office and asked what privileges he could suspend. They advised me that he could not do that. After that we were blackballed from attending any parties or activities that were for the Dental Corps. This was not a good working atmosphere and I decided that since I had already completed my 20 years of active duty and 25 towards becoming eligible to retire, I made an appointment with the Assistant to the Surgeon General for Dental Affairs, Col. Archambault, to explain my situation and to request retirement from active duty. I retired with honors and received my retirement papers at a nice ceremony where I was awarded the Meritorious Service Medal. My retirement was effective, February 1, 1980.

CHAPTER 45

EXPERIENCES IN PRIVATE PRACTICE

In Maryland at that time, home offices were allowed with the proper zoning permits. We had a large unfinished basement at our house, and after obtaining the necessary permits, we opened my office there in February of 1980. The house was built on a slope and had a direct door from the patient parking area to the reception room. It took several months for my dental practice to start to build up. Since we had no road frontage with signage or building visibility, we didn't get any exposure from the local area. The patients who came to the office often commented about how much they liked coming there. They liked the homey atmosphere. Two sides of the parking lot were fenced, one side was wooded with large trees and the other side was a pasture with a barn for our horse. One of our patients built a bench outside the door with a sign on it that said "Smokers Lounge". There were no other houses in view. The entrance road split in two, one side going directly to the office parking lot and the other to a circular drive that led to the garage or the front of the house. Since I had training as a children's dentist, I was fortunate to have a very good rapport with children, thus, I had a group of patients of a second age group. Many of them had their parents to bring them to their appointment early so that they could watch our horse, Whiskey, showing off in the middle of the field. Many of them brought carrots or apples to feed to the horse! Soon Whiskey would come galloping to the fence to get treats and be petted by the children. Sometimes, they would even stay a while after their treatment. We always had free hot coffee and hot chocolate available in the waiting room. During the holiday season Betty had hot spiced apple cider, egg nog and home baked treats available. Decembers were the busiest months for the practice at the home office!

Fortunately for me, I started getting some military referrals from both Andrews and Bolling Air Force Bases. Many of them were from families of military active duty patients. Military family members, Dependents as they are referred to, or military retirees are not treated at military dental facilities, therefore, they secure their care from local dentists.

Since my professional specialty is Prosthodontics, during my military career my clinical practice was limited to providing major restorative services only. Therefore, at the beginning of my private practice, I was only treating patients prosthetic needs, and referring the rest of their treatment to nearby general practitioners or specialists in other fields, as we customarily do in the military. It didn't take me long to realize that most of my civilian colleagues only referred patients to Orthodontists and Oral Surgeons, very seldom to Prosthodontists. I had a large pool of patients, but not enough to keep me busy or to have a laboratory technician on the premises.

So with the thought of continuing to limit my practice to my specialty, military style, I contacted some military specialists who were in the process of separating or retiring from active duty. I asked them to form a group that would offer all or at least several dental specialty services under one roof, where we would be able to have a common front office, receptionist and waiting room. After a few months, I had commitments from an Orthodontist, an Endodontist an Oral Surgeon and a General Dentist. I had also found an office space conveniently located half way between Andrews and Bolling on St. Barnabas Road near the Beltway. We leased the space and each one of us equipped our offices with top notch equipment. We opened our clinic under the name of "Alpha Dental Associates".

Our practices were going well until the owner with controlling interest of the building, an attorney, announced that the building was going to be sold. Most of the other owners were selling out their shares in order to invest in another of his projects in Upper Marlboro. The project was for a series of business town house buildings in an area called Melwood. It was about time to renew our lease for Alpha Dental and when the members of the group heard about the possible sale of the building, they started looking for places to move their practices. In an effort to keep our group together, I talked to some of the building owners, and found out that not everyone wanted to sell the building, but it was going to be a majority decision. I decided that I would buy the individual shares available and be able to have enough voting power to avoid the sale and keep Alpha Dental operating. In the meantime, the other members had found other locations and there were not enough of us to make it feasible to stay.

Unfortunately, the owner was determined to sell the building, thus putting an end to Alpha Dental Associates. Another lesson learned the painful way for me, never get into partnerships, unless you are a general partner.

Once again, I had my home office to fall back on. However, if I wanted to limit my practice to my specialty, I had to find a location in a commercial area. Based on my recent experience with a landlord, I wanted to own my office space. Since I was still part owner of the bank building on St. Barnabas Road, I was still in touch with the owner. He still had some townhouse office suites available in his new project at Melwood. He advised me that it was a great opportunity for me with all of the physicians investing there. So I opened an office there. While the area was probably good for a general practitioner, it was not suitable for me as a Prosthodontist. So I sold that office and returned full time to the home office.

In a short time, I found an office space in a building partially owned by an Oral Surgeon. This building had great road exposure and had an assortment of business offices occupied by physicians, attorneys and a couple of general dentists. I had become friends with the Oral Surgeon when I was his son's soccer coach when I was coaching some of our children in the Fort Washington Soccer Club.

My new office was a state of the art dental practice. All computerized and equipped with the best Sirona Units. I also had a full service fully equipped Crown and Bridge Dental Laboratory. It was then that I moved my practice out of our home completely.

I had been introduced to Dental Implantology by another Prosthodontist, Dr. Gerald Niznick, who was a graduate of the Prosthodontics Residency program at Indiana University School of Dentistry. He was the owner and developer of the Core-Vent System of Dental Implants. After taking some of his training courses, I decided to implement Dental Implantology into my practice. I prepared a Procedural Manual for his System for my office. I enrolled in one of Dr. Niznick's newest courses and I took my Manual with me to the course in order to get his opinion about it. After reviewing it, he liked it and offered to hire me to write a Manual for his company. I accepted his offer and I took Betty, as my typist, to California to do the typing work. After finishing the Manual, we returned home. I was impressed by the successful result I saw in his office, which needless to say, fueled my enthusiasm for dental implantology. I decided to share my knowledge in the local area. I made some presentations at some local study clubs, including the National Capitol Study Club, of which I was a member. This study club was founded by Dentists from all of the Military Service Branches, Georgetown University, Howard University and University of Maryland, members. I also took my presentations to Peru, Costa Rica and Hawaii and I gave a course to a group of Bolivian dentists at my office.

CHAPTER 46

THE HAUNTED HOUSE

My practice became very successful after my move to the new location. Elena was my dental hygienist and Betty was the General Office Manager. However, as time went by, office personnel problems and patient problems, among others began to weigh heavily on me. The three older children had already moved out of the house and Joe was the only one left at home.

Tony was the first to marry. He married MaryBeth,whom he met when she auditioned to be the female vocalist in the band. He was still in college studying Business Marketing. MaryBeth decided to go to Law School. They needed a place to live and it so happened I had just bought a small house in Fort Washington and was in the process of renovating it. We told them they could live there as soon as the renovations were complete.

During the course of the renovations, some unexplainable things happened. A handyman, who was working in the house, left his tools in the basement while he went out to eat lunch. When he returned to the house he couldn't find his tool box, so he assumed that I had picked it up. He came to my office to ask for his tools, but neither Betty nor I had been to the house that day. We immediately thought burglary, but we sent the man back to the house to check again before we called the police. When he went into the house his tools were there, right where he had left them! No one could come up with an explanation.

On a separate occasion, I had driven my laboratory technician to the house to do some painting. I told him that I would pick him up after I finished my last patient. It must have been about six p.m. when I arrived and found him on the front porch with an annoyed, or perhaps, frightened look on his face. I apologized for being a little late and he asked me why I had not come down to the basement, when I had been there earlier, to let him know that I was there. I assured him that I had not been there earlier. He kept looking around at me to see if I was joking and said that he had heard footsteps upstairs and heard voices coming from up there. He appeared very uncomfortable being there, so we left the house right away!

In the meantime, Tony had taken a year off from college to study cosmetology. He then finished college with a degree in Marketing and was offered a job in the D.C. area teaching cosmetology. MaryBeth was still in Law School and "Ignition" was still going strong. When the renovations were finished on the house they took us up on our offer and moved into the house. While they were living there unexplainable things continued to happen. Things that they had put away would appear in different places, and rolls of tape would be found in the middle of the floor. The TV would come on in the middle of the night when the game show "Password" was on. Once when Elena was there, she and Tony went to the kitchen for a few minutes and when they came back the TV had been changed from the program they had been watching to the World Series that was being played at that time.

The husband of the family that I had bought the house from had died suddenly. He had been heard to say that he would never live anywhere but that house. I told his wife about the strange things that had been happening, especially about the TV. She said "Oh, I hope the show wasn't "Password", that was my husband's favorite show other than sports!" So one day when Tony and MaryBeth came home bringing their groceries, the door wouldn't open no matter what they did, it wouldn't unlock. So

MaryBeth said "Come on Mr. Dillard, let us in". She tried the lock again and it unlocked!

After Tony and MaryBeth moved out we put the house on the market and sold it. Financially, we probably did not make any actual cash profit, but I felt that we still came out ahead by giving Tony and MaryBeth a place to live rent free, while they were still going to school and for me having some tax write offs.

Early on in my practice life, I realized that an investment in a place for my own business should be one of my priorities, independent from landlord manipulations and being my own tenant. I came across an individual who had a lot that he wanted to develop. I bought half interest in the lot and planned to build a professional building on it. Getting it rezoned and getting building permits was a long process and my partner became disillusioned and sold me his part. I went to an engineering firm and had plans drawn up and I had already gotten bank approval for a loan for the project. Just before I started the building process the entire country went into recession and the bank stopped making loans and increased interest rates on those already approved. My bank informed me that they were increasing the amount of the down payment. At first I considered a smaller building, but the bankers said it would be possible, but it would have to be a "bank participating loan" at a much higher interest rate. That essentially killed my project! Today, I still have the land, but to me, Prince George's County, Maryland is not the best county for business. I'll just keep the land for sale for a rainy day.

Nothing is easy or applicable to anyone in particular or everyone in general. Having basic business concepts has helped me to get involved with confidence into some real estate investment ventures. These have helped me to educate my four children and helped my family in general to live a little bit more comfortably than we would have been able to otherwise. I have learned that no matter in which area I have tried to invest, stocks, real estate or any other, I have been able to achieve some success. My biggest disappointments and losses have been in trusting people that I didn't know very well, whose shady actions caused my financial losses. The investments were sound, it was the unscrupulous people involved who caused the losses.

CHAPTER 47

CHILDREN MOVING ON

Time was continuing to move on and family needs and circumstances kept changing as the children grew older and became more independent. As time went by they started making their own plans. My dream plan for making a family compound on our four acres with a home for each child and their families wasn't feasible.

After Michael and Greg had finished medical school, their internships, and residencies, they decided that they would like to practice together somewhere in the South and started looking for opportunities. Betty had a friend from high school, Billie Hughes, who had moved to the Nashville, Tennessee area after they graduated. Billie's aunt was a friend of Betty's Mom, and when she heard that Michael was looking for a practice in the South, she told Billie about it. Billie just happened to work for a dentist whose practice was in a building that had a physician's office in it. This physician was looking for an associate, so Billie contacted Michael and introduced him to the physician. Michael and Greg liked the offer they were made and moved to Tennessee, where they bought a house on Old Hickory Lake, together.

After they moved into their house, the physician decided that he didn't want associates and withdrew his offer. Michael and Greg knew that their specialty was in great demand and were soon offered positions with an HMO in the area, which they decided to take until they found what they really wanted to do. Michael went on to open his own private practice and Greg became a consultant for the insurance company that owned the HMO.

After Elena started working in my office she decided that she wanted to be more independent and have her own home. I advised her that rather than renting a place, she should buy a house. I had bought a lot in a nearby neighborhood at a property auction and Elena and I decided that we could build a house for her there. After we had ordered a modular home to be placed on the lot, the neighbors obtained an injunction to stop us from doing so. They thought that a modular home was a double wide trailer, which it isn't, and they didn't want their property value to be lowered by that. We had to go to court and our attorney found a technicality that allowed us to build the modular home there. In the meantime, Elena found another new house nearby and bought it instead. She lived there for a few years and then decided to rent it out and move to Colorado. She loves to ski and of course Colorado is known for its beautiful ski resorts and scenery.

Now Joe was the only one of our children living in our home. He had decided to drop out of college and to pursue a career in music with the band. I had to have some serious father/son discussions with him about his long term plans for his future. I wanted him to realize that the band was probably not going to make him enough money to live on and he needed some kind of formal education at least as a back-up.

I would start by asking him to compare himself to the captain of a large powerful and well supplied boat, preparing for a life-long trip from Baltimore Harbor with either none or multiple stops to pick up his family along the way, to enjoy the rest of the journey. To start such a trip you should first identify your destination and have a navigation compass to guide your way. Unless you have your destination identified and a navigation chart to follow, you may get lost or start going in circles as soon as you get into the ocean and have no bearings to follow. I told him "Joe, you are the boat captain, Mom and I are the fuel suppliers. You have to choose what you would like to do to produce an income for your trip and get some training for that job. I am slowing down in my productivity and have to decide on Mom's and my own livelihood, but I will continue working until you can be decently self-supporting and not just a surviving person". Joe decided that some kind of work with computers would interest him. So he attended a Computer Training Program at a Technical School.

In the meantime, Michael had met Melinda Harris, a girl in his Sunday school class at his new church. The class went on a ski trip to North Carolina where he and Melinda became better acquainted. After a few weeks of dating they decided to become engaged. One evening Michael called us and asked Betty if she had any plans for her birthday, May 23rd. She said we had a few plans, but asked if there was something important happening on that date. He said "Well, we would like for you to come down here on that date to attend our wedding". So of course we changed our plans and attended on May 23, 1992.

Betty and I continued to live in our 7,000 square foot house in the middle of the woods with no neighbors or friends nearby. Tony and MaryBeth still lived in the haunted house and Joe lived with us, but they all were living their own lives and we didn't see much of them. We had met some Peruvian friends who owned a Peruvian restaurant, called "Cuzco" in Virginia. This restaurant became a night club with bands that played Peruvian and other Latin music for dancing after 10pm on the weekends. So we started going there every Friday and Saturday nights for dinner and dancing. I taught Betty how to dance my favorite Peruvian dances and we became pretty well known by the band members and other regular customers there. In fact one evening the band leader introduced Betty as "the American girl with a Peruvian heart". Many of the other patrons there actually thought she was Peruvian and were surprised when she didn't understand them when they spoke to her in Spanish.

Rolando and Betty dancing Huayno in Cuzco Restaurant, 1982

With my building project now cancelled, and the children gone, the fuel that ignited the fire of my ambitious plans was growing dim. I laid on my bed with my eyes closed pondering and praying in silence to the Lord for guidance as to where to go from here. My poor wife had her own health problems to deal with as well as the vacuum left by the gradual departure of our children. I felt that perhaps God was sending me a message to slow down and regroup. Perhaps Maryland or the D.C. area was not the place meant for me or my family to settle. Betty, the love of my life, had courageously undergone a lengthy battle with surgeries for breast cancer and post op treatments without burdening me or our children. We both pretended that the things that were happening were just bumps in the road that most people go through in the course of their lives. We never discussed our problems with the children. After all, we knew that at their tender ages, there was nothing they could do to help and we didn't want to distract them from their school work or their burgeoning careers.

In spite of all the things going on in that period of our lives, we tried to keep in close contact with each other. We celebrated the children's special occasions and had occasional family events, such as, vacation trips or anything that would keep the family connected. We never turned down an invitation to visit any of them. We visited Baltimore, Norfolk and Hendersonville several times. They also visited us sometimes. We missed our children a lot, but there was nothing we would not give up, including their nearness, as long as they were happy.

One of the occasions that we enjoyed was when Tony entered a Country Music contest on a TV show called "You Can Be A Star". Betty's Mom, brother, Garry and his wife Becky came from Indiana to see the show televised. Tony didn't win the contest, but it was a great experience.

While we were there we took the opportunity to visit the Opryland Amusement Park. It was very similar to Disney World except its theme was country music. There were country music shows in between all of the usual amusement park rides.

CHAPTER 48

DECISION TO LEAVE MARYLAND

Shortly before that show, Tony and MaryBeth had come to visit Michael. MaryBeth, who had just graduated from Law School and had not found a job anywhere yet, visited Vanderbilt University Law School and got some leads on jobs. She submitted an application to the U.S. Department of Labor in Nashville and got the job. So they moved to Nashville, too.

During this period of time, Joe had met a girl, Jennifer Rackey, and they decided to get married. They married on May 7, 1993. Joe had found a job, after graduating from the computer school, with an institution supported by government grants. There was constant uncertainty as to whether the grants would be renewed each year, so Joe was looking for a better job. Jen helped him send out resume´s and he got a job with a Temporary Agency which placed him with AOL, when AOL had only 10,000 customers. After six months as a temp they renewed his job for another six months and then offered him a permanent job. At first he was reluctant to take it because it didn't pay very well. However, they offered him stock options in addition to his regular salary. After consulting with Jen, us, and his siblings he decided to take it. That was probably one of the best decisions of his life! He and Jen were then able to buy a nice townhome in Virginia.

Betty and I still had the big house on 4 acres of land that had become difficult to maintain without appropriate help and equipment. It had become expensive to continue to live there for just the two of us. So I put my dental practice up for sale. Selling the practice was an emotional transition for me because my patients had become my friends. They came from everywhere, from southern Maryland to Northern Virginia, Washington, D.C., Florida, Missouri, and Seattle. Socially, many of my immediate local area friends were also moving to other faster growing, and better communities. Professionally speaking, there were many opportunities for Prosthodontists throughout the country, from teaching positions to private practice, but nothing in particular attracted me at the time.

Betty and I wanted to be at a closer distance to where the children settled. After closing the sale of the practice, I was obligated to stay for one year after to make transition smoother to the new owner. After the year was over, I still had not made up my mind as to what to do after stopping private practice. So when I saw an advertisement from Meharry Medical College School of Dentistry in Nashville, TN, regarding a position as Associate Professor in the Department of Prosthodontics, I answered it. I had been involved in post graduate education to a good extent in the Air Force with internship and residency programs. But, I was not familiar with undergraduate education, and there is a great difference. After I flew to Nashville for an interview with Dr. William Butler, who was chairman of the Department of Prosthodontics, I decided to take the job.

Our house had been on the market for some time and had not sold. Meharry wanted me to start my job in August, so reluctantly Betty and I decided that she would stay in the house and I would move to Nashville. We wanted to live in the Nashville area because our family there was growing. Michael and Melinda now had two children, Michael Rolando, Jr. who was born in 1994 and Caleb Nathaniel, who was born in 1995. Tony had one child, Alexandra Elena, who was born in 1995. We were sorry that we had to leave Joe and Jen who had one child, Haley Susan, who was born in 1996 and Elena who was still single, behind in the D.C. area.

Tony and Michael had each offered a place for me to stay with them until we sold our house and bought a new one in the Nashville area. I stayed with Tony and MaryBeth the first few months. Then so as not to overstay my welcome, I stayed with Michael and Melinda. I flew to Maryland frequently on the weekends to visit Betty and she flew to visit me sometimes too. I spent my spare time looking for condominiums in Nashville. I couldn't find any in the downtown area. I was told that zoning ordinances didn't allow them to build high rise buildings downtown. (Boy, have things changed!) As time passed I decided to look for houses for sale on Old Hickory Lake. There were a few, but none that we could afford. That pushed me to consider looking for lakefront lots and I found one that I liked in Gallatin. It was also relatively close to Michael's house. I decided to buy it and I wanted to build a Peruvian style house. While visiting Lima with Betty, we had an architect to draw us a plan for our lot in Gallatin. After contacting a couple of local area builders, we realized that they had mostly negative comments, about Mediterranean style houses (Peruvian houses are similar to Mediterranean). Mediterranian style was not common at all in the South and we were told that we might encounter difficulties obtaining bank financing. I was discouraged, but, negative news had never deterred me before, so I continued my search. Unfortunately, things were not moving on the sale of our house in Maryland, either.

CHAPTER 49

FINDING A HOME IN TENNESSEE AND HEART PROBLEMS

Betty and I decided that we were tired of living apart and if the house had not sold by Christmas, we would lower the price and seriously look for a place in the Nashville area. So I gave up on building a Peruvian style house and started looking for a house. I came across a new, very small neighborhood being developed by Phillips Builders, which had 10 lake-front lots. There were only four on which they were planning to build. Of those four there was only one on which they didn't have a contract. They already had plans for the house they were going to build there and would not accept any modifications. They would accept a few small upgrades, such as, a full basement, an enlarged driveway, a walkway to the rear of the house and a large patio in the back. They would only do these things if they were paid in advance in addition to the down payment. Since the house in Maryland had not yet sold, we had to scrape together all the cash we had, including all of the change I had saved over the years. Betty spent a lot of time sorting and counting it while she was living alone in our big house. But, it was all worthwhile, because we could now live together again and be close to at least part of our family, which was growing every year. In May of 1997, Michael and Melinda had their first daughter, Rachel Eliza. And in September of 1997, Joe and Jen had their second daughter, Rachel Lee.

We still had the lot in Gallatin, so we put it on the market. While looking for a builder for that lot, I had met a builder by the name of Bob

Goodall, whose company, Goodall Homes, was building subdivisions in the area. He wasn't interested in building custom homes, but in talking to him one day he asked me if I would be interested in trading that lot for partial payment on one of his homes in a subdivision in White House, Tennessee. He was thinking of building a waterfront home for himself on the lake lot. So I took him up on his offer bought the house and rented it out. The person who rented it eventually bought it from me.

Hendersonville home

Preparing to move from a large house to a smaller house presented some problems. Betty had two yard sales and sold many items that none of the members of the family wanted. She had to have the yard sales in the front yard of Elena's house, since we had no road frontage in front of ours. After we moved into our new house, on July 4, 1997, we had to go back to visit the house in Maryland periodically. So we had left a few things in the house, such as a bed and bedding and some kitchen utensils.

In the meantime, Elena had become engaged to George Roy, who she met just before she moved to Colorado. He flew to Colorado to visit her several times and on one of those trips he proposed. The only problem was she had to move back to Maryland because he had three sons who he couldn't bring with him if he moved to Colorado. So she came back and got married on September 20, 1997. Since we still had the house there, the family members who came for the wedding all stayed with us. Some were on beds and some in sleeping bags. We all had a good time though and the wedding was beautiful.

In July of 1998 Melinda and Michael had their second daughter, Hannah Francesca. In April of 1999, Tony and MaryBeth had their second daughter, Olivia.

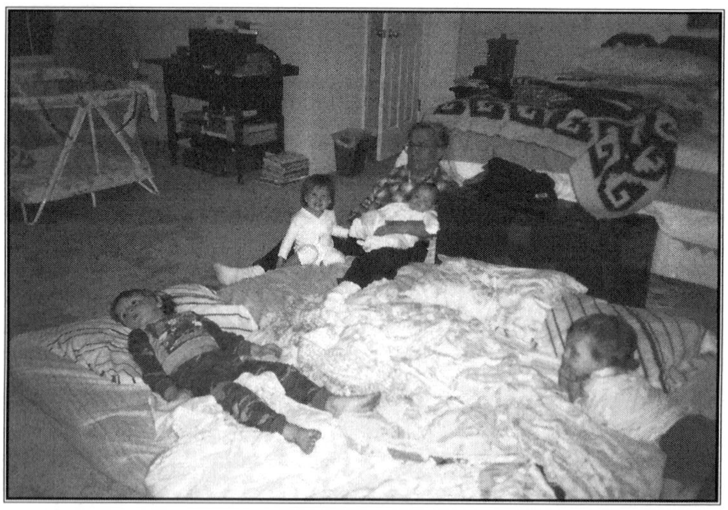

Michael, Rachel, Rolando, Hannah, and Caleb, 1998

Living in Nashville made it also easier to go to Indiana to visit Betty's mother and her brothers and their families. We used to go early on Friday morning and return on Sunday afternoon. On one occasion, on a Friday morning, I didn't feel very well. It appeared to me that I might be coming down with the flu. So I suggested that we stop at Michael's office on our way so that he could give me a prescription for some kind of flu medication.

What was planned as a brief stopover, ended up by becoming a big event! After we had called him to tell him we were going to stop at the office, he ordered the staff to get an EKG, while we waited for him to get there. When he saw the EKG, he thought he saw an abnormality and sent it to a cardiologist in the same office building at the hospital. He asked Betty if we had any copies of previous EKGs. She told him that we might have one in his Air Force medical record that we had at home. So he sent her home to get it. Before she left, the nurse came in to the examination room with two aspirins and told me to chew them. That was the first indication that this could be a heart problem. When Betty returned, I was in the admitting room filling out forms in order to be admitted. The cardiologist had called Michael and told him that the EKG indicated that something was wrong and I needed to have a cardiac catheterization immediately. The results were that they discovered that five cardiac arteries were from 95% to 99 % obstructed and needed immediate intervention. I was taken to the Cardiac Intensive Care Unit until they could take me to Centennial Medical Center in Nashville on Monday. There a well-known heart surgeon performed quintuple bypass surgery on February 7, 2000, our 41st wedding anniversary. What an anniversary gift! I was warned that the smallest diameter artery bypassed might not stay open, but I should function well with the other four corrected. My recovery, although it appeared to me long and slow, was considered fast for a 70 year old individual. The staff at Meharry was very kind to me and gave me all the time I needed for my recovery.

One of the things that helped speed up my recovery was that Elena had announced that she and George were expecting their first child in March. I knew that I had to be well enough by then to go see the new baby. In March of 2000, Zachary Bernui Roy was born. The doctor said that we could drive to Maryland if we stopped every two hours for me to walk around for 15 minutes. So that is what we did.

I returned to work at Meharry and developed a course for teaching Implant Dentistry, about which I wrote a book entitled, *Basics of Implant Dentistry*.

I continued to work there until June of 2013. When, due to a change in the administration, I decided to retire once again.

CHAPTER 50

MEETING MOTHER'S SIDE OF THE FAMILY

In 2002, Betty and I went back to Peru for the wedding of my niece, Magali, the daughter of my cousin Meche. We went a week early in order to travel up to Huaraz, Carhuaz and Parihuanca to see what had happened to our property there. We found that it had been taken over by squatters and there was no way we could get it back! So it was a bittersweet trip. When we returned to Lima, we had a very nice time seeing many family members and friends whom we had not seen for many years.

The following year, Sarah was born in February to Michael and Melinda. The next year, Maria was born in July and in November of the next year Joelle was born. Joelle's birth was an exciting experience! Michael and I had gone to a seminar in Virginia two weeks before her due date. On the last evening of the seminar, at the dinner for the ending of the event, Michael got a call from one of the children that Melinda's water had broken and she was in labor. I tried to call Betty, but, she was at church and didn't get the call right away. Finally, when I called her again she was on her way home. When I told her what was happening she turned around and went to their house, where the children were all relieved to see her. Melinda insisted on driving herself to the hospital with Betty behind her with all of the children. Michael, Jr. helped her get into the hospital. In the meantime, Michael, Sr. and I went to the airport and got the first flight that was available to Nashville. We arrived in time for Michael to be with Melinda when Joelle was born the next morning. It was all very exciting!

The next year, Michael and Melinda presented us with our 14th grandchild, Joshua who was born in March. He is their 9th child, the third boy.

In 2008 we went to Peru again and spent two weeks just visiting with family and friends. My cousin, Hugo Palacios, from my Mother's side, organized a party for me at the Ancash Club in Lima. I was able to see many of my Cousins, Uncles and Aunts, and their children, from Mother's side of the family. At the end of the party an Ancash Club executive escorted us to the club's office to sign the "Golden Book". Every distinguished guest they have is invited to write something and sign the Book. I was honored to know that they put me in that category.

One of the relatives who attended the party was my Uncle Samuel Vidal, who was the man who came to Huaraz to take me back to Yauya, after my Mother passed away. He came up to me and asked me if I would speak to him. He thought I had been angry with him for all those years for taking me away. I told him that I had not been angry at all, in fact, at that time I thought it was a great adventure! We kept in touch with each other until 2015 when he passed away at over 100 years old.

A few days later, another cousin from my Mother's side of the family came to see us and invited us to his home for lunch the next day. When we arrived there were two other couples there. One of them was the Police Chief of Lima and his wife and the other was another distant cousin and his wife. After a delicious lunch of Peruvian food the police chief told me he wanted to have a serious conversation with me. So I listened to what he had to say. He told me that they would like for me to run for President of Peru! I was shocked and surprised! I told him that I wouldn't have the money to embark on something like that and besides that there weren't enough people in Peru who knew me and would vote for me. He said that money wouldn't be a problem and that they could gather enough people to vote for me and that he felt I would have a good chance of winning. Since the whole conversation was in Spanish, I told Betty what they were offering me and she was as shocked as I was. In the end I told them that I was happy doing what I was doing living in the USA and I turned down their offer.

All in all it was a very nice visit.

Rolando's mother's family

CHAPTER 51

OUR TRIP TO PERU WITH GRANDCHILDREN

In 2010 I decided it would be a good time to take some of our children and grandchildren to Peru to see where I grew up. So I asked all of our children if any of them or the older grandchildren could go with us. Elena said she couldn't go and Zachary was too young. Michael said that they couldn't go but their four oldest children, Michael, Jr., Caleb, Rachel and Hannah could. Tony said they couldn't go and MaryBeth said that Alex couldn't go unless one of her parents went. Joe said they couldn't go and their children couldn't go either. So Betty and I contacted a travel agency, "Peru For Less" to make arrangements for a trip. We definitely wanted to go to Lima, Machu Picchu, Cuzco, and Huaraz. Michael, Jr. had seen a documentary about the Uros Islands in Lake Titicaca, near Puno and wanted to go there. I had been told by my nephew, Tulio Obregon, about the Colca Canyon, the deepest canyon in the world, where you could look down and see Condors flying below you. Since I had never been there, I wanted to see it. So we made our plans and departed on Thursday, June 24. We flew from Nashville to Ft. Lauderdale, Florida. From there we flew to Bogota, Colombia and then on to Lima, arriving at midnight. The next day, Friday, we had a nice luncheon at the home of Magali and Scott Crutchfield, with my cousins, Meche, Polo and his wife, Nelly. It was so nice to visit with them after several years.

The next day we flew to Arequipa, the second largest city in Peru, where we had a tour of the city, which included a tour of a convent. From

Arequipa we traveled by minivan for a 5 hour drive to the small town of Chivay. On the way we saw a chain of eight volcanoes, and fields of Vicuñas, Llamas and Alpacas. After arriving in Chivay, and checking into our hotel, Pozo Del Cielo, we were taken to La Calera, where we bathed in the hot springs. They had a zip line there that went from the top of a mountain down to a field next to the hot springs. It was so fast that each person had a parachute to slow them down for the landing! The boys wanted to do that but it was too late for them to climb up the mountain and get down before dark. After arriving back at the hotel we rested for an hour and then were taken for dinner to a restaurant that had a folk dancing show. When we arrived back at the hotel we found that they had put hot water bottles at the foot of our beds to keep our feet warm because there was no heat in our rooms and it gets rather cool at night in the mountains.

The next day we traveled by minivan for the one hour drive to the Colca Canyon. We saw the awesome Condors flying everywhere below us in the Canyon. They are huge birds, some with 16 foot wingspans! On the way back we stopped at two small towns where there were beautiful views of the terraces and lagoons. There was also a place where they had a large hawk and some Alpacas with which we had our pictures taken. After returning to Chivay, we had lunch at the hotel and then left for the return trip to Arequipa.

The next day we almost missed our flight to Puno because the tour agency had the wrong time for our pick up. After I called them they rushed us to the airport in a thrilling ride! Puno lies on the shore of Lake Titicaca, the highest navigable lake in the world. During the Spanish period, Puno was one of the continent's riches cities, because of its proximity to the Laaykakota silver mines. Lake Titicaca was once the most sacred body of water for the Inca and still holds many traces of that rich culture, including the Uros, the floating reed islands where many continue to live. As I mentioned, Puno is at a very high altitude and when we arrived at the hotel some of us experienced a bit of altitude sickness. The hotel had oxygen available so I called for it and after a few deep breathes of that we all felt back to normal and didn't need it again. The hotel was very nice and each of our beds were decorated with animal figures fashioned from the towels and washcloths. The children, especially Hannah, were fascinated with how they were made, so I made arrangements with the maid to come and give us a lesson on how to make some of the animals. We videotaped the lesson so that they could remember how to make them when we arrived back home.

The next day, Betty wasn't feeling well, so the children and I embarked on our trip to the Uros Islands and Taquile Island. The Uros Islands are thirty floating islands in the middle of Lake Titicaca. We visited two of them, they are made of reeds and when you step onto them it feels like stepping on a water bed. The houses and boats and everything on the island are made of reeds, so they are not allowed to have fire for anything. All of the heat is from the sun. We were given a demonstration of how they make and maintain the islands and how they weave blankets and rugs. We also had a ride in one of the reed boats. It was all very interesting to me, as well as the grandchildren, because I had never been there before either. After leaving those islands we proceeded to Taquile Island, where we had a 2 km hike up to the main town where we had a lecture about the importance of Taquile in the history of Peru. We also had lunch there. After seeing their woolen and alpaca clothing and colorful handicrafts, we had a long hike down to the other side of the island where our boat was to pick us up. It was a very rough trail with steps of stones that were very uneven, from a step of six inches to a step of a foot or more. Hannah was very sweet to me and took my arm to make sure I didn't fall, and we made it to the boat safely for our three hour trip back to our hotel in Puno.

The next day we boarded a bus to Cuzco, the capitol of the Inca Empire, which included present day Peru, Ecuador, Chile, Argentina and Bolivia. As we were boarding the bus, I decided to go into the terminal to buy some bottled water for the trip. It took me a little longer than I expected and the bus was just pulling out of the station when I came outside! Of course, Betty was trying to communicate to the driver that I wasn't on the bus and that I was right outside, but they didn't understand what she was saying even though she was speaking Spanish! Finally, I managed to flag them down and was able to board the bus! On the way we stopped at some pre-Inca ruins, an Inca temple and a church, and crossed the highest pass on the route. We stopped half way and had a buffet lunch. After arriving in Cuzco, we were taken to our hotel.

The following day we took the Cuzco City and Ruins tour. We saw the Cathedral with its amazing golden altar and art masterpieces, the Koricancha Temple and some of the ruins surrounding Cuzco. Then we went to Sacsayhuaman, which the children jokingly renamed "sexy-woman". Sacsayhuaman is a fortress built with giant stones, some larger than a house, put together with no mortar, to form a wall around a large open area. No one knows how the Incas were able to bring these giant stones to this area. This is where they have a festival every year called the Inty Rymy. They recreate an Inca festival to honor the sun. It is a very interesting place. We then traveled to the fortress of Puka Pukara, the Inca Baths at Tambomachay and the temple of Qenqo. At the Inca Baths there is a waterfall that comes out of the rocks and then disappears. No one knows where it goes!

The next day we left Cuzco, which is the gateway to Machu Picchu, one of the Seven Wonders of the World. It was a religious center and fortress built in one of the most inaccessible and wildest terrains, on the peak of a mountain. No one knows how the Incas were able to bring the huge rocks up to that location to build it, either. So the next day after we arrived, we had to be at the train station at seven o'clock in the morning to catch the train to Machu Picchu. It was one of the first trains that was allowed to go, after a rock slide that had blocked the tracks for several months. It was a beautiful ride with lunch included. After arriving in Aguas Calientes, we transferred to a bus that took us up to Machu Picchu. That was a thrilling ride, on a narrow road with hairpin turns and steep grades, Rachel commented, "Grandma, do you realize that our lives are in the hands of this bus driver?" We had a great tour of the city with our guide, Fabrizio, who explained all of the buildings, the terrace farming, and the water system that somehow brought water from the river below and circulated it throughout the city. It is an amazing place and we were happy that we all were able to see it.

Rolando, Michael, Hannah, Rachel, Betty, and Caleb at Machu Picchu, 2010

That evening we were transported to the train station for our trip back to Cuzco. After about an hour and half the train slowed down and came to a halt. We sat there for about half an hour and then the train started backing up. Finally, someone came through the train and told us that there had been a small rock slide that had blocked the tracks and we were going back to the last stop, Piscaycucho, where they would put us on buses to take us back to Cuzco. The train was full and by the time we were off of it the lines for the buses were long. Betty heard an announcement, in Spanish, for any elderly people or children to come over to another place with a much shorter line. So we figured that we qualified on both counts and we went to the shorter line! Unfortunately, Betty had put our Peruvian cell phone in her jacket pocket and somehow during the ride it slipped out of the pocket and wasn't missed until the next day, so we were without a phone for the rest of the trip.

After spending the night in a bed and breakfast in Lima, we departed early in the morning to go to Callejon de Huaylas. My niece, Magali, had arranged transportation for us with a company called, "Peru's Golden Shuttle". We were in an eight passenger minivan with the owner of the company, Branimir, as our driver. After several hours we stopped at a gas station along the way for a rest stop. Across the road from the station was a small market where they were selling fruit. I had wanted to have a fruit called Chirimoya, so I went there and sure enough they had it. So I bought some for all of us to try. Everyone really liked it, especially Caleb. When we were ready to leave one of the young girls there told me that we could leave Caleb there and he could have all the Chirimoya he wanted! I laughed and told her that was a nice offer but Caleb couldn't stay! We did, however, bring more of the fruit with us.

After we arrived in Huaraz, we had time to drive up to Pariahuanca, so that I could show the children the property that had belonged to my family. We stopped at the small general store in town and the owner remembered me. He was very nice and told me a little bit about what had happened to various people from the area that I had known during my childhood, since I had left. We then returned to Huaraz and had dinner at a local restaurant. While there I asked the waitress if she knew my cousin, Hermalinda, the daughter of my Uncle Moises. She said she did, but she didn't know her phone number or the exact address, but she knew the name of her street. So after dinner, we took Betty and the children to the Hotel Columba, and Bran and I set out to see if we could find Hermalinda. The hotel had an internet cafe, so the children went there to make their daily Skype call to Michael and Melinda, while Betty went to our room to rest. We did find Hermalinda and she wanted to meet the children, so I told her where we were staying and she said she would come to the hotel to meet them. When Hannah and Rachel went to our room to let Betty know, she was in bed, sound asleep, so they woke her up and told her that I wanted her to come to the Lobby because the family was coming. She, half asleep, told them to tell me that she was asleep. So I sent them back to tell her that they really wanted to see her. So she got dressed and came out to see them. Hermalinda had brought three of her daughters, her son-in-law and some of her grandchildren, so it was a large reunion. They also brought us some Peruvian pottery gifts. Betty was happy that she didn't miss it!

The next day we drove to Carhuaz and Matacoto, where we visited with, Raquel and Phil Krebs, she is another relative of mine who is married to an American. Their home is up high on a mountainside with a full view of the Huascaran. What an awesome location! Then we went up to the base of the Huascaran, where we stayed for a while at Lake Llanganunco. It is a beautiful lake with unbelievably blue water and is at a very high altitude, about 20,000 feet. We really wanted to go on to Yauya, but, were told that the road was bad and we wouldn't have time to get there and back that day. After that we went back on a different route through Yungay, a town that was destroyed by a mud and rock landslide in the '60s. It has a huge statue of Jesus with His arms stretched open overlooking the cemetery and the area where the town had been. We then returned to our hotel for the night.

The next day we traveled back to Lima. After spending the night in the hotel "El Carmel" we had breakfast and Magali picked us up and gave us a nice tour of Lima. It happened to be July 7th, Hannah's 12th birthday, so we went to a restaurant, Pardo's Pollo ala Brasa, for lunch. Without telling anyone, I asked our waiter to prepare a birthday cake for Hannah. So after we finished eating our chicken, here came all of the waiters and waitresses carrying a big cake, they then put a big hat on Hannah and everyone in the whole restaurant sang Happy Birthday in English and Spanish! You should have seen the look on Hannah's face when they put that big hat on her, it was priceless! Unfortunately, since I hadn't told Betty about the cake she wasn't prepared to take a picture so that look was not recorded, but none of us will ever forget it!

The next day we had to check out of the hotel, but our flight wasn't until one o'clock in the morning. So Magali and Meche picked us up and took us to the Indian Market to shop for souvenirs. The children had a great time bargaining with the proprietors of the small shops located in the Market and got some really good buys. From there we had a nice buffet of Peruvian foods for lunch. Afterward we went to Magali's home, where we stayed until the car came to take us to the Airport for our flight home.

CHAPTER 52

MORE TRAVELS AND MORE HEART PROBLEMS

Since I retired from Meharry in 2013, many more things have happened to us.

In 2013, we traveled back to Hawaii and visited our friends the Taogoshi's and the Ah Moos. Tony, Jeanne, Alex, and Olivia went with us. When we went to Aiea, we saw our former next door neighbors, the Oda's. Tony and their daughter, Rae, were friends when we lived there and we have kept in touch with Rae, Harry and Harriet ever since then.

We stayed at the Hale Koa Military Hotel at Fort DeRussey and while we were there I decided to make reservations to go back the following year for Betty's birthday in May.

In December of 2013, I was having pain in my chest and went to the cardiologist. He did some tests and found that one of my bypass arteries was blocked and I needed to have a stent inserted. So just before Christmas I had that procedure done and recovered well.

Since I was doing well, instead of going to Hawaii in May, we returned to Hawaii with Joe and his daughter, Rachel in July of 2014. About a month before the trip, I had not been feeling well again, so I went to the doctor and was diagnosed with pneumonia. I had just finished taking my antibiotics a week before our trip. When we changed planes in Chicago I had trouble keeping up with Betty on our way to our gate. I told her that my chest hurt. We both thought it was due to the fact that I was just recovering from pneumonia. So Betty ask a gate agent for wheelchair assistance because it was still a long way from our gate. We continued on and arrived in Honolulu about a half hour before Joe and Rachel arrived. We rented a car at the airport and drove to the Hale Koa and everything was beautiful. We were there for two weeks, but every time we walked anywhere my chest hurt and I had to sit down and rest. I continued to take my daily walk on the beach, but had to sit down now and then. We had a great time other than that. Once again we visited with our friends the Taogoshis and the Ah Moos. David took us out for lunch or dinner almost every day. Earl and Arlene took us to the Kahala Country Club for lunch where we were joined by their daughter Reine. Joe and Rachel left on the tenth day of the vacation, so we were there for four more days after they left.

When we returned home Betty insisted that we call Michael and tell him about my chest hurting. He told us to come in to the office right away. He took an EKG and called his friend, Dr. Tracy Callister, a cardiologist, to take a look at the EKG. Dr. Callister immediately told us that I needed to have a Cardiac Catheterization as soon as possible. So the next morning I had that procedure done and was sent immediately to the CCU at Centennial Medical Center in Nashville. My cardiac arteries were all almost completely blocked and I needed to have bypass surgery as soon as possible. The Cardiovascular surgeon, Dr. Pass, told me that because of my age he was going to give me a choice as to whether I wanted to have stents put in or have bypass surgery. He said that normally there was no choice because bypasses were the best way to treat my condition. The problem was that bypass surgery is more painful, has a longer recovery time and is more life threatening than having stents inserted. I decided that since my previous bypasses had lasted 14 years and the stent had only lasted 6 months, I would go with the bypasses. I had been through this before so I knew what I was getting into! Fortunately, I survived the surgery and recovered, slowly but well.

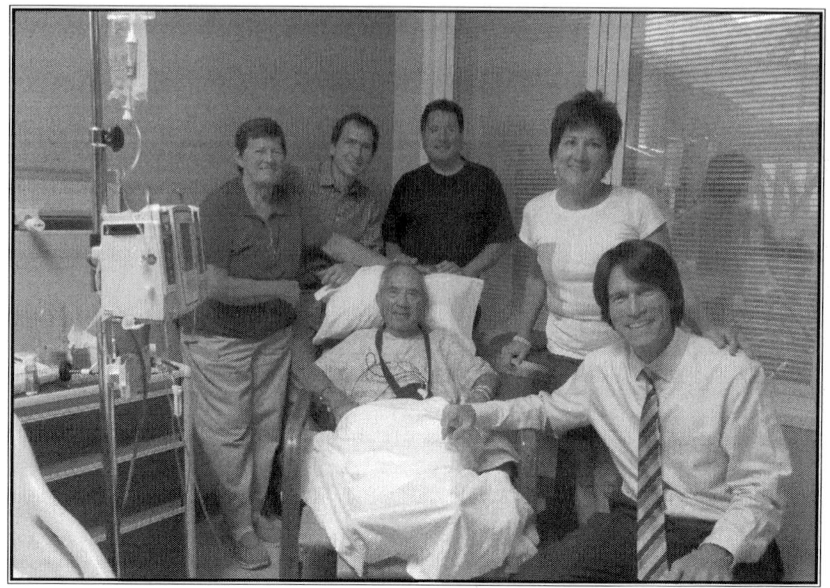

Rolando with Betty, Tony, Joe, Elena, and Michael before heart surgery, 2014

CHAPTER 53

ANOTHER TRIP TO PERU

After I fully recovered from my heart surgery Tony and Jeanne expressed an interest in going to Peru. So we all got together and planned a trip. On May 27, 2016, Tony, Jeanne, Alex and Olivia and we, departed on our trip. We were met at the airport in Lima by my Peruvian Dental School classmate, Mario Bermejo and his son, who drove us to our apartment. We stayed in a VRBO apartment in Miraflores. It was a very comfortable apartment with 3 bedrooms, 2 baths a full kitchen, washer and dryer and it was centrally located for most of the things we wanted to do. While we were there the Bermejos provided us with transportation just about anywhere we wanted to go around Lima.

My nephew, Tulio Obregon, invited us to have dinner with him at his beautiful apartment twice. The first time was a family dinner with his brothers and sisters and their spouses. The second time was with the Ambassador from Egypt. Both dinners were prepared by his personal gourmet chef. The meals were delicious!

While Tony and family went to Cuzco, we stayed in Lima and visited with my family members. We had lunch with my cousins, Meche, Polo, Polo's wife Nelly and Meche's daughter Jessica. My cousin Romulo and his wife came to visit us at our condo. I hadn't seen him for over 50 years! So it was a nice reunion. My cousin Hermalinda Obregon Ortega, Romulo's sister, and her daughter Liz, who live in Huaraz, happened to be in Lima and heard that we were there, so they also came to visit us. I am so happy that we were able to visit with them because Hermalinda passed away about six months after we saw her there. She always made it a point to see us every time we were in Huaraz. I lived with her family for a year when I was growing up and since she was about my age, we became close then.

After Tony and family returned from Cuzco, we traveled by bus to Huaraz. The bus service is very good. The buses are two level, have comfortable seats that can become beds at night, and restrooms. It's just like traveling on an airplane with a cabin attendant who serves meals and drinks. In Huaraz we stayed in an Air B & B that was actually a small hotel. The person who booked us into it also arranged for us to have a driver who had a mini-bus. He took us everywhere we wanted to go. Including up beyond the Huascaran where the altitude was 22,000 feet. The road was very winding and we went through the new tunnel that was built to make it easier to get to the other side of the mountains toward the jungle.

Chacas is the first large town after we went through the tunnel. I hadn't been there since I was in high school and went for a soccer tournament. Chacas is also the town where the mines are, where my father and grandfather were killed. I saw an old man sitting on a bench on the plaza, so I asked him if there were any Bernuis living there anymore. He said no but there were some who lived farther down the road toward Yauya. He also told me that the mines had been closed for many years and the owners had moved to Lima. We were hoping to visit Yauya, but the road between Chacas and Yauya was all gravel and it would have taken us another two hours to get there. Since that would have made it dark for our trip back to Lima, we decided to just visit Chacas for a while so that we didn't have to drive on that perilous road in the dark! Chacas has a beautiful Cathedral with a golden altar. Betty decided to just take a look inside and was completely surprised at how beautiful it was inside. She told Tony that he should take a look and he was impressed. They took several pictures of it. After looking around for a while and having lunch we headed back to Huaraz by way of Carhuaz and Yungay.

While in Carhuaz I showed everyone where my Uncle Samuel's home and office had been when I lived there with his family. In Yungay we visited the cemetery where many victims of the landslide there were buried. There is a beautiful statue of Jesus overlooking the town. We then returned to Huaraz. The next day we took a walking tour of the city and saw the neighborhood where I lived and the church where I attended Mass. Pariahuanca is nearby so we also went there, where I showed the family where I used to live on the farm. The next evening we returned to Lima by bus. It wasn't as nice an experience as the trip up there had been! We were on the upper level, so there was a lot more motion and since it was dark we couldn't see out. To make a long story short, the next time we go up to Huaraz we will fly or hire a minivan and driver to drive us there!

CHAPTER 54

LIFE AFTER HEART SURGERY

Since then I have started being a consultant to some of the other dentists in town about dental implants. I still keep up with new advances in dentistry and share my knowledge with others.

We have been travelling to Indiana once a month to visit Betty's Mother. Unfortunately, Betty's Mom passed away on March 22, 2019, after celebrating her 100th birthday on Feburary 2, 2019.

Our children have been successful in their chosen professions. Elena is a Dental Hygienist, Michael is a Physician, Tony is a Physician Assistant, and Joe retired from AOL and is now living his dream, playing guitar and singing in many venues in Virginia and Maryland in the D.C. area.

Betty and I enjoy visiting with our children and especially our grandchildren. Five of them have gone to college, one, Caleb went on to obtain his Master's degree in Cell and Molecular Biology and since the Fall of 2018 is going to medical school at Debusk Osteopathic School of Medicine. Another one, Alex, graduated from Oberlin College and works in theatre in New York City. Michael, Jr. graduated from the University of Tennessee in May, 2018 and has a job as a Demand Chain Analyst at Dollar General's Corporate offices in Goodlettesville, which is very near Hendersonville. Hannah has opened her own Photography and Videography business last year. She worked in Michael's office to learn to be a Medical Assistant. She recently decided to go to Nursing school. After finishing two years studying Computer Science at the College of Southern Maryland, Zachary is now studying Information Systems at the University of Maryland Baltimore County. Haley has graduated from college with a degree in Art and in English. Rachel E. graduated from College and Nursing School in May of 2019 and as of July is a Registered Nurse. She recently started working at Vanderbilt Medical Center in Nashville. Olivia is working towards a degree in Journalism and Spanish at Western Kentucky University. Rachel L. is working in the restaurant and retail business. She and Haley have moved to Florida where their mother lives. Haley recently bought a house there. Eliza has graduated from High School and took a gap year off. She is now attending Welch College in Hendersonville and is studying Business Marketing. The others are all in elementary or high school. They are all the joy of my life!

Betty and I enjoy living here on Old Hickory Lake. We enjoy each other's company and try to keep healthy. I have started taking Tai Chi classes and I also walk and work out at the gym. Betty has decided not to coach soccer anymore, but is planning on continuing to play golf. I might even join her in that. She is thinking about joining the gym to work out on the machines and walking. We both want to stay healthy so that we can enjoy watching our family grow.

I'm very happy that I became a "Citizen by Choice" of the United States of America and that I am living the American Dream!

Fiftieth wedding anniversary with family, 2009.

Sunset from our sunroom

AFTERWORD

A few simple rules for success in America:

1. Love all Americans, respect and learn their language

2. Love the country geographically, respect the territorial integrity (borders).

3. Respect all elected officials, obey the laws

4. Live with Americans. No segregated communities of any country.

If you are invited to their homes, be polite, eat their food, drink their beverages. Laugh when they laugh (Learn their culture).

If you invite them into your home, be patient and polite, tell them about your traditions. You will be surprised to see that they will want to know more and you will all have a good time.

While in this country live the American life, not in settlements of foreigners or enclaves where you will keep on living as you did in your native country. Don't try to impose the lifestyle in your country on others.

If you find it intolerable to live in the USA, then go where you can live more happily. Go home and make changes at home. You will find a great number of people who think and feel like you do.